UNDERSTANDING TERENCE

UNDERSTANDING
TERENCE

BY

SANDER M. GOLDBERG

PRINCETON UNIVERSITY PRESS

PRINCETON, NEW JERSEY

COPYRIGHT © 1986 BY PRINCETON UNIVERSITY PRESS
PUBLISHED BY PRINCETON UNIVERSITY PRESS, 41 WILLIAM STREET
PRINCETON, NEW JERSEY 08540
IN THE UNITED KINGDOM
PRINCETON UNIVERSITY PRESS, GUILDFORD, SURREY

ALL RIGHTS RESERVED

LIBRARY OF CONGRESS CATALOGING IN PUBLICATION DATA WILL
BE FOUND ON THE LAST PRINTED PAGE OF THIS BOOK

ISBN 0-691-03586-5

PUBLICATION OF THIS BOOK HAS BEEN AIDED BY GRANTS FROM
THE HENRY A. LAUGHLIN FUND OF PRINCETON UNIVERSITY PRESS
AND THE EUGENE M. KAYDEN FUND OF THE UNIVERSITY OF COLORADO

THIS BOOK HAS BEEN COMPOSED IN LINOTRON JANSON

CLOTHBOUND EDITIONS OF PRINCETON UNIVERSITY PRESS BOOKS
ARE PRINTED ON ACID-FREE PAPER, AND BINDING MATERIALS
ARE CHOSEN FOR STRENGTH AND DURABILITY

PRINTED IN THE UNITED STATES OF AMERICA
BY PRINCETON UNIVERSITY PRESS
PRINCETON, NEW JERSEY

J. W. H.

SCHOLAR   TEACHER   FRIEND

CONTENTS

ABBREVIATIONS AND TEXTS
ix

PREFACE
xi

I   THE CONTEXT   3

II   THE PROLOGUES   31

III   THE WELL-MADE PLAY   61

IV   *Contaminatio*   91

V   THE *duplex comoedia*   123

VI   THE PRICE OF SIMPLICITY   149

VII   THE *purus sermo*   170

VIII   THE DEATH OF COMEDY   203

SELECTIVE BIBLIOGRAPHY
221

INDEX
Passages Cited
227

General
228

ABBREVIATIONS

The titles of periodicals appear in the abbreviated forms recommended by the *American Journal of Archaeology* 69 (1965) 201–06, supplemented as necessary by the list in *L'Année philologique*. The citation of Latin authors and works follows the practice of the *Oxford Latin Dictionary*. Some frequently cited books are abbreviated as follows:

Büchner, *TT*	K. Büchner, *Das Theater des Terenz* (Heidelberg 1974)
Denzler, *Monolog*	B. Denzler, *Der Monolog bei Terenz* (Zurich 1968)
Duckworth, *NRC*	G. Duckworth, *The Nature of Roman Comedy* (Princeton 1952)
Fraenkel, *EPP*	E. Fraenkel, *Elementi plautini in Plauto* (Florence 1960)
Garton, *PA*	C. Garton, *Personal Aspects of the Roman Theatre* (Toronto 1972)
Goldberg, *MMC*	S. M. Goldberg, *The Making of Menander's Comedy* (Berkeley 1980)
Leo, *GRL*	F. Leo, *Geschichte der römischen Literatur I* (Berlin 1913)
Leo, *PlF*	F. Leo, *Plautinische Forschungen*, 2 ed. (Berlin 1912)
Norwood, *AT*	G. Norwood, *The Art of Terence* (Oxford 1923)
Wright, *DiC*	J. Wright, *Dancing in Chains* (Rome 1974)

TEXTS

Plautus and Terence are cited from the Oxford editions of Lindsay (1904–1905) and Kauer, Lindsay, and Skutsch (1958), except for *Casina* and *Adelphoe*, which follow the Cambridge texts of, respectively, Willcock (1976) and Martin (1976). Menander is cited from the Oxford text of Sandbach (1972). Except as noted, all translations are my own.

PREFACE

> Shakespeare's name, you may depend on it, stands absurdly too high and will go down. He had no invention as to stories, none whatever. He took all his plots from old novels, and threw their stories into dramatic shape, at as little expense of thought as you or I could turn his plays back again into prose tales. That he threw over whatever he did write some flashes of genius, nobody can deny: but this was all.
> —LORD BYRON TO JAMES HOGG
> ("The Ettrick Shepherd") 24 March 1814

It has been enough. Shakespeare's reputation has not gone down. Adherence to a different standard has made the truth of Byron's criticism somehow beside the point. Modern readers prize those flashes of genius, distinguish newness of content from artistic merit, and avoid judging the whole by the limitations of a part. Scholars use and value the insights of source criticism without ignoring other lines of inquiry and other dimensions of Shakespeare's art. Studies of imagery, theme, outlook, and background all have their place. The literary critic has free rein. Not all the resulting scholarship may be equally good, but a wide field of investigation inevitably broadens our understanding and deepens our appreciation.

As a group, we Latinists are not so eclectic, and the study of Roman comedy has generally followed a narrower path. Our philological training leads us to concentrate on the origins of things. Because Plautus and Terence derived their plays from a Greek comic tradition, we therefore wonder most about their originality. We try to reconstruct their lost Greek models from the Latin copies and then to compare the Roman comic tradition with its Greek forerunner. This is source criticism without the sources, and we have not done badly at it. Close attention to the conflicting details of Terence's text—the minutiae of exposition, characterization, pacing and tone as measured against Greek practices—has produced rich and abundant results. We know much more about his dramatic technique than ever before. Yet the very success of this analytic approach has fostered a certain narrowness in the enterprise. We have learned so much that we more readily mistake one aspect of his achievement for the whole. Our focus on the "how" of Terence's art has slighted the "why."

What Terence accomplished on the Roman stage is too often discussed primarily in terms of what his models Menander and Apollodorus achieved before Greek audiences. The comparison can be telling, but it is not complete. The picture of Terence that emerges is, like Byron's critique of Shakespeare, not so much wrong as inadequate. We need a broader base for our opinions. His debt to the Greek theatrical tradition must not distract us from another fact of equal significance: Terence's primary place is among the seminal figures of *Latin* literature. This book therefore approaches Terence through the Latin tradition of New Comedy and focuses on his contribution to the Romans' literary development. It will not deal directly with Menander and Apollodorus, and it will not engage in that analysis of structural incongruities so common in Terentian studies. "Terence" in the following pages will always mean the author of the Latin text under discussion, even when he is not necessarily its originator. We need not distinguish what is uniquely Terentian in these plays from what may also have appeared in his Greek models in order to demonstrate how they work on the stage and how they came to influence subsequent Roman literature. They are entirely Terentian in that the language, the action, and the characters are what the Roman dramatist himself chose to present to Roman audiences. I have therefore relegated to footnotes and parentheses problems of alterations and origins that are often central to scholarly discussion. Given the recondite convolutions, disagreements, and dead ends to which that scholarship so frequently brings us, most students of Terence and of drama in general will probably be relieved. A few specialists may be perplexed, though I hope not angered at my refusal to address their concerns. My reasons for slighting them are set out in detail in Chapters 1, 3, and 4. Readers can judge for themselves if the methods I substitute and the alternative questions I raise are any more helpful to their understanding of Terence.

Those methods and questions do not simply substitute literary for philological interests. My aim throughout is not to ignore philology, but to point it toward wider issues in the criticism of Roman drama. I have added to the literary interpretation of individual plays only as means toward this larger end, which is to understand the nature of the interpretative problem Terence presents to modern critics and to suggest new ways to approach it. How I prefer to read *Adelphoe*, what I think is wrong with *Hecyra* and right about *Eunuchus*, will no doubt come clear in the following chapters, but my goal is to encourage debate about individual plays rather than to end it.

This is, then, an opinionated, though I hope not a willful, book. Those opinions are my own, or at least my own responsibility, but the debts incurred in forming them are nevertheless both a duty and a pleasure to acknowledge. The work began and ended with fellowship support, an A. W. Mellon Post-Doctoral Fellowship at Stanford University that got it going in earnest and a research fellowship from the National Endowment for the Humanities that provided leave to complete it. I have also been helped by a generous travel grant from the University of Colorado's Council for Research and Creative Work, a fruitful and expedient alternative to interlibrary loan. Parts of the work have been read before a variety of audiences and improved by their comments. The bulk of Chapter 2 appeared in *Classical Philology* for 1983; an early version of Chapter 8 appeared, albeit with a different conclusion, in *Comparative Drama* for 1982–1983.

Even more pleasant to recall because more personal are my debts to individuals. Special thanks go to Mrs. Lucy Walker and the members of Denver's EDEN Theatrical Workshop, whose invitation to advise their production of *Adelphoe* provided the most practical of tests for many ideas. The experience enables me to say with confidence that while details of the original productions of all six plays are beyond recall, the interpretations and stagings suggested here are indeed in the text and readily come to life in actual production. Among scholarly debts, the keenest is to scholars I never knew but wish I had, Friedrich Leo and Eduard Fraenkel, my greatest teachers and silent companions. Those who can and have quite often talked back include my former Berkeley colleagues William S. Anderson and Erich S. Gruen, who dealt firmly yet sympathetically with some of my wilder notions; Elaine Fantham of the University of Toronto, a rigorous but supportive critic; and especially James W. Halporn of Indiana University, who first posed on a doctoral examination the questions this book tries to answer. I hope he likes the book better than he liked the exam, but its dedication is in any case truly *pietatis causa, non ambitionis.*

UNDERSTANDING TERENCE

[1]

THE CONTEXT

The comedies that entertained Roman crowds at a festival like the *ludi Romani* bore only superficial resemblance to the Greek plays on which they were modeled. While the authors of Greek New Comedy had put the characters and situations of their own time on a stage and before audiences steeped in an old and respected dramatic tradition, playwrights and producers at Rome were adapting a foreign art form to quite different conditions. Roman theatre people had to be adroit and aggressive professionals, seeking contracts from public officials to perform plays on makeshift stages amid the bustle of large and diverse public shows.[1] To attract the necessary crowds, they turned the fourth-century Greece of their models into a comic fantasy land populated by absurd Greeks who spoke highly stylized Latin and whose broad comic effects and elaborate songs imposed native Italian tastes upon Greek dramatic structures. The resulting form of comedy was extremely successful. Between 240 B.C., when a Greek from Tarentum named Livius Andronicus first presented plays in Latin at the *ludi Romani*, and Plautus' death in about 184, a Roman theatrical tradition grew rapidly and well. The steady addition of new festivals and the growing tendency to include plays in the public celebration of military victories, temple dedications, and state funerals created more theatrical opportunities for Plautus than the dramatists of fifth-century Athens had known.[2] With this increase in quantity came a corre-

---

[1] E. J. Jory, "Association of Actors in Rome," *Hermes* 98 (1970) 224-253; Garton, *PA* 51-72.
[2] L. R. Taylor, "The Opportunities for Dramatic Performance in the Time of Plautus and Terence," *TAPA* 68 (1937) 284-304.

sponding increase in quality. Cicero found the plays of Livius not worth a second reading; Plautus' comedies quickly became objects of admiration, imitation, and study.[3] They reflect a time of great creativity and growing technical skill. As a later producer of Plautus was to claim,

> ea tempestate flos poetarum fuit,
> qui nunc abierunt hinc in communem locum.
> sed tamen apsentes prosunt pro praesentibus.
>
> That was a time when poets flowered,
> poets now gone to their just reward,
> but though absent they profit us as if present.
> (*Casina* 18–20)

Yet the development of Roman comedy did not end with Plautus. As Rome learned more about Greece and as the Roman aristocrats who sponsored *ludi scaenici* learned more about literature, the character of Roman comedy and its performance changed.

Signs of that change show clearly in the six plays of Terence, which date from the 160's. The bold and brilliant style of Plautus and his successor Caecilius has been replaced by something calmer and less fantastic. The plays seem more recognizably Greek, or at least less blatantly Roman. Such a change in style and outlook presents special problems of interpretation, for these plays mark both a departure from the traditional values of Roman comedy and also the end of productive experiments on the comic stage. Neither Plautus nor Menander is exactly comparable, and the fragments of Roman comedy after Terence are too

---

[3] Cic., *Brut.* 71: "Livianae fabulae non satis dignae quae iterum legantur." The tragic poet Accius (b. 170) was the first Plautine scholar; Cicero's older contemporary Varro worked to establish a corpus of authentic comedies from a mass of forgeries, fit testimony to the commercial value of Plautus' name. See A. Ronconi, "Sulla fortuna di Plauto e di Terenzio nel mondo romano," *Maia* 22 (1970) 19–37.

scanty to complete the perspective. Yet his plays are not isolated monuments. The cultural forces that worked upon Roman literature in the second century have left their mark, and the contrast with his predecessors can reveal how Terence modified familiar devices of his genre. A review of this social and literary context, along with some necessary reappraisal of traditional beliefs concerning them, will provide the perspective for forming our own understanding of Terence.

I

Back in 189 B.C., while Plautus still dominated Roman comedy, the development of Latin literature took a new turn. When Marcus Fulvius Nobilior, consul in that year, embarked on a campaign against the Greek city of Ambracia, he included the poet Quintus Ennius in his entourage. Hellenistic kings had long known the value of court poets. Alexander the Great took an epic poet as well as a historian with him to the east. Attalids and Seleucids had poems written in their honor. Nobilior's act, however, was unprecedented at Rome. As a group, the early Roman poets occupied the lower rungs of an increasingly class-conscious society and did not mix with the aristocracy. Their professional association, the so-called *Collegium poetarum*, was organized as an artisans' guild; Cato likened poets to vagabonds.[4] Livius had in fact come to Rome as a slave and Plautus as an Italian provincial on the make. Caecilius was a Gaul. Naevius, from Campania, perhaps ranked higher on the social scale, but his legendary quarrel with the powerful Metelli is our only example, and that a negative one, of contact between a poet and a public figure.[5] Roman

---

[4] "Poeticae artis honos non erat. Si quis in ea re studebat aut sese ad convivia adplicabat, 'grassator' vocabatur," Cato, *Mor.* 2 (Gel. 11.2.5). The organization and function of the *collegium* is imperfectly understood, but see N. Horsfall, "The Collegium Poetarum," *BICS* 23 (1976) 79–95.

[5] That quarrel, like most "facts" of early Roman literary history, defies sure interpretation. Naevius may have been imprisoned for slander, but the

comedy generally avoided specific political references; Naevius' epic on the Punic War is a poem without a patron. What favoritism influenced the award of contracts for the various *ludi* and the commissioning of public hymns has left no trace.[6]

With Ennius' career we can document an important development. He too was a foreigner, a Calabrian rather than a Roman, but he came to Rome in 204 at Cato's urging. He lived modestly but moved in high circles. Later tradition linked him not only with Cato and Nobilior, but with such other notables as Scipio Nasica and Servius Sulpicius Galba.[7] He gave elegant recompense for the company he kept. The siege of Ambracia occupied a prominent place in Book 15 of Ennius' epic masterpiece, the *Annales*, and Nobilior's eventual claim to a triumph in the face of strong political opposition at Rome was perhaps aided by a second work entitled *Ambracia*, which was most likely a play.[8] En-

---

circumstances are beyond recall. Recent discussions of the problem include H. B. Mattingly, "Naevius and the Metelli," *Historia* 9 (1960) 414–439, and H. D. Jocelyn, "The Poet Cn. Naevius, P. Cornelius Scipio, and Q. Caecilius Metellus," *Antichthon* 3 (1969) 32–47. On the general problem of interpreting such evidence, see J. H. Waszink, "Anfangsstadium der römischen Literatur," *ANRW* 1.2 (Berlin 1972) 869–927. W. Suerbaum, *Untersuchungen zur Selbstdarstellung älterer römischer Dichter* (Hildesheim 1968), is the best modern study of Livius, Naevius, and Ennius.

[6] Yet surely there was some. Compare the uproar when Cato, as censor, tried to regulate the awarding of contracts for public works (Plut. *Cat. mai.* 19.1–2, *Flam.* 19.3; Liv. 39.44.5–9) and the revolt of the corrupt *publicani* as described at Liv. 25.3–4.

[7] E. Badian, "Ennius and His Friends," *Fondation Hardt Entretiens XVII: Ennius* (Vandoeuvres-Geneva 1971) 151–199. Badian, 155–163, endorsed by J. S. Ruebel, "Cato, Ennius, and Sardinia," *LCM* 2 (1977) 155–157, questions the traditional association of Ennius with Cato, but his arguments have convinced few. See the discussion, pp. 200–202. M. Martina, "Ennio 'poeta cliens,' " *QFC* 2 (1979) 15–74, sees Ennius as a supporter of Nobilior's interests exclusively, a difficult position to maintain when so little of Ennius' poetry survives.

[8] Only four unconnected lines of *Ambracia* survive. Ribbeck thought the work a *fabula praetexta*; Vahlen is less confident. It could conceivably have

nius also wrote a poem entitled *Scipio*, in honor of Africanus, and he extended the *Annales* beyond its original fifteen books in order to include the valiant deeds of more contemporary Romans. Sometime in the 170's, Cato attacked Nobilior for having taken Ennius to Ambracia, but his perception of poetry's political power had come too late.[9]

This patronage of Ennius belongs in the larger context of cultural developments in the second century. As Rome increased its meddling in Greek affairs and as Greeks increasingly found themselves drawn to Rome, cultural contact between them grew rapidly. Roman nobles, often bilingual and always confident travelers to the east, found themselves not simply with the power to appropriate Greek books, Greek art, and Greek tutors for their sons, but with the leisure to appreciate their appeal. Scipio Africanus, while commanding a Roman army at Syracuse in 205, walked about the gymnasium in Greek dress and read Greek books. Fulvius Nobilior used spoils from Ambracia to decorate a temple at Rome to Hercules of the Muses. After the battle of Pydna in 168, Aemilius Paullus put the royal Macedonian library at his sons' disposal.[10] With this growing appreciation of Greek culture came an increased awareness of literature's power to influence public opinion. The first Roman historical writing dates from this period, originally in Greek but soon after in Latin, and

---

been performed as part of Nobilior's victory games in 186. For his political problems over the triumph, see Liv. 38.43–44.6 and 39.4–5.

[9] Cic., *Tusc.* 1.3 (= Cato, fr. 149M) refers to an "oratio Catonis, in qua obiecit ut probrum M. Nobiliori, quod is in provinciam poetas duxisset: duxerat autem consul ille in Aetoliam, ut scimus, Ennium." Malcovati identifies this with the speech *In M. Fulvium Nobiliorem* dated no earlier than 178. See H. H. Scullard, *Roman Politics 200–150 B.C.*, 2 ed. (Oxford 1973) 266–267, and Suerbaum (above, n. 5) 201–204.

[10] Scipio at Syracuse, Liv. 29.19.12 and V. Max. 3.6.1; Nobilior's temple, Plin., *Nat.* 33.66; Paullus and the library, Plut. *Aem. Paul.* 28.6. For these and many other examples see "Philhellenism: Culture and Policy," Chapter 7 in E. S. Gruen, *The Hellenistic World and the Coming of Rome*, vol. 1 (Berkeley 1984), esp. 255–260.

the public entertainments expanded in number and scope. The two curule aediles, who had charge of the *ludi Romani* and the *ludi Megalenses* (established in 204, drama added by 194), quickly learned the political value of lavish entertainments. The festivals grew longer, which was certainly good for the acting profession, and the aediles grew popular. All of those identified between 217 and 187 went on to higher elected office. Victorious generals adopted the same course. As thanks to Jupiter for the victory at Ambracia, for example, Nobilior celebrated *ludi* for ten days in 186 and imported actors and athletes from Greece, as well as lions and panthers, for the occasion. The Senate found it necessary to limit the expense.[11] This aristocratic involvement in the sponsorship of literary activity, especially activity of the public sort, is crucial for understanding the next such documented case, the patronage of Terence.

The prologues to Terence's plays suggest a career dogged by hostile rumor and innuendo, and among these is the insinuation that his success owed more to friends than to his own talent ("amicum ingenio fretum, haud natura sua," *HT* 24). In *Adelphoe* he deftly turned such an accusation to his advantage.

> nam quod isti dicunt malevoli, homines nobilis
> hunc adiutare adsidueque una scribere,
> quod illi maledictum vehemens esse existimant,
> eam laudem hic ducit maximam quom illis placet
> qui vobis univorsis et populo placent,
> quorum opera in bello, in otio, in negotio,
> suo quisque tempore usust sine superbia.
>
> Now as to what the spiteful say, that certain
> nobles help him out and always share the writing,

---

[11] Liv. 39.5.10. The same limit was imposed on the consul Q. Fulvius Flaccus in 179 (Liv. 40.44.10). For the growing political importance of *ludi*, see Scullard (above, n. 9) 23–25, and A. E. Astin, *Scipio Aemilianus* (Oxford 1967) 339.

>   this charge they think a powerful slander
>   he deems an honor, since he pleases men
>   who please you all and please the Roman people,
>   whose deeds in war, in peace, in politics
>   we all enjoy in need and without arrogance.
>   (*Adelphoe* 15–21)

Who were these *homines nobilis*? Since *Adelphoe* was performed in 160 at the funeral games of Aemilius Paullus, an association with his son Scipio Aemilianus, the most famous philhellene of the second century, has long provided an easy answer. Suetonius, whose earliest sources date from late Republican times, records this identification as fact, and Cicero mentions a rumor that the comedies had been written by Scipio's close friend Laelius.[12] It is all guesswork, though, and involves an awkward problem of chronology. Though Scipio distinguished himself at Pydna in 168, he was only seventeen at the time. He did not enter the Senate until 152, and his famous career *in otio, in negotio* can hardly date to the 160's.[13] Laelius was scarcely older. Yet the presumed association with Scipio and Laelius has often colored critical thinking about Terence.

Belief in a philhellenic coterie surrounding the younger Scipio

---

[12] Suet., *Vit. Ter.* 11 (Rostagni): "Hic cum multis nobilibus familiariter vixit, sed maxime cum Scipione Africano et C. Laelio . . ." Cic., *Att.* 7.3.10: "Terentium, cuius fabulae propter elegantiam sermonis putabantur a C. Laelio scribi." Quint., *Inst.* 10.1.99, makes the rumored author Scipio. Suetonius actually reports conflicting accounts of Terence's relations with various *nobiles*, leading W. Beare, "The Life of Terence," *Hermathena* 59 (1942) 20–29, to doubt them all. Badian (above, n. 7) 185, discussing the Ennian biography, rightly warns of "how little was really known by the first century B.C., even where much was asserted." The fact of Terence's association with *nobiles* seems certain, but not their identity.

[13] H. B. Mattingly, "The Chronology of Terence," *RCCM* 5 (1963) 12–61, redates Terence's career into the 150's, but his argument is not persuasive.

occasionally tempts scholars to see Terence as the first elegant spokesman for the enlightened *humanitas* with which this "Scipionic Circle" assailed a chauvinistic archaism often identified with Cato the Censor. At the very least, the dramatist's rhetorical polish has been read as the reflection of "Scipionic interests."[14] Others have cast him as a poet with a mission and used that mission to explain certain oddities of his life and work. His break with the traditional comic style, for example, and the quarrel reported in the prologues with such older contemporaries as Luscius Lanuvinus became evidence for his adherence to a consciously philhellenic program. "Thus the hostility of Luscius," wrote one supporter of this view, "was motivated not so much by artistic concerns or by professional jealousy . . . as by a more profound social and political motive: the need to obstruct the re-evaluation on the stage of that Greek world which Plautus had known so well how to make ridiculous."[15] The plays of Terence are thus read as the first systematic attempt to bring Greek values to rude Latium, and such critics see in him that wrestling with Greek form and content later manifest in the work of authors like Cicero and Horace.

A Scipionic *humanitas* also appeals to critics who would prefer apparent defects in dramatic technique to be thought virtues. There is, for example, Terence's handling of the specifically Greek references in his originals. He might have left them in place, perhaps with a joke about their oddity (e.g., Plautus' "licet haec Athenis nobis," *Stich.* 448), or he might have substituted Roman equivalents. Instead, he usually generalizes. A passage

---

[14] Most recently advanced by G. Calboli, "La retorica preciceroniana e la politica a Roma," *Fondation Hardt Entretiens XXVIII: Éloquence et rhétorique chez Cicéron* (Vandoeuvres-Geneva 1982) 41–99, esp. 50–71, but see the comments of Winterbottom and Stroh, 100–105.

[15] I. Lana, "Terenzio e il movimento filellenico in Roma," *RFIC* 75 (1947) 44–80, 155–175. The quotation is from p. 59.

from *Heauton timorumenos* is often cited in this context, for the Greek original survives.

πρὸς τῆς Ἀθηνᾶς, δαιμονᾷς, γεγονὼς ἔτη
τοσαῦθ'· ὁμοῦ γάρ ἐστιν ἑξήκοντά σοι,
⟨ὡς ὑπονοῶ⟩· καὶ τῶν Ἅλησι χωρίον
κεκτημένος κάλλιστον εἶ, νὴ τὸν Δία,
ἐν τοῖς τρισίν γε, καὶ τὸ μακαριώτατον
ἄστικτον.

By Athena, you are mad, and at
your age! You're nearly sixty,
I would guess. You've bought
the finest farm in Halai. It ranks
in the top three, by God, and best of all,
It's got no mortgage.
      (Menander, fr. 127K–T)

nam pro deum atque hominum fidem, quid vis tibi aut
quid quaeris? annos sexaginta natus es
aut plus eo, ut conicio; agrum in his regionibus
meliorem neque preti maioris nemo habet.

For heaven's sake, what do you want?
What do you seek? You're sixty, maybe
more, I'd guess. No one hereabout has
better land, or land worth more.
      (Terence, *HT* 61–64)

Terence has generalized the oath. He has replaced the pointed δαιμονᾷς with a bland expostulation and the Athenian deme name with the vague *in his regionibus*, and he has dropped the Attic concern with mortgages. The effect, from the purely dramatic standpoint, is to take the edge off Chremes' inquisitiveness. The details in the speech Terence gives him could all be the result of his own observation; Menander's fragment suggests far more aggressive a busybody. Some might find in such softening of characterization Terence's notorious lack of *vis*, but for others he has raised his art above the level of petty detail in quest of the universal. "The aim for the universally valid," wrote Karl Büchner, "seems to me to be the chief intention in the alteration of Greek formulations."[16]

Such broad philosophical concerns may also assuage critics convinced that literature, especially drama, must be rooted in and speak to its own time. Readers of Terence might otherwise be stymied, for the plays seem to lack a sense of period. Terence makes no references to living people, Greek or Roman. His language is not rich in the vocabulary of Roman law, nor does he play on the political significance latent in such words as *gloria* and *virtus*.[17] Thraso, his one *miles gloriosus*, is the apparent exception that illustrates the rule. In *Eunuchus*, Thraso deploys centuries and maniples before the house of Thais. He finds inspiration in Pyrrhus, and his follower Sanga knows well the *imperatoris virtutem et vim militum*. But Thraso, for all this Roman jargon, is hardly a character drawn from life. He is the product of a purely literary tradition, lifted from Menander's *Kolax*, and his greatest scene finds its parallel, not in the plays of Plautus, but in the *Perikeiromene* of Menander when Polemon prepares to assault the house of Glykera.[18] But if Terence has refused to be directly topical, the "Scipionic program" can at least show him to be themat-

---

[16] K. Büchner, "Terenz in der Kontinuität der abendländischen Humanität," *Humanitas Romana* (Heidelberg 1957) 50. W. Ludwig, "The Originality of Terence and His Greek Models," *GRBS* 9 (1968) 169–182, esp. 174–176, deals firmly with such impressions.

[17] D. C. Earl, "Terence and Roman Politics," *Historia* 11 (1962) 469–485, in significant contrast to his earlier study, "Political Terminology in Plautus," *Historia* 9 (1960) 234–243.

[18] *Eun.* 771ff. ~ *Perik.* 467ff. For the comparison, see Goldberg, *MMC* 48–50.

ically topical. His comparative fidelity to his Greek models, his sympathetic portrayal of women, his uniquely urbane diction, and his quiet humor have all been taken to prove his role as a conscious popularizer of Greek values. Thus *Hecyra* has been praised for its refusal to pander to Roman taste. *Adelphoe* has been read as a philosophical struggle between Paullus and Cato played out by surrogates, and the legalism of *Phormio* has been called "a kind of Scipionic inside joke."[19] Such readings are very convenient, but we can no longer accept them uncritically.

For one thing, historians have disbanded the "Scipionic Circle." Scipio Aemilianus doubtless formed significant friendships with literary figures like Polybius and Lucilius, but the notion of a *salon* centered around him has been revealed as little more than a fiction of Cicero's dialogues.[20] We have also lost that useful dichotomy between Scipio and Cato. The complex cultural issue between them can no longer be explained by the old stereotypes. Under scrutiny, the career of Aemilianus has turned out to be something less than uniquely enlightened, and a reappraisal of Cato's attitude toward the Greeks reveals nearly as great an interest in their heritage as a distaste for their contemporary character. It has been a misleading simplification to speak, at least in cultural terms, of phil- and antihellenic factions in second-century Rome. Both Cato *and* Polybius mocked A. Postumius Albinus for writing history in a Greek poor enough to require its author's apology, while Cato himself, though always writing Latin, admired Demosthenes and was steeped in the work of

---

[19] G. Norwood, *Plautus and Terence* (New York 1931) 160–169; P. MacKendrick, "Demetrius of Phalerum, Cato, and the *Adelphoe*," *RFIC* n.s. 32 (1954) 18–35; E. Segal and C. Moulton, "*Contortor legum*: The Hero of the *Phormio*," *RhM* 121 (1978) 276–288.

[20] H. Strasburger, "Der Scipionenkreis," *Hermes* 94 (1966) 60–72; Astin, *Scipio* (above, n. 11) 294–296; J.E.G. Zetzel, "Cicero and the Scipionic Circle," *HSCP* 76 (1972) 173–179.

Xenophon.[21] Finally, we have lost the comforting idea of a new *humanitas*. Both the word and the concept in Latin date only from Cicero's time, and that widely cited statement of Terentian *humanitas*, "homo sum: humani nil a me alienum puto" (*HT* 77), is only a busybody's excuse for his prying.[22]

Belief in an exclusively Scipionic Terence is untenable, for no single faction used him as its spokesman; not all the aediles who bought his plays were Cornelii and none was an intimate of Scipio Aemilianus. Marcus Fulvius Nobilior, the elder son of Ennius' patron, was aedile in 166, the year *Andria* launched Terence's career at the *ludi Megalenses*. His brother Quintus was aedile in 160, when *Hecyra* was performed at the *ludi Romani*. In 161, when *Eunuchus* was performed at the *Megalenses* and *Phormio* at the *Romani*, one of the aediles was Lucius Postumius Albinus, a cousin of that Aulus Postumius whose philhellenism was to irritate Cato and Polybius. Neither the Fulvii nor the Postumii were close political allies of the Scipionic faction, but all shared that interest in literary activity increasingly typical of Roman *nobiles* in the second century. And to support Terence was both good politics and good business. All but one of the aediles who financed these productions eventually reached the consulship, and Ambivius Turpio, a professional impresario whose livelihood depended on furnishing them with popular plays, continually brought them Terence. The sniping attacks of Luscius Lanuvinus evidently came to nothing. *Eunuchus* earned a record fee and an unprecedented encore performance. Even *Hecyra*, which had trouble holding its audience, was backed for a second and fi-

---

[21] On Postumius, Polyb. 39.1 and Plut., *Cat. mai.* 12.5; Cato and the Greeks, A. E. Astin, *Cato the Censor* (Oxford 1978) 157–181, and J. S. Ruebel, "Cato and Scipio Africanus," *CW* 71 (1977) 161–173.

[22] Astin, *Scipio* (above, n. 11) 302–306; H. D. Jocelyn, "Homo sum: humani nil a me alienum puto," *Antichthon* 7 (1973) 14–46. P. Grimal, "Térence et Aristote à propos de l' *Héauton timorumenos*," *BAGB* (1979) 175–187, is not an effective reply.

nally a third, successful, showing. Terence died quite young in 159 and never had the opportunity to develop the following Plautus enjoyed, but he was always a commercial success.

Nevertheless, the new values reflected in his adaptation of Greek models created problems for Roman comedy. Though the dramatic tradition was extremely flexible, there were some forms it could not take without showing signs of strain, and it did not long survive his innovations. We shall eventually want to ask how and why this was so, but we need first to examine those literary changes that form the second part of the interpretative problem Terence presents.

II

By Terence's day, Latin comedy in Greek dress, the so-called *comoedia palliata*, had been performed at Rome for some seventy years and had developed an elaborate array of favorite characters and stage devices. Terence was as much heir to that tradition as he was the product of increasingly Hellenized tastes. How to use the traditional forms to reflect contemporary concerns posed a constant challenge. He himself often calls attention to it. The prologue to *Eunuchus*, for example, defends his appropriation of a soldier and parasite from Menander's *Kolax* with these words on the limitations dramatists face.

> quod si personis isdem huic uti non licet:
> qui mage licet currentem servom scribere,
> bonas matronas facere, meretrices malas,
> parasitum edacem, gloriosum militem,
> puerum supponi, falli per servom senem,
> amare odisse suspicari? denique
> nullumst iam dictum quod non dictum sit prius.

> For if he's not allowed to use these figures,
> how then can he introduce the running slave,
> create good matrons, greedy whores,

a hungry parasite, the braggart soldier,
foundling child, old man tricked by
slave, love, hate, suspicion? After all,
nothing's said that's not been said before.
(Eun. 35-41)

Terence quarrels here with contemporary dramatists, but he is neither lamenting nor rejecting the characters and situations available to him. His plays use all of them frequently and with enthusiasm. What he does reject is their repetition for the same stereotyped effects. Though recognizing and embracing the usefulness of stock elements, he refuses to accept them at face value. Thus *Eunuchus* surprises us with a boastful soldier rewarded for his foolishness. *Andria* and *Hecyra* present slaves too clever for their own good, familiar characters whose actions nevertheless run counter to our expectations. Whole scenes from the tradition can also be modified and given new point. Consider the *servus currens*.

The hurrying messenger too busy to notice his master and too exhausted to deliver a coherent message was such a stage favorite that Plautus put two of them in *Epidicus*, the first a genuine messenger (1ff.) and the second a sham (192ff.).[23] Such figures frequently threaten violence to those in their way. Curculio, for example, uses flailing arms and legs to repel an imaginary crowd.

Date viam mihi, noti [atque] ignoti, dum ego hic officium meum
facio: fugite omnes, abite et de via secedite,
ne quem in cursu capite aut cubito aut pectore offendam
   aut genu.

---

[23] G. E. Duckworth, "The Dramatic Function of the *Servus Currens* in Roman Comedy," *Classical Studies Presented to Edward Capps* (Princeton 1936) 93-102; T. Guardì, "I precedenti greci della figura del 'servus currens' della commedia romana," *Pan* 2 (1974) 5-15. Among the fragments of Roman comedy, Caecilius 132-3 R³ and Turpilius 69-70 R³ also suggest the *currens*.

Out of my way, strangers and friends, while I do my
job: everyone run, scoot, and clear a path,
or I'll send someone headlong by head or elbow, shoulder
   or knee.
                              (*Curc.* 280–282)

Eighteen lines of threats and abuse precede Curculio's eventual recognition of his master Phaedromus, who has been present from the beginning. Terence seems impatient with such foolishness, ridiculing a rival dramatist,

> qui nuper fecit servo currenti in via
> decesse populum: quor insano serviat?
>
> who recently had a crowd in the street yield place
> to a running slave: Why would it indulge a madman?
>   (*HT* 31–32)

The logic of this criticism strikes at the very heart of the *currens'* comic appeal; Curculio's entrance is so funny precisely because it is so absurd. Arrant foolishness of this type does not suit Terence, but neither does he wish to sacrifice the comic potential of such scenes. There are five running slaves in his six plays. Geta of *Adelphoe* is the most colorful, rushing on stage with a flurry of words to rival Curculio's (*Ad.* 299ff.). He is too preoccupied to notice his mistress, and he has sharp words for imaginary bystanders.

> nil est quod malim quam illam totam familiam dari mi obviam,
> ut ego iram hanc in eos evomam omnem, dum aegritudo haec
>   est recens.
> satis mihi id habeam supplici dum illos ulciscar modo.
> seni animam primum exstinguerem ipsi qui illud produxit
>   scelus;
> tum autem Syrum inpulsorem, vah, quibus illum lacerarem
>   modis!

18   CHAPTER I

  sublimem medium primum arriperem et capite in terra
     statuerem, ut crebro dispergat viam;
  adulescenti ipsi eriperem oculos, post haec praecipitem darem;
  ceteros ruerem agerem raperem tunderem et prosternerem.

  There's nothing I'd like more than getting that whole family in
     my way,
  so I could spit my anger out at them, especially now when
     fresh.
  I'd take my knocks so long as I could give a few to them.
  First I'd bash the old man breathless, the one who caused the
     crime.
  Then that instigator Syrus, how I'd tear him into bits!
  First I'd grab him 'round the middle, stand him on his head,
     and stain the street with brains;
  I'd tear that young creep's eyes and fling him headlong;
  the rest I'd bash, bang, pluck, pound, and grind to pulp.
                                              (311–319)

The repetition and homoioteleuton of Geta's last line is typical of the *palliata* style. So is the violence of his speech, but Terence has transferred the generalized aggression of the typical *currens* to the specific situation. These are not just *any* imaginary bystanders, and Geta wants to encounter them. He imagines using the license of his role to attack Micio, Syrus, and Aeschinus, the people he holds responsible for the bad news he is bringing. Terence capitalizes on the expected behavior of the running messenger, using its traditional comic value but giving it added dramatic point.

  He may also build upon basic conventions of the comic stage. The limited settings of New Comedy, for example, confined dramatized action to a public street or other open place. When pregnant girls go into labor, people on the stage can hear their cries. Thus, at *Aulularia* 682ff., Plautus' young man Lyconides stands outside Euclio's house, begging his mother to help him marry the miser's daughter, Phaedria. The offstage cries of the girl in childbirth punctuate his appeal and move Eunomia to action.

> EUN. et caussa iusta est, siquidem ita est ut praedicas,
> te eam compressisse vinolentum virginem.
> LY. egone ut te advorsum mentiar, mater mea?
> PH. perii, mea nutrix. opsecro te, uterum dolet.
> Iuno Lucina, tuam fidem! LY. em, mater mea,
> tibi rem potiorem video: clamat, parturit.
> EUN. i hac intro mecum, gnate mi, ad fratrem meum,
> ut istuc quod me oras impetratum ad eo auferam.

> EUN. Your case is strong, if it is as you say, that you
> were drunk and got his daughter pregnant.
> LY. Mother, am I the sort to lie to you?
> PH. I'm done for, nurse. Please! The pain begins.
> Juno of Childbirth, help me! LY. There, mother,
> is an even stronger reason: she cries, she's giving birth.
> EUN. Come inside with me, son, to my brother.
> I'll ask him to do what you require.
>
> (688–695)

There is a similar moment in Terence's *Andria*, but old Simo reacts quite differently. Believing Glycerium's pregnancy to be a sham, he takes her sudden cry as proof of Davus' trickery.

> SI. haec primum adfertur iam mi ab hoc fallacia:
> hanc simulant parere, quo Chremetem absterreant.
> GL. Iuno Lucina, fer opem, serva me, obsecro.
> SI. hui tam cito? ridiculum: postquam ante ostium
> me audivit stare, adproperat. non sat commode
> divisa sunt temporibus tibi, Dave, haec.

> SI. This is the first step in the plan to trick me.
> They pretend she's giving birth to frighten Chremes off.

GL. Juno of Childbirth, help! Save me, please!
SI. What? So fast? Absurd: no sooner does she hear
I'm by the door than now she hurries. Your timing,
Davus, is not so good.

(471–476)

In the very next scene he overhears the midwife's instructions to her charge, and again he challenges the likelihood of the situation.

> non imperabat coram quid opus facto esset puerperae,
> sed postquam egressast, illis quae sunt intus clamat de via.
> o Dave, itan contemnor abs te?

> She didn't order in person what the childbirth requires,
> but once outside she yells from the street to those within.
> Davus, do you think me such a fool?

(490–492)

Terence seems to be mocking the conventions of offstage birth and intimate conversations in the street, but he is also turning such skepticism to dramatic advantage.[24] The birth is genuine, and the laugh is on Simo, who throughout the play makes trouble for himself by refusing to accept the clear evidence of his senses.

In each case Terence has preserved the structural function of the convention and given it a comic twist, but he carefully integrates its humor into his overall design. These scenes always ad-

---

[24] A. W. Gomme, "Menander" in *Essays in Greek History and Literature* (Oxford 1937) 260 n. 1, faults Terence for simultaneously mocking and using this convention. Büchner, *TT* 75, is more tolerant of Terence's irony, though he misses its specific dramatic relevance. Terentian characters make similar allusions to the convention at *Ph.* 818 and *Eun.* 894–895. A. G. Katsouris, *Tragic Patterns in Menander* (Athens 1975) 156–162, discusses offstage childbirth in New Comedy and its tragic roots. To date, all the comic examples are Latin, and only at *Truc.* 462f. is the birth really a sham, presented there as a *fait accompli* without offstage shouts.

vance, never retard, the action. Such streamlining not only distinguishes Terence from Plautus, but runs counter to the established practice of *palliata* comedy, which was to embellish stock elements. Roman dramatists readily turned the entrance of a running slave into a show-stopping monologue or an expository prologue into a comedian's stand-up routine because the humor and spectacle of such scenes played especially well before the raucous and mobile crowds at Roman *ludi*. By refusing to follow suit, Terence sacrificed a traditional formula for success, but he evidently had to take this risk. Though the Plautine style of elaboration could be very funny, it distorted the original shape and focus of Greek New Comedy. By avoiding fantasy and exaggeration, Terence freed himself to present characters rather than caricatures and to develop rather than obscure the genuine problems of family relationships and social obligations on which his comic material was based. Menander's style of comedy, more often wry than farcical and poignant rather than riotous, was his regular model for doing so. Unlike Plautus, who borrowed more often from Philemon and Diphilus, Terence based four of his six plays on Menandrean originals and two on plays by Menander's closest successor, Apollodorus of Carystus. Menander, too, avoids having individual characters or stock scenes distort the basic structure of a play. The only certain *servus currens* in the new papyri, for example, is Pyrrhias of *Dyskolos*, who has no trouble finding his master and wastes barely five lines of dialogue before getting to his message (81ff.). Davus of Terence's *Andria* is just this kind of running slave, with only a perfunctory show of breathlessness and confusion (338ff.). Yet Terence, though suggesting Menandrean standards of humor and dramatic focus, remained a Roman dramatist working in the Roman tradition. He may struggle with Roman conventions and stereotypes, but he does not abandon them. To read Menandrean subtleties into him, to think he could turn Greek plays into Latin ones without allowing for the requirements of his own tradition and culture, creates serious difficulties of interpretation for the modern critic.

Consider the ways a dramatist signals his meaning to the audience. He may want to tell them where their sympathies should lie, or what to think about a character. Monologue is one of Menander's most effective ways to do this. Smikrines' monologue at *Aspis* 149ff. quickly confirms our suspicion that he is a miser; at *Samia* 616ff. Moschion makes clear why he will pretend to leave home. Terence can make similar use of short monologues. The action of *Eunuchus* looks rather different if we see Thais as simply the *meretrix mala* of comic stereotype (a view encouraged in the opening scene) or as someone more complex and sympathetic. Terence recognized the need for clarity on this point and soon has Thais reveal her motives.

>   me miseram, fors[it]an hic mihi parvam habeat fidem
>   atque ex aliarum ingeniis nunc me iudicet.
>   ego pol, quae mihi sum conscia, hoc certo scio
>   neque me finxisse falsi quicquam neque meo
>   cordi esse quemquam cariorem hoc Phaedria.

>   Alas, perhaps he has little faith in me
>   and judges me by other women's characters.
>   But I, who know myself, know this for sure:
>   I have never told a lie, nor is
>   anyone dearer to me than Phaedria.
>   (197–201)

Thus assured of her sincerity, we watch the play with a certain sympathy for her and ironic amusement at the agonies of her admirers. The monologue orients us clearly and effectively, but its appeal for our good will is hardly subtle.

The dramatic power and effectiveness of Knemon's great speech in *Dyskolos* illustrates a much more sophisticated use of monologue, for in that scene Menander both advances the plot and shapes our understanding of it (*Dys.* 702ff.). The mechanics of Knemon's entrance, the change of meter, and the very length of the monologue after only brief glimpses of the title figure signal its importance and seize our attention. The plot turns on his sudden change of heart and the delegation of responsibility for his daughter's marriage. A famous moment toward the end of Terence's *Adelphoe* may appear comparable. After playing the coarse, obstructive country brother with consistent verve, Demea suddenly renounces his severity and frugality.

age age, nunciam experiamur contra ecquid ego possiem
blande dicere aut benigne facere, quando hoc provocat.
ego quoque a meis me amari et magni fieri postulo:
si id fit dando atque obsequendo, non posteriores feram.

When then, now I'll see if I can top him
in sweet talk and generosity, since he provokes it.
I too want my family to think me loving and important.
If giving's what it takes, and saying yes, I won't be left behind.
(877–880)

The subsequent action of *Adelphoe* seems to turn on this monologue just as Knemon's *apologia* settles the course of *Dyskolos*. But how should we interpret this change? If Demea means what he says, his apparent victory over his brother Micio at the end becomes a punishment of Micio's leniency. If he is only affecting a change to punish his brother, the ending is simply a joke at Micio's expense. Each interpretation has found scholarly exponents.[25] What signals of his meaning does Terence provide?

---

[25] A representative sample of modern opinions includes J. N. Grant, "The Ending of Terence's *Adelphoe* and the Menandrian Original," *AJP* 96 (1975) 42–60; N. A. Greenberg, "Success and Failure in the *Adelphoe*," *CW* 73 (1979/80) 221–236; V. Pöschl, "Das Problem der Adelphen des Terenz," *SHAW* 4 (1975) 5–24; and H. Tränkle, "Micio und Demea in den terenzischen Adelphen," *MH* 29 (1972) 241–255. Each includes full bibliography.

Since *Adelphoe* is based on a Menandrean original, critics wise in the ways of Menander might build a reading on the following points.

First is the monologue form itself, especially this kind of monologue where an old man announces a discovery by making a general statement and then applying it to himself.

> Numquam ita quisquam bene subducta ratione ad
>   vitam fuit
> quin res aetas usus semper aliquid adportet novi,
> aliquid moneat: ut illa quae te scisse credas nescias,
> et quae tibi putaris prima, in experiundo repudies,
> quod nunc mi evenit.

> Nobody ever reckons his accounts in life in such a way
> that circumstances, time, experience don't bring him some-
>   thing new,
> have something new to teach: what you thought you knew,
>   you don't,
> and what seemed most important, you cast aside in practice.
> That's what I've discovered.
>
>   (855–859)

A Menandrean Demeas begins a speech with the same device, and he had many successors.

>   ]. δρόμου καλοῦ
> χειμὼν ἀπροσδόκητος ἐξαίφνης [
> ἐλθών. ἐκεῖνος τοὺς ἐν εὐδίαι ποτὲ
> θέοντας ἐξήραξε κἀνεχαίτισεν.
> τοιοῦτο γὰρ καὶ τοὐμόν ἐστι νῦν.

>   while sailing easily
> a sudden storm comes up . . .
> It shatters and tips those who once

were calmly running free.
That's exactly my position now.

(*Sa.* 206ff.,
cf. Pl. *Cas.* 563ff., *Merc.* 225ff.)

Not all these monologues are equally serious, but in each case an old man is at least telling the truth.[26] A second possible clue is Demea's echo of Micio's words from the first scene.

MICIO: ego hanc clementem vitam urbanam atque otium
secutus sum et, quod fortunatum isti putant,
uxorem numquam habui. ille contra haec omnia:
ruri agere vitam; semper parce ac duriter
se habere; uxorem duxit; nati filii
duo

I've pursued an easy life in town,
enjoyed my leisure and, what some think lucky,
never had a wife. He's been just the opposite:
a country life, always being hard and
tight. He married. Had two
sons.

(42–47)

DEMEA: ille suam semper egit vitam in otio, in conviviis,
clemens placidus, nulli laedere os, adridere omnibus;
sibi vixit, sibi sumptum fecit: omnes bene dicunt,
amant.
ego ille agrestis saevos tristis parcus truculentus tenax
duxi uxorem: quam ibi miseriam vidi! nati filii,
alia cura.

---

[26] Greek dramatic monologues (as distinct from prologues) do not generally mislead the audience. See W. Schadewaldt, *Monolog und Selbstgespräch* (Berlin 1926) 28–31 and especially O. Rieth, *Die Kunst Menanders in den "Adelphen" des Terenz* (Hildesheim 1964) 111–113.

> He's always spent his life in leisure, parties,
> easy, relaxed, with scowls for none, laughs for all:
> lived for himself, spent for himself. Everyone
>   loves and praises him.
> I'm the hick, rough, gruff, tight, mean, firm.
> I married. What misery I saw there! Sons were born,
> another trouble.
>
> (863–868)

We believed Micio, and this repetition might encourage us to believe Demea as well. Third is a point of diction.

> illum amant, me fugitant; illi credunt consilia omnia,
> illum diligant, apud illum sunt ambo, ego desertus sum;
> illum ut vivat optant, meam autem mortem exspectant scilicet.

> Him they love, me they flee. Him they trust completely.
> Him they choose. They're both with him. I'm deserted.
> They hope he lives. No doubt they'd like to see me dead.
>
> (872–874)

The anaphora here has a distinctly tragic sound, as in this line from Ennius' *Alexander* (40 J):

> men obesse, illos prodesse, me obstare, illos obsequi.

> That I oppose, they defend, I obstruct, they concede!

Demea's frustration and bitterness gain in power from the dignity of their expression. Last is a curious point of meter.

> ἐγὼ δ' ἄγροικος ἐργάτης σκυθρός πικρός
> φειδωλός.

> I'm a farmer, a workman sullen, harsh,
> tight.
>
> (Menander, fr. 11 K–T)

This fragment is generally regarded as the original of Demea's line 866 quoted above.²⁷ If this identification is correct, Terence has deliberately changed the iambic trimeters of his original to trochaic septenarii, the Latin equivalent of the catalectic trochaic tetrameters of Knemon's parallel speech in *Dyskolos*.

This sounds, then, like a serious monologue with calculated approximations to the tragic echoes that make Knemon's speech poignant and convincing. Form, diction, and meter all suggest that Demea is speaking honestly and that his speech marks a dramatic climax. These are certainly the Menandrean signals, and this is how we would read them there. But as students of *Adelphoe* know only too well, believing Demea here causes difficulty at the end, when a bemused Micio asks what has come over him.

>   dicam tibi:
> ut id ostenderem, quod te isti facilem et festivom putant,
> id non fieri ex vera vita neque adeo ex aequo et bono,
> sed ex adsentando indulgendo et largiendo, Micio.
>
>   I'll tell you:
> I want to show that what these boys may think your free and easy life
> comes not from honest living and a truly generous heart,
> but from saying yes, indulgence, and extravagance, Micio.
>   (985–988)

The play has a final twist that contradicts Demea's earlier declaration. Donatus therefore believed that Demea only pretended to

---

²⁷ Photius attributes the line to Menander, but assignment to *Adelphoi B'* is modern, based upon this affinity to Terence. Note, however, that the rustic grouch was a common figure of the Greek stage and often prone to expressions of this kind. Cf. Men., *Dys.* 724–727 and Phrynichos, *Monotropos*, fr. 18K: ζῶ δὲ Τίμωνος βίον / ἄγαμον, ἄδουλον, ὀξύθυμον, ἀπρόσοδον / ἀγέλαστον, ἀδιάλεκτον, ἰδιογνώμονα. Kock compares Arist., *Nub.* 43ff. For the type, see W. Görler, "Knemon," *Hermes* 91 (1963) 268–287.

change his values. Some modern critics prefer to deny Demea's apparent meaning in the monologue or to suggest that his actions simply take him further into extravagance than he had originally planned.[28] Whichever explanation we prefer, the critical problem remains the same: close reading of Demea's monologue leads to difficulties with the ending of *Adelphoe*. The speech is either less true or less definitive than its Greek equivalent. Terence has created ambiguity where Menander so often created clarity.

There is an important lesson in this. The Greek aesthetic that Terence suggests is often only superficial. Sometimes, as here, a device with good Greek parallels nevertheless fails to function in the Greek way. Terence may also make structural changes in his model that affect the form and meaning of the new Latin play: replacing monologue with dialogue, interpolating characters and whole scenes from a second model, doubling the love motif. Such overt changes, more often revealed by his own prologue or the comments that Donatus aimed at schoolboys of the fourth century A.D. than by glaring flaws in the dramatic structure, have encouraged an analytic approach to Terence that reconstructs the lost originals from these clues and then measures his achievement by comparison with them. The best practitioners of this method avoid circularity and have taught us much about his dramatic technique. Yet there is more to understanding Terence than this. We can learn by looking forward as well as back. Early in this century Friedrich Leo recognized in Terence's "neue römische Urbanität" the beginning of new literary developments, and there is much to be gained by discussing Terence in his own Roman context.[29] His position near the beginning of a new Latin

---

[28] Don., *ad Ad.* 992: "hic ostendit Terentius magis Demeam simulasse mutatos mores quam mutavisse." In his edition of *Adelphoe* (Cambridge 1976) 26–29 and 240–241, R. H. Martin argues that Demea changes his mind again without telling anyone. For still other explanations, see Greenberg (above, n. 25) 233–236 and further references there.

[29] Leo, *GRL* 253. He is thinking primarily of diction. For the analytic

tradition is at least as significant as his culmination of an old Greek one. How are we to understand that contribution?

We now know enough about the development of Roman experience and taste in the second century and about the capabilities of *palliata* comedy to recognize that Terence altered his models not simply to appeal to a semi-literate rabble, but because he cared for the subtleties of his originals and sought effective Roman equivalents for them. Though close translation might have reproduced the outward form of a Greek play, it would have failed to convey its original meaning and excellence.[30] It would have made a bad Latin play, and Terence in fact castigates a rival for just that fault.

> qui bene vortendo et easdem scribendo male
> ex Graecis bonis Latinas fecit non bonas.
>
> who, through careful translation and terrible writing,
> made bad Latin plays from good Greek ones.
> (*Eun.* 7–8)

Terence had to reproduce the significance of his models using the techniques of his own tradition, and our aims and methods for measuring his success cannot ignore the nature of that task. It is necessary to think of Terence first in Roman terms. We must measure the plays against his own goals, limiting our recourse to reconstructed Greek standards or to a modern sense of dramatic excellence. We must also recognize that the plays are products of constant experiment. Each has its own focus and interest. Not

---

method and its contributions, see S. M. Goldberg, "Scholarship on Terence," *CW* 75 (1981) 84–86 and 100–102.

[30] Not that "faithful" translation in the modern sense would have been likely at Rome. See S. Brock, "Aspects of Translation Technique in Antiquity," *GRBS* 20 (1979) 69–87, and B. Gentili, *Theatrical Performances in the Ancient World* (Amsterdam 1979) 89–105. W. R. Chalmers, "Plautus and his Audience" in *Roman Drama*, ed. T. A. Dorey and D. R. Dudley (London 1965) 21–50, discusses the sophistication of the Roman audience.

every play follows the same pattern; not all their innovations in style and structure may work equally well. How to distinguish success from failure and how to establish appropriate criteria for judging them are the main challenges that Terence presents to modern readers. A fair response to them will produce the understanding that we seek.

[11]

THE PROLOGUES

Because Terence's prologues answer charges leveled at him by jealous rivals, they affect a contentious tone reminiscent of Aristophanes' more combative *parabaseis*. Yet while Aristophanes would tuck his polemic into the middle of a play, by which time the audience was safely engaged in its comedy and might well savor the resulting change of pace, Terence thrusts his quarrel to the front and abandons entirely the expository prologue so common in Greek New Comedy. This is a new technique for beginning a play, and also a risky one. Modern historians of literature are understandably intrigued by the tantalizing glimpse he thus provides of old aesthetic arguments. An audience just settling into place amid the bustle of a Roman public festival could well have reacted differently. The lack of formal exposition might not itself have taxed their patience. Such Plautine comedies as *Curculio* and *Epidicus* have come down to us without any prologues at all, and while it is possible that introductory speeches have been lost in transmission, they are not really necessary. The opening scenes of these plays are themselves designed to meet the needs of a new and uninformed audience.[1] In other plays, the prologues avoid exposition. The *Trinummus* prologue does so explicitly.

---

[1] E. Fantham, "Plautus in Miniature. Compression and Distortion in the *Epidicus*," *Papers of the Liverpool Latin Seminar* 3 (1981) 1–28, esp. 5–10, suggests that the Greek originals of *Epidicus* and *Curculio* had delayed prologues that Plautus has suppressed. *Mostellaria*, *Persa*, and *Stichus* also lack prologues; we cannot tell about *Bacchides*. Duckworth, *NRC* 211–218 surveys Plautus' varied practice in prologues.

> sed de argumento ne exspectetis fabulae:
> senes qui huc venient, i rem vobis aperient.
>
> Don't expect the plot of this play:
> The old men coming out will explain things to you.
> (*Trin.* 16–17)[2]

Plautus can address the crowd this way because Roman audiences did not necessarily expect or require expository prologues. It was neither difficult nor unusual for the dramatist to introduce characters and situations in the course of his play. What is remarkable about Terence's prologues, then, is not that they too avoid explanatory introductions. Only *Hecyra* is seriously affected by the absence of omniscient exposition, and it, as we shall later see, is in many ways a special case. The true oddity lies in Terence's substitution of arcane literary polemics. What models did he have for such an innovation, and what led him to think that audiences would accept it?

I

Once when Diphilus dined with the hetaira Gnathaena, she served him wine cooled by snow. When the startled dramatist asked what had made his wine so cold, she replied that she had poured some of his prologues into it (Ath. 580). Formal prologues, especially formal prologues of the expository sort, easily grow cold and a little tedious. A touch of Diphilus' ψυχροτής survives in the long prologue of Plautus' *Rudens*, and audiences no doubt felt grateful to the speaker in an unidentified comic fragment who promised not to be such a μακρολόγος θεός.[3] Menan-

---

[2] Cf. Ter., *Ad.* 22–23: "dehinc ne exspectetis argumentum fabulae, / senes qui primi venient, ii partem aperient." This sounds like a formula, and thus hardly a surprise to the audience.

[3] P. Argent. 53 = n. 252 in C. Austin, *Comicorum Graecorum fragmenta in papyris reperta* (Berlin 1973). A heavily restored text was published by D. L.

der seems to have avoided tedium in his prologues by restricting their expository content and often by delaying their appearance. When Tyche interrupts the action of *Aspis* to deliver a prologue, for example, she says little that is essential for understanding the plot. We learn nothing from her that we could not learn in a different way or at another time, but her revelations so early in the play shape our attitudes toward the action and its characters. Menander creates a thematic rather than purely expository link between prologue and play. Though sophisticated and effective, however, his prologues are rather bloodless little speeches that deliberately put distance between audience and characters.[4] Rarely humorous and never fantastic, they do their work with a smooth and calculated precision.

The Latin prologues of the Plautine corpus offer a different answer to the problem of expository tedium. Consider the case of *Asinaria*:

> Hoc agite sultis, spectatores, nunciam,
> quae quidem mihi atque vobis res vortat bene
> gregique huic et dominis atque conductoribus.
> face nunciam tu, praeco, omnem auritum poplum.
> age nunc, reside, cave modo ne gratiis.   5
> nunc quid processerim huc et quid mi voluerim
> dicam: ut sciretis nomen huiius fabulae;
> nam quod ad argumentum attinet, sane brevest.

Page as no. 60 in vol. 3 of his Loeb *Select Papyri* (Cambridge and London 1962). Despite the famous disclaimer, the prologue-speaker still provides ample expository information. See O. Bianco, "Il frammento della *Poiesis* di Antifane ed un prologo anonimo," *RCCM* 6 (1961) 91–98.

[4] The technique was perhaps learned from Euripides. Compare R. Hamilton, "Prologue, Prophecy, and Plot in Four Plays of Euripides," *AJP* 99 (1978) 277–302, and S. M. Goldberg, "The Style and Function of Menander's *Dyskolos* Prologue," *SO* 53 (1978) 57–68. For a survey of Menander's prologues, see S. Ireland, "Prologues, Structure, and Sentences in Menander," *Hermes* 109 (1981) 178–188.

> nunc quod me dixi velle vobis dicere
> dicam: huic nomen graece Onagost fabulae;   10
> Demophilus scripsit, Maccus vortit barbare;
> Asinariam volt esse, si per vos licet.
> inest lepos ludusque in hac comoedia,
> ridicula res est. date benigne operam mihi
> ut vos, ut alias, pariter nunc Mars adiuvet.   15
>
> Pay attention now, spectators, if you please:
> I heartily hope it will benefit me and you,
> this company, its managers, and producers.
> Herald, give this whole crowd ears now.
> All right, that's enough. Be sure to send a bill.   5
> Now as to why I've come here and what I want;
> I want you to know the name of this play.
> As for the plot, that is quite simple.
> Now I shall say what I said I wanted to
> say: this play is called Onagos in Greek.   10
> Demophilus wrote it. Maccus turned it barbarian.
> He wants to call it Asinaria, if you agree.
> There's wit and fun in this comedy,
> an amusing subject. Kindly give me your attention
> so that now, as ever, Mars will be with you.   15

This speech reveals another kind of calculation. Though extravagant and funny, it is no less studied in its effects than the prologues of Menander. Its verbosity is deliberate. The expanded objects of line three form a tricolon of ascending stature in the theatrical hierarchy. *Omnem auritum poplum* is an imaginative locution for the more usual *animum advortere*. The indirect questions of line six are synonymous, and the *dixi . . . dicere dicam* sequence in lines nine and ten makes repetition itself a joke. The stage business with the herald that goes on between lines four and five would further protract the prologue's delivery. Nearly every one of these devices has a parallel elsewhere among the

Plautine prologues. *Menaechmi* has a similar opening. *Poenulus* has the same play with a herald, another version of the *auritus* locution, and a similar conclusion. The *vortit barbare* joke reappears in *Trinummus* and has echoes in *Mercator* and *Casina*.[5] Yet the cumulative effect of these formulae is ease and spontaneity. The short sentences, the seemingly artless repetition of *nunciam* (1, 4) and *nunc* (5, 6, 9, 15), and the frequent imperatives suggest the choppy redundancies of colloquial speech. At the same time the ironic petition of *sultis* and *si per vos licet* reveals the speaker's mastery of his task and his situation. Although an actor himself, he sets himself apart from both audience and *grex*, and his joke on *barbare* plays with the convention of Latin comedies presented with Greek settings and dress. He also knows precisely where his speech is going: nine lines to bring the crowd to order, a four-line announcement, and a brief *captatio* whose final words echo the opening.

No Greek parallels for such a prologue exist. Sections of expository material from the Greek originals are no doubt embedded in the longer prologues to such plays as *Aulularia*, *Captivi*, and *Rudens*, but this naming of title and author and this kind of verbal play appear first in Plautus. The Roman dramatist had to win his audience in a way that Greek poets did not have to do, and Plautus responded to the different requirements of his theatre with this different emphasis in his prologues. In doing so he drew upon the distinct qualities of the Roman comic style. The prologues share the diction and the humor of the plays as a group, while Plautus tailors the approach of each prologue speaker to the requirements of the individual play.[6] Thus, while

---

[5] Specific parallels are *Asin.* 1–3 ~ *Men.* 1–2; *Asin.* 4–5 ~ *Poen.* 11–15; *Asin.* 6–12 ~ *Trin.* 16–20 (cf. *Cas.* 30–34, *Merc.* 9–10); *Asin.* 13–15 ~ *Cas.* 21–22, *Poen.* 128.

[6] Useful works on the Plautine prologues include Leo, *PlF* 188–247; W. Kraus, "*Ad spectatores* in der römischen Komödie," *WS* 52 (1934) 66–83; and K. Abel, *Die Plautusprologe* (Frankfurt 1955). For the similarity of form

Arcturus speaks with a dignity that befits the exotic romanticism of *Rudens*, the *Amphitruo* prologue casts Mercury as a stand-up comedian, because Plautus must establish his gods as comic characters to prevent his play from becoming a grotesque melodrama. Mercury's singularly long prologue gives Plautus the time he needs to create a comic role for the god, and the result, as in many of these prologues, is a masterpiece of practical writing for the comic stage.

The stylistic unity of introduction and play is the key to its success. Each prologue speaks in a language audiences know and enjoy, thus securing their good will and binding them closer to the play that will follow. Plautus works for his audiences' attention, but he is confident that they will grant it. Because Roman audiences liked his plays, even a later producer can be sure of acceptance.

> haec quom primum acta est, vicit omnis fabulas.
> ea tempestate flos poetarum fuit,
> qui nunc abierunt hinc in communem locum.
> sed tamen apsentes prosunt pro praesentibus.
>
> This play, when first produced, beat all the rest.
> Those were the days when poets flowered,
> poets now gone to their just reward.
> But though absent, they profit us as if present.
> (*Cas.* 17–20)

These lines were added to the original prologue for a revival of *Casina* sometime after Plautus' death.[7] Their alliteration and

---

between Plautine and Greek prologues, see R. B. Lloyd, "Two Prologues: Menander and Plautus," *AJP* 84 (1963) 146–161, and for the unique requirements of the Roman stage, E. W. Handley, "Some Thoughts on New Comedy in Latin," *Dioniso* 46 (1975) 117–132.

[7] See Abel (above, n. 6) 55–61. The authenticity of other Plautine prologues is also questionable. For example, H. D. Jocelyn, "Imperator histricus," *YCS* 21 (1969) 95–124, argues that the extant *Poenulus* prologue is ac-

wordplay reflect familiar mannerisms of Roman comic diction, and the speaker's assurance stems from the knowledge that audience, actor, and playwright share the same tastes and the same dramatic values. A dramatist less willing to exploit traditional devices, and thus less sure of his audience, will not be able to introduce a play this way. Terence was certainly such a dramatist, and this was a problem he had to face.

The need to bring an unruly outdoor audience to order was as pressing for Terence as it had been for his predecessors, but he went about the task rather differently. The first prologue to *Hecyra*, uncommonly short but characteristically artful, makes the difference clear.

> Hecyra est huic nomen fabulae. haec quom datast
> nova, novom intervenit vitium et calamitas
> ut neque spectari neque cognosci potuerit:
> ita populus studio stupidus in funambulo
> animum occuparat. nunc haec planest pro nova,   5
> et is qui scripsit hanc ob eam rem noluit
> iterum referre ut iterum possit vendere.
> alias cognostis eius: quaeso hanc noscite.

> This play is called Hecyra. When first offered,
> uncommon bad luck and disaster intervened,
> preventing it from being seen and appreciated.
> The crowd, struck dumb with desire, wanted a
> tightrope walker. Now the play is good as new,   5
> and its author doesn't want you to think
> he's brought it back simply to sell it twice.
> You know his other plays. Meet this one, too.

---

tually a conflation of three separate acting scripts. Such an argument, if true, would support the view that the surviving texts represent traditional norms for the writing of *palliata* prologues, not just the unique genius of Plautus, and would lend further support to the arguments for a stylistic unity in the genre presented by Wright, *DiC*.

This little speech is perfectly symmetrical. The short announcement of title, set off by a hiatus rare in Terence, is balanced by the two short sentences of the concluding *captatio*. At the center is a simple core sentence (*ita populus . . . occuparat*) surrounded by two longer sentences which are themselves parallel. They have similar beginnings (*haec quom datast nova* ~ *nunc haec planest pro nova*), and each ends with an *ut*-clause. The central sentence explaining why the first production of the play failed is also the prologue's central idea. Terence's diction is as careful as his structure. The repeated demonstratives are emphatic. He plays quite effectively on *nova*, *novom* and *cognostis*, *noscite*, creates the memorable phrase *populus studio stupidus*, and pairs infinitives (*spectari* and *cognosci*, *referre* and *vendere*). The deliberately grandiose words *vitium* and *calamitas* have overtones of augury and grave misfortune, to suggest that external obstacles, not lack of merit, thwarted the first production.

The prologue's stark announcement of title, its alliteration and wordplay, and its avoidance of the *argumentum* can easily be paralleled in the Plautine corpus, but its departures from the Plautine norm are even more striking. Consider the matter of verbosity. Both this speech and the *Asinaria* prologue turn simple statements into long ones.

> quae quidem mihi atque vobis res vortat bene
> gregique huic et dominis atque conductoribus.
> (*Asin.* 2–3)
> haec quom datast
> nova, novom intervenit vitium et calamitas
> ut neque spectari neque cognosci potuerit.
> (*Hecyra* 1–3)

Plautus' multiplication of datives makes a logical progression but adds nothing significant to his sense. He is marking time, waiting for his audience to settle down and realize that the performance in this curtainless theatre has begun. He is even willing to win attention by making the prologue itself a comic routine: thus the herald. Each of Terence's accretions adds nuance to his basic sense. *Vitium* and *calamitas* are not synonyms, and Donatus takes *spectari* closely with the former and *cognosci* with the latter: "vitium quod non spectata est, calamitas quod non cognita" (Donat. *ad loc.*). Donatus, who had his own schoolman's notion of elegance, may be reaching a little far here, but Terence has clearly chosen his words with care to unfold the picture of a performance so plagued by bad luck that the audience could neither see the play nor appreciate it. When he does simply repeat words (*neque . . . neque, iterum . . . iterum*), he uses them to clarify his argument, not complicate it (cf. *Asin.* 9–10). Terence wastes no time and makes every line count. At the heart of this stylistic difference is a fundamental difference in attitude toward the audience. *Asinaria* treats the crowd with familiarity, reaching out from the very first line with easy and entertaining banter. Terence is comparatively stiff. His speaker simply states the facts of the case and does not address the audience directly until the last line. Nor does he take their acceptance for granted. The prologue is extraordinarily contentious. In eight lines Terence disparages an earlier audience, defends himself against the charge of reviving a turkey for financial gain, and asks the present audience for better treatment. This is a daring strategy. The composition of his new audience was unlikely to differ much from the one that preferred the tightrope walker, and any defense of *Hecyra* cannot help but recall earlier doubts about its quality.[8] Why does Terence take

---

[8] The second surviving prologue to *Hecyra* reveals that Terence did not in fact run this risk successfully. After an auspicious beginning, the second production was stopped when the audience abandoned the play for gladiators (*Hec.* 39–41). The structural integrity of this first prologue, incidentally, tells against the recurring suggestion that it is either fragmentary or late. For discussion of its authenticity, see D. Klose, *Die Didaskalien und Prologe des Terenz* (Bamberg 1966) 71–78, who argues for its "absolute Vollständigkeit."

this risk? Why does he give his audience not a joke or an *argumentum*, but an argument? This kind of prologue is neither Menandrean nor Plautine. Terence's model for it is not dramatic.

II

Drama was not the only oral art to develop sophistication in the middle years of the Republic, and not the only available source of literary models. Though later tastes found the oratory of this period a little harsh and uncouth, it had nevertheless developed a style well suited to the requirements of oral argument and oral delivery.[9] Its methods were comparatively simple. Clarity and emphasis came largely from the repetition of words, syntactic structures, and ideas. The sound patterns of assonance and alliteration, homoioteleuton, the *figura etymologica*, and the like were the predominant aids to delivery, and orators worked pairing, parallelism, and tricola very hard. Word choice too owed much to sound. Thus the elder Cato liked the resonance of nouns in *-tudo*, adjectives in *-bundus* and *-osus*, and the short perfect in *-ere*. He preferred *mortalis* to *homo* and *atque* to *et* and *ac*.[10] Such devices, however obvious, could be extremely effective, as the following example will show.

In 190 B.C. Cato denounced the high-handed tactics of the consular Q. Minucius Thermus, who was claiming a triumph for campaigns in Liguria.[11] The surviving fragment of his speech *De falsis pugnis* runs as follows (frag. 58 M.):

There is a bibliography in H. Gelhaus, *Die Prologe des Terenz* (Heidelberg 1972) 8, n. 1, but Gelhaus himself does not discuss the text.

[9] "Antiquior est huius sermo," says Cicero of Cato, "et quaedam horridiora verba. ita enim tum loquebantur." (*Brut.* 68) This did not stop Cicero from admiring his illustrious predecessor: cf. *Orat.* 20, *Brut.* 65–66. There is a fine appraisal of Cato as orator in Leo, *GRL* 284–290.

[10] Full discussions of Cato's diction are M. T. Sblendorio, "Note sullo stile dell' oratoria Catoniana," *AFLC* 34 (1971) 5–32, and R. Till-C. de Meo, *La lingua di Catone* (Rome 1968). There is also a helpful chapter on Cato's oratory in A. E. Astin, *Cato the Censor* (Oxford 1978) 131–156.

[11] Liv. 37.46.1–6. For the background, see Astin (above, n. 10) 34, 63, 65.

dixit a decemviris parum bene sibi cibaria curata esse. iussit vestimenta detrahi atque flagro caedi. decemviros Bruttiani verberavere, videre multi mortales. Quis hanc contumeliam, quis hoc imperium, quis hanc servitutem ferre potest? nemo hoc rex ausus est facere: eane fieri bonis, bono genere gnatis, boni consultis? ubi societas? ubi fides maiorum? insignitas iniurias, plagas, verbera, vibices, eos dolores atque carnificinas per dedecus atque maximam contumeliam, inspectantibus popularibus suis atque multis mortalibus, te facere ausum esse? set quantum luctum, quantum gemitum, quid lacrimarum, quantum fletum factum audivi! servi iniurias nimis aegre ferunt: quid illos, bono genere gnatos, magna virtute praeditos, opinamini animi habuisse atque habituros, dum vivent?

He said his provisions had not been sufficiently well arranged by the decemvirs. He ordered their clothes stripped and a beating with the lash. Bruttiani beat the decemvirs. Many people saw it. Who could endure this insult, this tyranny, this slavery? No king has dared do this. Should such things be borne by good men, born of good families, of good intentions? Where is our alliance? Where is our ancestral honor? What glaring wrongs, blows, lashes, stripes, these pains and tortures with outrage and gravest insult as their fellow citizens and many people looked on have you dared to do? But what grief, what groans, what tears, what weeping have I heard! Slaves bitterly resent injuries. What feeling do you think these men, born of good families, outstanding in character, had and will have as long as they live?

The passage is a famous example of Cato's ferocity in attack and bears familiar hallmarks of early oratorical style. Alliteration and parallelism are exploited from the outset, and Cato's repetitions are as plain as they are effective. Yet the passage also shows fea-

---

All fragments of Roman oratory are cited from the third edition of E. Malcovati, *Oratorum romanorum fragmenta* (Turin 1967).

tures of real sophistication. Most apparent is the careful word order: the resonant chiasmus of *Bruttiani . . . mortales* and the interlocked phrase *nemo hoc rex*, which emphasizes the emotionally charged word by delaying it. *Opinamini animi* is a deliberate jingle caused by the hyperbaton of *quid . . . animi*. The parallelism in *nemo . . . facere* and *te facere ausum esse* emphasizes the sudden shift to the second person and encourages the insidious association of *rex* and *te*. Equally skillful is the use of the tricolon, which amounts to something more than the weighty verbosity of what is sometimes called the "padded style." *Contumelia, imperium, servitus* creates an ascending order of outrage. *Servitus* is the climax, and Cato echoes it in the last line, "servi iniurias nimis aegre ferunt." He is also adept at varying his grammatical subjects. There is the dramatic shift from third to second person in addressing Thermus, and a sense of rising indignation as the indefinite *quis* becomes the personal *audivi* and then shifts to the second plural as Cato shifts his own reaction to the reaction of his audience. Yet, though their mistreatment by Thermus provided the very substance of this passage, only in the last sentence are the *decemviri* themselves a grammatical subject. Attention centers on Thermus' action and our response to that action, not on his victims, and Cato's syntax reflects that emphasis.

There are suggestive stylistic parallels between this fragment and the first *Hecyra* prologue. We find the same fondness for paired infinitives and for developing an idea by a progression of near synonyms. There are also similar tricks of word order: chiasmus (*decemviros . . . mortales; haec . . . calamitas*) and parallelism for emphasis (*nemo hoc rex ~ te ausum esse; haec quom data nova ~ nunc haec planest pro nova*). And both authors respect the power of the short sentence. The crucial difference is on the syntactic level, and this leads us to some of the limitations of early oratorical style. Consider first the opening sentence of Cato's famous speech in 167 B.C. urging clemency for the Rhodians, who had leaned the wrong way in the Macedonian war.

> scio solere plerisque hominibus rebus secundis atque
> prolixis atque prosperis animum excellere atque super-
> biam atque ferociam augescere atque crescere.

> I know it is customary for many men, when things are
> favorable and successful and prosperous, to puff up,
> and for their pride and arrogance to grow and swell.
>
> (frag. 163 M.)

The connective *atque* here is doing triple duty. It links adjectives (*secundis . . . prosperis*) and nouns (*superbiam atque ferociam*). It pairs infinitives (*augescere atque crescere*), and it joins the two parts of the predicate, *animum excellere* and *superbiam . . . crescere*. The sentence rambles before the eye, but the sense comes easily to the ear as the speaker's inflection marks the significant units of meaning.[12] This reliance on voice rather than vocabulary or structure can, however, lead to the kind of syntactic diffuseness we find later in the speech, as Cato seeks to excuse the Rhodians' conduct.

> atque ego quidem arbitror Rodienses noluisse nos ita depug-
> nare, uti depugnatum est, neque regem Persen vinci. sed non
> Rodienses modo id noluere, sed multos populos atque multas
> nationes idem noluisse arbitror atque haut scio an partim
> eorum fuerint qui non nostrae contumeliae causa id noluerint
> evenire: sed enim id metuere, si nemo esset homo quem ve-
> reremur, quidquid luberet faceremus, ne sub solo imperio nos-

---

[12] Thus Astin (above, n. 10) 145: "There is a dependence on inflexions of the voice and slight pauses in delivery to make clear relationships which are not fully conveyed, as they would have been in a Ciceronian speech, by more complex grammatical structures." For discussion of *Pro Rodiensibus*, see Gel. 6.3, Astin 273–281, and especially the text and commentary of G. Calboli, *M. Porci Catonis Oratio Pro Rhodiensibus* (Bologna 1978). There are also helpful discussions in A. D. Leeman, *Orationis ratio* (Amsterdam 1963) 44–47, and M. von Albrecht, *Meister römischer Prosa* (Heidelberg 1971) 24–37.

> tro in servitute nostra essent. libertatis suae causa in ea sententia fuisse arbitror. . . .

> And I really think that the Rhodians did not want us to end the war as we did and have King Perses be defeated. But not only the Rhodians did not want that, but many peoples and many nations, I think, did not want the same thing, and I suspect there were some who did not want this to happen not to disgrace us, but because they feared this: if there were nobody whom we feared, we would do whatever we wished. They would be under our sole rule in slavery to us. For the sake of their own freedom I think they held this opinion. . . .
>
> (frag. 164 M.)

Here the repetition *noluisse . . . noluere . . . noluisse . . . noluerint* requires Cato to limit each negative with a corresponding, but not very graceful, *sed*. Even more striking is the use of *id . . . idem . . . id* first referring back to the events marked by the initial *ita*, and then followed by another *id* that looks ahead to the following *si-* and *ne-* clauses. He wisely follows this rambling sequence with a short sentence, but the vague *in ea sententia* adds neither special power nor point to what has gone before.

Cato's sequence of thought is not always so roughly marked, but a fragment of his *Suasio legis Voconiae*, dated to 169 B.C., offers connectives that are at least as naive.

> principio vobis mulier magnam dotem adtulit; tum magnam pecuniam recipit, quam in viri potestatem non conmittit, eam pecuniam viro mutuam dat; postea, ubi irata facta est, servum recepticium sectari atque flagitare virum iubet.

> Originally the woman brought you a large dowry. Then she withdraws a large sum which she does not entrust to her husband's care. This money she gives her husband as a loan. Later, when she grows angry, she orders her personal slave to hound and dun her husband.
>
> (frag. 158 M.)

This dependence on redundant pronouns and temporal adverbs to link sentences is characteristic of early prose. We find it, for example, in Ennius' translation of Euhemerus and in the fragments of Cato's *Origines*. Comedy often affects this style when telling stories, as, for instance, at *Andria* 220–224.

> et fingunt quandam inter se nunc fallaciam
> civem Atticam esse hanc: "fuit olim quidam senex
> mercator; navim is fregit apud Andrum insulam;
> is obiit mortem." ibi tum hanc eiectam Chrysidis
> patrem recepisse orbam parvam. fabulae!

> Now between them they're inventing a certain story
> that she's an Attic citizen: "Once on a time there was
> an old merchant. He was shipwrecked on Andros;
> He died." Then that Chrysis' father
> took in the orphaned girl. Fables!

Here the slave Davus is probably mimicking the innocent style of fables and children's stories, and in the next century the *Rhetorica ad Herennium* expressly advises against this kind of repetition in oratorical *narratio*, illustrating the point with lines in comic verse:

> Athenis Megaram vesperi advenit Simo;
> ubi advenit Megaram, insidias fecit virgini;
> insidias postquam fecit, vim in loco adtulit.

> Simo came to Megara from Athens in the evening;
> When he came to Megara, he plotted against a girl;
> When he carried out his plot, he got violent.
>   (*Rhet. Her.* 1.9.14)[13]

[13] The verses are Ribbeck's *Incerta* II but might as easily have been composed by the rhetorician to illustrate his point. This repetitive style can be traced back to Ennius' translation of Euhemerus, for which see E. Fraenkel, "Additional Notes on the Prose of Ennius," *Eranos* 49 (1951) 50–56.

The contrast between the obvious strength of Cato's oratory and the roughness of its syntax and diction is reflected in the ancient opinions of him, which are curiously divided. Early in *Brutus*, for example, Cicero equates Cato with Lysias, praising his acuity, precision, wit, and brevity: "Quis illo gravior in laudando, acerbior in vituperando, in sententiis argutior, in docendo edisserendoque subtilior?" (63) This is primarily a judgment of content, or at most of style as determined by the effectiveness of content, because it suits Cicero's purpose at this point in his dialogue to cite a worthy predecessor for his own goals in oratory. Later, however, Cicero's Atticus makes clear the absurdity of comparing Cato and Lysias in absolute terms: "orationes autem eius ut illis temporibus valde laudo: significant enim formam quandam ingeni, sed admodum impolitam et plane rudem" (*Brut.* 294). This judgment on the purely stylistic level is echoed by Quintilian, who thinks boys should not read too much of Cato and the Gracchi. Their own style, he fears, will become too harsh and bloodless (*horridus atque ieiunus*) if they fail to put the antique *vis* in historic perspective (*Inst.* 2.5.21). Yet Cato was certainly a pioneer in the right territory, and his achievement offers some justification for Aulus Gellius' more grandiose claim that "Catonem contentum eloquentia aetatis suae non fuisse et id iam tum facere voluisse quod Cicero postea perfecit" (*NA* 10.3.16). Cato's command of rhetorical figures and his powers of structure and argument are evident from the fragments, but when compared to the taut elegance of the Terentian prologues his diction is undeniably harsh. What kind of model was he for the dramatist? What links the prologues to this antique style of argument?

III

The pairings and parallelism, chiasmus and alliteration, of the first *Hecyra* prologue have offered some clues. A closer look at a longer speech will begin to show the extent of Terence's debt to contemporary oratory. His first effort was the prologue to *Andria*, produced the year after Cato's speech *Pro Rodiensibus*.

> Poeta quom primum animum ad scribendum adpulit,
> id sibi negoti credidit solum dari,
> populo ut placerent quas fecisset fabulas.
> verum aliter evenire multo intellegit;
> nam in prologis scribundis operam abutitur,   5
> non qui argumentum narret sed qui malevoli
> veteris poetae maledictis respondeat.
> nunc quam rem vitio dent quaeso animum adtendite.
> Menander fecit Andriam et Perinthiam.
> qui utramvis recte norit ambas noverit: 10
> non ita dissimili sunt argumento [s]et tamen
> dissimili oratione sunt factae ac stilo.
> quae convenere in Andriam ex Perinthia
> fatetur transtulisse atque usum pro suis.
> id isti vituperant factum atque in eo disputant   15
> contaminari non decere fabulas.
> faciuntne intellegendo ut nil intellegant?
> qui quom hunc accusant, Naevium Plautum Ennium
> accusant quos hic noster auctores habet,
> quorum aemulari exoptat neglegentiam   20
> potius quam istorum obscuram diligentiam.
> de[h]inc ut quiescant porro moneo et desinant
> male dicere, malefacta ne noscant sua.
> favete, adeste aequo animo et rem cognoscite,
> ut pernoscatis ecquid spei sit relicuom,   25
> posthac quas faciet de integro comoedias,
> spectandae an exigendae sint vobis prius.

> When first our poet turned his mind to writing,
> he thought his only job was that
> the plays he made should please the public.
> Now he knows how differently things work:

> he has to squander time in writing prologues 5
> not to sketch the plot but to reply to
> slanders from a poet old and mean.
> Consider, if you please, the bone they pick.
> Menander wrote an Andria and a Perinthia.
> Anyone who knows one well will know them both: 10
> they differ not so much in plot, but in their
> treatment of events and in the diction used.
> Our poet grants he transferred from Perinthia
> what suited Andria and used it as his own.
> They pick on this and argue that 15
> plays must not be contaminated.
> Does not such sensibility show lack of sense?
> Accuse him thus and Naevius, Plautus, Ennius
> all stand accused, whom our poet takes as models
> and whose negligence he'd rather emulate 20
> than carping critics' abstruse diligence.
> I recommend they now be still and quit their
> slander, or they'll hear their own faults catalogued.
> Now please be kind and fair and judge the case.
> See whether any hope remains 25
> that you will watch new plays he makes
> through to the end, or hiss them off the stage.

This prologue is the oldest example of Roman rhetorical argument to survive intact.[14] Its diction builds on Cato, not Plautus.

---

[14] The rhetorical quality of the Terentian prologues was first appreciated in detail by F. Leo, *Analecta plautina: De figuris sermonis II* (Göttingen 1898) = *Ausgewählte kleine Schriften* (Rome 1960) 135–149 and *GRL* 251–252. I owe much to his analysis. The prologues earn a place in histories of ancient rhetoric, e.g., Leeman (above, n. 12) 24–25, but the ramifications of Leo's work have not yet been developed. See also H. Haffter, *Untersuchungen zur altlateinischen Dichtersprache* (Berlin 1934) 99–101. A. Ronconi, "Analisi del pro-

Its persona is the courtroom pleader, and its content is shamelessly manipulated. Consider its mode of argument (5–7):

> nam in prologis scribundis operam abutitur,
> non qui argumentum narret sed qui malevoli
> veteris poetae maledictis respondeat.

Terence implies here that there are two kinds of prologues, one of acknowledged dramatic value and the other a veritable waste of effort. His rivals force him to write this second type and are therefore to blame if he is tedious. This artful distinction turns an ostensible excuse into an attack on the opposition and signals at the very outset a writer well skilled in debate.[15] His ability to turn a phrase, already noted in the first *Hecyra* prologue, is responsible for some famous lines unmistakably colored by rhetoric (13–16):

> quae convenere in Andriam ex Perinthia
> fatetur transtulisse atque usum pro suis.
> id isti vituperant factum atque in eo disputant
> contaminari non decere fabulas.

Here Terence says first what he has done, then records the fact of opposition to it, and finally puts his opponents' charge in ringing terms. Why does he make the accusation so memorable, especially since he does not really intend to refute it? The reason is rhetorical, and Cato's use of the same device makes its purpose clear.

---

logues," *PhQ* 6 (1927) 235–269, and H. B. Mattingly, "The Chronology of detail.

[15] Terence is perhaps adapting here the rhetorical *schema synkritikon* illustrated by Hermogenes, *Progymnasmata* (L. Spengel, *Rhetores Graeci II* [Leipzig 1854] 5): Μήδεια ἡ Αἰήτου θυγάτηρ ἀντὶ μὲν τοῦ σωφρονεῖν ἠράσθη, ἀντὶ δὲ τοῦ φυλάττειν τὸ χρυσόμαλλον δέρας προύδωκεν, ἀντὶ δὲ τοῦ σώζειν τὸν ἀδελφὸν Ἄψυρτον ἐφόνευσε.

> Rodiensis superbos esse aiunt id obiectantes quod mihi et liberis meis minime dici vellem. sint sane superbi. quid id ad nos attinet? idne irascimini, si quis superbior est quam nos?

> They say the Rhodians are proud, leveling a charge I would hardly want made against me or my children. Well, let them be proud. What is that to us? Should we be angry, if someone is more proud than we?

(frag. 169 M.)

Aulus Gellius, who marvels at this "mirifica et prope divina" evasion, explains Cato's strategy: "Absolutely nothing could be said with greater force or weight than this apostrophe against men proud of their deed, loving pride in themselves, but condemning it in others" (*NA* 6.3.51). The speaker phrases the accusation as extravagantly as possible so its absurdity may fall back with maximum weight upon the accusers. This is precisely what Terence does. *Contaminari* is deliberately chosen to inflate and obscure the nature of his deed. It is as colorful and hyperbolic a verb as Terence can find to mean "spoil," and he uses it to ridicule his opposition.[16] Having inflated their accusation to the point of parody, he then proceeds to evade it. "If I have spoiled plays," he argues, "so have Naevius, Plautus, and Ennius. I would rather imitate their *neglegentia* than my accusers' kind of *diligentia*." It is hardly clear from this passage that interpolation, Terence's own way of "spoiling" plays, was indeed the kind of *neglegentia* to be found in Naevius, Plautus, and Ennius, but Terence does

---

[16] This meaning for *contaminari*, first argued convincingly by W. Beare, "Contaminatio," *CR* 9 (1959) 7–11, now seems beyond question. Cf. M. Simon, "*Contaminatio* und *furtum* bei Terenz," *Helikon* 1 (1961) 487–492, and O. Kujorę, "A Note on *Contaminatio* in Terence," *CP* 69 (1974) 39–42. Ronconi (above, n. 14) 1137–1138 nevertheless revives the old notion of a technical sense, "to spoil by mixing" (*sconciare intrecciando; cose malamente unite*), but his arguments are unconvincing.

not want to be clear. He has created an antithesis as false as it is artful.

Terence makes a simple enough contrast between *diligentia* and *neglegentia*, but he reverses the expected value of each term. The addition of *obscura* makes *diligentia* pejorative, while mention of distinguished predecessors gives *neglegentia* an unexpectedly positive sense. In Terence generally, the word simply means "neglect"; for example, Chremes' neglect of his Lemnian family (*Phorm.* 571), or the failure of Chrysis' Andrian relatives to provide for her (*An.* 71). Only in the prologues, here and at *Adelphoe* 14 ("locum reprehensum qui praeteritus neglegentiast"), does it seem to mean "carelessness." Both of these passages refer specifically to the process of writing a play, and *neglegentia* in the context of composition means the studied ease of the careful writer. Cicero, for example, in discussing the appeal of the plain style, praised the *non ingrata neglegentia* of its diction with a warning against unwise separation of *neglegentia* and *diligentia*: "Illa enim ipsa contracta et minuta non neglegenter tractanda sunt sed quaedam etiam neglegentia est diligens" (*Orat.* 77–78).[17] Terence, keenly aware of the relationship between *elocutio* and *inventio*, knows as well as Cicero that literary *neglegentia* is a studied effect. The *Andria* prologue makes a false distinction between *neglegentia* and *diligentia* because Terence wants, not to clarify his method of composition or to advance a literary theory, but to abuse his opponents. He attributes to himself the easy grace of a master, not the labored fidelity of a pedantic copyist.

The essentially argumentative quality that runs throughout the prologue finds further confirmation in Terence's vocabulary,

---

[17] The same sentiment reappears in Quint., *Inst.* 8.3.87: "nam ipsa illa ἀφέλεια simplex et inadfectata habet quendam purum, qualis etiam in feminis amatur, ornatum, et sunt quaedam velut e tenui diligentia circa proprietatem significationemque munditiae." On *neglegentia* and the plain style, see C. Henderson, Jr., "Cato's Pine Cones and Seneca's Plums," *TAPA* 86 (1955) 256–267.

which has consistent legal overtones. Such words as *maledicta* and its echoes, *disputare, accusare, favere, cognoscere* and *fateor, aequus, isti* referring to the opposition, the shortened perfect *convenere*, and the connective *atque* all suggest the law court.[18] The material and structure of the speech are also forensic. Aristotle had observed that the *exordium* of a forensic speech must win the good will of its hearers just as a dramatic prologue does (*Rh.* 1415a), and the author of the *ad Herennium*, following Aristotle closely on this point, sees four ways to do so: "benivolos auditores facere quattuor modis possumus: ab nostra, ab adversariorum nostrorum, ab auditorum persona, et ab rebus ipsis" (1.4.8). Terence uses all four. He speaks of his own obligations and literary standards (1-3, 18-21), and he attacks his opponents as spiteful, foolish, and flawed in their own work (6-7, 15-17, 21-23). He addresses the particular point at issue (8-14), and he compliments the audience by alluding to their own power and acumen (24-27). All this is done in a tightly structured speech that is itself no simple *exordium* but, like a full-scale oration, divides neatly along oratorical lines into *exordium* (1-8), *narratio* (9-16), *argumentatio* (17-23), and *conclusio* (24-27).[19]

Terence's need to win his audience has led to an oratorical prologue. This whiff of the court is a common device in the *palliata* tradition. Plautus had demonstrated time and again that audiences loved to hear the language of contracts, litigation, and politics turned to new and unexpected purposes. Pseudolus enters

---

[18] Most of these examples are discussed by G. Focardi, "Linguaggio forense nei prologhi terenziani," *SIFC* 44 (1972) 55-88. A subsequent article, "Lo stile oratorio nei prologhi terenziani," *SIFC* 50 (1978) 70-89, points to the recurrence of certain figures of speech, e.g., alliteration and paranomasia, in the prologues and oratory.

[19] This is the discovery of Gelhaus (above, n. 8) 32-40, who then attempts to find similarly clear divisions in the other prologues, too. The task is unfortunately not so simple; see the review of E. Lefèvre, *Gnomon* 48 (1976) 346-353.

into a formal *stipulatio* with his master Calidorus; the prologue-speaker of *Poenulus* calls himself *imperator histricus* and affects the language and manner of a magistrate with *imperium*. The comic incongruity of such Roman elements created a special bond between audience and play, but this came only at the expense of the dramatic illusion that Terence himself worked hard to maintain.[20] He generally avoided Roman allusions in the body of a play. In the prologues, however, Terence needed a certain closeness with his audience and a new way to create it. The ornately raucous banter of the Plautine prologues did not suit him, and his decision to avoid exposition meant he could find no help in his Greek models. The developing art of Roman oratory offered a convenient alternative. To introduce *Andria* Terence therefore embroiled his audience in a controversy, casting his arguments in rhetorical form using the structure and vocabulary of the court. Yet, despite the vehemence of its argument, the resulting speech is also rather cold. This is not, perhaps, the notorious $\psi\upsilon\chi\rho\acute{o}\tau\eta\varsigma$ of Diphilus, but the prologue yet manages to sound aloof and impersonal. The play's title is announced indirectly. Neither the poet nor his rival has any clear identity. We need Donatus to tell us that the *malevolus vetus poeta* was Luscius Lanuvinus, and the true nature of his quarrel with Terence remains something of a mystery.[21] The poet's spokesman also lacks a distinct *persona*. He speaks anonymously and almost entirely in the third person. Terence, feeling his way in a new form of prologue, develops a

---

[20] For this distinction between Plautus and Terence, see G. Williams, *Tradition and Originality in Roman Poetry* (Oxford 1968) 285–294, and H. Haffter, "Terenz und seine künstlerische Eigenart," *MH* 10 (1953) 80–93.

[21] Garton, *PA* 41–139 discusses Luscius and the possible grounds for his quarrel with Terence. Other accounts of value include P. Fabia, *Les prologues de Térence* (Paris 1888) 101–109; M. R. Posani, "Osservazioni su alcuni passi dei prologhi terenziani," *SIFC* 37 (1965) 85–113; and P. Grimal, "L'ennemi de Térence, Luscius de Lanuvinum," *CRAI* (1970) 281–288.

tone for his speech without creating an identity for its speaker. With the next prologue in the corpus he takes that second step.

The prologue to *Heauton timorumenos* again casts the speaker as a courtroom pleader and the audience as judges of the case, but this time Terence does not deprive his advocate of personality. The speaker begins by calling attention to his age.

> Nequoi sit vostrum mirum quor partis seni
> poeta dederit quae sunt adulescentium,
> id primum dicam, deinde quod veni eloquar.
>
> So none of you wonders why our poet
> has given young men's parts to an old one,
> I'll explain that first, then say why I've come.
>   (1–3)

He proceeds to announce the play's title in the next lines, but by making only oblique reference to the Latin author and his Greek model, he quickly frees himself to develop his own role.[22]

> oratorem esse voluit me, non prologum:
> vostrum iudicium fecit; me actorem dedit.
> sed hic actor tantum poterit a facundia
> quantum ille potuit cogitare commode
> qui orationem hanc scripsit quam dicturus sum.
>
> He wanted me as an advocate, not a prologue:
> He's made you the judges, me the pleader.
> I only hope this pleader's eloquence can match
> the skill he had when thinking up
> this speech which I'm about to speak.
>   (11–15)

---

[22] A. Primmer, "Zum Prolog des *Heautontimorumenos*," *WS* 77 (1964) 61–75, makes clear that the speaker does indeed explain his own role before introducing the play. Lines 4–9 are a parenthesis; *nunc* of line 10 means "this being the case" and is not a transition to a new point (cf. Pl. *Bacch.* 412, *Ps.* 7, Cic., *Tusc.* 3.2).

The speaker carefully distinguishes himself from the poet, and, though this is to be a courtroom speech, he is well aware that it is spoken on the stage. *Me actorem . . . hic actor* plays on the double sense of *actor* as advocate and player; his *oratio* is both an oration and a dramatic speech.[23] The speaker here is presumably Ambivius Turpio, Terence's producer, and the poet calls upon both his forensic skill and his knowledge of the stage.

Accusations and refutations come first. These begin with another charge of *contaminatio* that is answered even more boldly than in *Andria* and with another appeal to the *bonorum exemplum* (16–21). Then comes a charge that the poet has had outside help. He writes drawing not on his own talent, but with the help of friends (*amicum ingenio fretus*, 22–24). The prologue evades this charge with an appeal to the audience's good sense that uses repetition, chiasmus, and alliteration in the familiar way.

> arbitrium vostrum, vostra existumatio
> valebit. quare omnis vos oratos volo,
> ne plus iniquom possit quam aequom oratio.
>
> Your judgment, your opinion will
> decide. That's why I want to urge you all
> to let no slander but an honest speech prevail.
> (25–27)

Last comes an attack on the poet's critic. The *Andria* prologue had threatened to catalogue the faults of rivals, and Terence now holds his critic's *servus currens* up to ridicule. Though his own plays are *sine vitiis*, much more can be said *de illius peccatis* and will be said if the attacks do not stop (28–34). A transition brings the prologue back to the present play.

---

[23] Primmer (above, n. 22) 71–72 observes the deictic sense of *hic*. Strictly speaking, we might expect Terence to use *patronus* to denote a defender, as in Pl. *Vid.* 62: "qur, malum patronum quaeram, postquam litem perdidi?" The choice of *actor* preserves the ambiguity of the speaker's role.

> adeste aequo animo, date potestatem mihi
> statariam agere ut liceat per silentium
>
> Be well disposed. Give leave to me
> to stage a quiet play in silence
>
> (35–36)

This is now theatrical language. *Adeste aequo animo* is a formulaic *captatio* in dramatic prologues. *Agere* is used in the technical sense of "perform," and with *mihi* the speaker reverts to his role as producer of the play (cf. 5). *Stataria* itself may also be a technical term; it certainly became one later.[24] Terence makes this change in vocabulary because the *actor* who began by pleading the poet's case is now pleading his own. Ambivius is an old man. Plays full of broad action no longer suit him, and he is glad to offer a play whose appeal depends not on action, but on dialogue: *in hac est pura oratio* (46).[25] The oddity of having a *senex* speak the prologue thus has a dual purpose. His age lends *auctoritas* to the poet's plea and explains his own preference for the present play. By developing a distinct *persona* for his advocate, Terence has broadened his prologue's appeal. To artistic arguments about his own methods and abilities he adds expert testimony about his play's unique merits.

For the third attempt to produce *Hecyra*, Terence had special need of that expert advocate. The play presented a unique problem, for it had failed twice when disturbances in the theatre dis-

---

[24] The only other classical appearances of the term *stataria* refer to the manner of a speaker's delivery, not his subject (Cic., *Brut.* 30.116 and 68.239). Donatus and Evanthius are the ones who categorize plays as *stataria*, *motoria*, and *mixta*. See G. K. Henry, "The Meaning of *Stataria* as Applied to the Comedies of Terence," *SP* 13 (1916) 72–80.

[25] *Oratio* here must refer to the use of speech itself, not to the purity of the author's style. Note Terence's own distinction at *And.* 12: "dissimili oratione sunt factae ac stilo." See D. A. Kidd, "Terence, *Heaut.* 46," *CR* 62 (1948) 13.

rupted its performance.[26] The producer therefore speaks in his own person. He is pleading his own case for a hearing, not primarily his poet's, but the prologue Terence gives him wins that hearing with the familiar devices. There are the same distinctions between *orator* ~ *prologus* and *senex* ~ *adulescens* (9-13, cf. *HT* 1-3), and the same progression from the speaker's role in general to the particular case at hand. Even the transition between these parts is familiar.

> nunc quid petam mea causa aequo animo attendite.
>
> Now, for my sake, listen fairly to my plea.
> (*Hec.* 28)

> mea causa causam hanc iustam esse animum inducite.
>
> For my sake, understand this cause is just.
> (*HT* 41)

In this prologue, however, the first person verbs are genuine.

> quia scibam dubiam fortunam esse scaenicam,
> spe incerta certum mihi laborem sustuli
>
> Since I've always known that Fortune's fickle on the stage,
> I've propped my certain labor with uncertain hope
> (16-17)

We share with Turpio the frustration of yielding place to tightrope walkers and gladiators (33-42), and he credits us with important powers of discernment (*potestas condecorandi ludos scaenicos*, 45). Yet his poet is not entirely forgotten. Turpio is the man who had produced the plays of Caecilius and made them popular (14-15). He now has Terence in his charge.

[26] F. H. Sandbach, "How Terence's *Hecyra* Failed," *CQ* 32 (1982) 134-135; D. Gilula, "Who's Afraid of Rope-Walkers and Gladiators? (Ter., *Hec.* 1-57)," *Athenaeum* 59 (1981) 29-37.

> sinite impetrare me, qui in tutelam meam
> studium suom et se in vostram commisit fidem,
> ne eum circumventum inique iniqui inrideant
>
> Allow me to insure that one who's put
> his future in my charge and trusts in you
> will not be thwarted and mocked by captious critics.
> (52–54, cf. vv. 21–23 of Caecilius)

The stridency of the *Andria* and *Heauton timorumenos* prologues is gone. Turpio seeks to raise Terence above the carping of his critics and to imply equality with the acknowledged master Caecilius. He has also reminded his audience that he brings them plays they like. Once again the cases of poet and advocate are intertwined.

Between the courtroom pose of *Andria* and *Heauton timorumenos* and the more theatrical arguments of *Hecyra* II lie three more refutations of Terence's anonymous critic. In the *Eunuchus* prologue Terence attacks the writer,

> qui bene vortendo et easdem scribendo male
> ex Graecis bonis Latinas fecit non bonas
>
> who, through careful translation and terrible writing,
> made bad Latin plays from good Greek ones.
> (7–8)

He singles out the rival's *Phasma* and *Thesauros* for special ridicule, then defends his own *Eunuchus* against a charge of plagiarism. For *Phormio*, the poet assumes the role of an injured party who attacks his rival only from necessity.

> ille ad famem hunc a studio studuit reicere:
> hic respondere voluit, non lacessere.
>
> He's tried to cast our man from work to want:
> We want now to respond, not to provoke.
> (19–20)

The prologue to *Adelphoe* is a straightforward defense against a charge of unfair patronage and a new charge of *contaminatio*. Yet, while the quarrel Terence records no doubt took place, these prologues are hardly a trustworthy record of it.[27] Their function was neither to report the controversy accurately nor even to win it for their author. The place for Terence to fight *that* battle was before the magistrates who commissioned his productions (cf. *Eun.* 20–24). The prologues have a more immediate purpose: to capture the attention of the Roman crowd and secure its good will. The matter at hand for Terence's *orator* is not one of literary theory, but of practical dramaturgy. The audience must be summoned to order and convinced that the forthcoming play is worth seeing. The quarrel with Luscius is used as a device to pique their interest.

Ancient critics appreciated the diverse requirements of dramatic prologues. In his general remarks on comedy, for example, Donatus defined four distinct types: *commendativus* praising the author or his play, *relativus* attacking his rivals or winning his audience, *argumentativus* giving the *argumentum*, and the combination of these, the *mixtus*. These categories are hardly discrete; nearly every prologue of Plautus and Terence would have to be called *mixtus*.[28] Taken together, however, they describe fairly

[27] Attempts to read the prologues as true documents of literary history have not been convincing. Cf. R. C. Flickinger, "A Study of Terence's Prologues," *PhQ* 6 (1927) 235-269, and H. B. Mattingly, "The Chronology of Terence," *RCCM* 5 (1963) 12–61.

[28] Don., *de comoedia* 7.2 and Eugraphius' introduction to *Andria* (p. 3.8w): "omnis prologus triplici inducitur causa, vel ut argumentum fabulae possit exhibere vel poetam populo commendare vel ut a populo audientiam postulet." Leo, *PlF* 234–238, discusses the artificiality of Donatus' categories. The roots of such critical thinking are perhaps more rhetorical than theatrical. The term *relativus* is itself rhetorical (e.g. *relatio criminis*, Cic. *Inv.* 1.15), and cf. *Rhet. Her.* 1.4.8 on the *exordium*. Was Terence himself schooled in rhetoric? The *vita* is silent on this point, but his style of argument in the prologues certainly smacks of rhetoric. Elaine Fantham suggests to me that he might have acquired such training as a favored slave in the household of Ter-

well the peculiar requirements of prologues in Roman comedy. At the start of a performance, the Greek predecessors of Plautus and Terence could take the attention of an audience more or less for granted. Menander's prologues, for example, needed only perfunctory *captationes*.[29] He was free to develop expository speeches that shape in quite sophisticated ways his audience's understanding of the play to follow. Plautus and Terence had different needs. At the Roman *ludi*, where plays were only one of the available attractions and only an improvised stage was furnished for their performance, dramatists had to work much harder to secure their audiences. Plautus therefore added to the expository function of a prologue the trappings of a comic routine calculated to settle the crowd and make it tractable. Terence's technique, though different, was no less determined by theatrical exigencies. He won the attention of his audience by embroiling them in a controversy, presenting the quarrel with Luscius Lanuvinus in a form to arouse and intrigue them. The technique evidently worked. Only that first, short prologue to *Hecyra* failed to win a hearing for its play. The rhetorical model served him well. Terence won the struggle with his contemporaries, but, as we shall now see, his texts faced new difficulties with modern critics.

---

entius Lucanus. This would be our earliest example of a rhetorical education at Rome. The hypothesis is attractive but difficult. Cf. Astin's doubts about Cato's formal training, (above, n. 8) 147–153, and, in general, G. Kennedy, *The Art of Rhetoric in the Roman World* (Princeton 1972) 60–71.

[29] Thus *Dys.* 45–46: ταῦτ' ἐστὶ τὰ κεφάλαια, τὰ καθ' ἕκαστα δὲ / ὄψεσθ' ἐὰν βούλησθε—βουλήθητε δέ. The idea is apparently repeated at *Sikyonios* 23–24. The fragments of other fourth-century comic prologues are too scanty to support generalizations. They include the anonymous speech of P. Argent. 53; Antiphanes, fr. 73 and 168; Alexis, fr. 107; Eubulus, fr. 68; and Heniochus, fr. 5.

[III]

THE WELL-MADE PLAY

> We have . . . as it were nothing but a shadowy outline left of the object of our wishes, but that very indistinctness only awakens a more earnest longing for what we have lost, and we study the copies of the originals more attentively than we should have studied the originals themselves, if we had been in full possession of them.
> —J. J. WINCKELMANN,
> *A History of Art* (1764)

Until well into the nineteenth century, Plautus and Terence enjoyed reputations as essentially original writers. Terence's delicacy of diction and characterization—traits by their very nature his own—had long made him an admired mainstay of the school curriculum, and even Plautus, who had to be rediscovered in the Renaissance and whose text presented greater difficulties to readers, was appreciated in his own right, if not necessarily on what we would call his own terms. Lessing, who knew perfectly well that Roman comedy was based upon Greek models, nevertheless praised Plautus' *Captivi* as the greatest of comedies, without troubling to disentangle the Latin text from its Greek original. In a monograph of 1837, Wilhelm Adolph Becker, a well-known popularizer of classical antiquity, compared Plautus' technique as an adapter of Greek comedy to Molière's freedom in turning *Aulularia* into *L'Avare*, and he used the Terentian prologues as evidence for Terence's own freedom in handling his models. As late as 1851, *Rheinisches Museum* printed anonymously a sensitive and astute appreciation of Plautus and Terence that attributed all but free creation to them, and no less an authority than Friedrich Ritschl endorsed this view by reprinting the article in his own

Opuscula Philologica of 1868.¹ By then, however, this admiring opinion of the Roman dramatists was already losing favor as a quite different critical approach reached maturity.

In rediscovering the greatness of Greek art, Johann Joachim Winckelmann had envisioned a Greece of unmatched splendor. His ancient Greeks, with their perfect bodies and flawless tastes, captured the fancy of the age, and neither Roman art nor literature could equal them. The shield of Aeneas as Lessing came to see it in his *Laokoon* of 1766 is a pallid, even tawdry trinket when placed beside its Homeric model. Aeneas' shield, wrote Lessing, is "a sheer interpolation, simply and only intended to flatter the national pride of the Romans.... The shield of Achilles, on the other hand, is a rich, natural outgrowth of the fertile soil from which it springs."² The independent reputations of Plautus and Terence could not long survive Winckelmann's inspired reconstruction of Greek aesthetics and Lessing's doubts about the quality of Vergil. August Wilhelm Schlegel put Roman comedy firmly in its place in his famous *Lectures on Dramatic Art and Literature* of 1809 when he set out to discuss Greek New Comedy.

¹ The mysterious article in *RhM* 8 (1851) 51–69 is reprinted under the title "Zur Charakteristik des Plautus und Terentius" in F. Ritschl, *Opuscula Philologica*, vol. 2 (Leipzig 1868) 752–764. Its authorship remains uncertain. O. Ribbeck, *Fr. W. Ritschl*, vol. 2 (Leipzig 1881) 416, refers to "eine nahverbundene weibliche Feder"; W. M. Calder III suggests the lady may be Frau Ritschl. Compare pages 76–86 of Becker's monograph *De comicis romanorum fabulis maxime Plautinis quaestiones* (Leipzig 1837). Becker is best known for two popular books on ancient social history, *Charikles* (Leipzig 1840) and *Gallus* (Leipzig 1838). On Lessing, see M. E. Agnew, "Lessing's Critical Opinion of the *Captivi* of Plautus," *CW* 39 (1945/46) 66–70 and, for his views on Terence, J. G. Robertson, *Lessing's Dramatic Theory* (New York 1965) 318–330.

² G. E. Lessing, *Laokoon*, tr. W. A. Steel (London 1930) 69. For the rediscovery of Greece by Winckelmann and Lessing, see E. M. Butler, *The Tyranny of Greece Over Germany* (Boston 1958) 9–70 and H. Levin, *The Broken Column* (Cambridge, MA 1931).

"We may safely affirm," he declared, "that in the graces and elegances of execution, the Greek poets have always lost in the Latin imitations. We must use our imagination to retranslate these into the finished elegance which we perceive in the Greek fragments."[3] Just as Winckelmann had recreated the elegant canons of Greek sculpture beneath the coarser surfaces of Roman copies, so Schlegel hoped to recapture the qualities of the lost New Comedy by analytic study of Latin texts. Lessing had been willing to value Plautus and Terence as dramatists in their own right, largely because they represented a tradition in which he himself saw continuing possibilities; his own career as a dramatist took him from translation, through adaptation, to the incorporation of Roman comic motifs into his own independent creations.[4] To Schlegel's more scholarly mind, the study of Roman drama was the means to a quite different end. Plautus and Terence are seen, like Winckelmann's Roman statues, as only the rough outlines of lost originals, and Schlegel's harsh criticism of them is the inevitable consequence of his own longing for the thing lost. This condescending view of the Romans continues to shape the study of their comedy, but it could not have done so were it not for compatible developments in living theatre.

The nineteenth century was also the age of what the French, who pioneered the style, called *la pièce bien faite*, "the well-made play." Its founder was Eugène Scribe, and his disciples included Eugène Labiche, Victorien Sardou, and ultimately Georges Feydeau.[5] Although classical French drama, with its adherence to

---

[3] I have revised the translation of J. Black in A. W. Schlegel, *Lectures on Dramatic Art and Literature* (New York 1879) 189. The relevant portions of the original are reprinted in E. Lefèvre, ed., *Die römische Komödie: Plautus und Terenz* (Darmstadt 1973) 21–24.

[4] J. Kont, *Lessing et l'antiquité* (Paris 1894) 64–88; V. Riedel, *Lessing und die römische Literatur* (Weimar 1976) 31–85.

[5] For the history of the well-made play, see T. F. Driver, *Romantic Quest and Modern Query. A History of the Modern Theatre* (New York 1980) 45–57,

64   CHAPTER III

the three unities and to what Corneille called *la liaison des scènes*, had certainly valued careful plotting, only in the nineteenth century was structure prized so greatly over probability and were characters so completely subordinated to the details of dress and accidents of time, place, and the post office that determine their actions. Had Maurice de Saxe, for example, not worn roses in his lapel during the first act of Scribe's *Adrienne Lecouvreur*, misunderstanding and jealousy would not have led so inexorably to his ruin in Act IV and to Adrienne's death in Act V, when she sniffs those same roses, now doused with poison by Maurice's former mistress. Such a play had to be deft. It did not have to be deep. The charm of the well-made play comes from the cleverness with which its action is first complicated and then resolved, not from the richness of its characterizations or the depth of its thought. The critic Francisque Sarcey, for example, defended Sardou's *Nos Intîmes* in the following way:[6]

> At the sixth performance, I met, during the first interact, a man of infinite taste who . . . complained of the lengthiness of this first act: "What a lot of details," he said, "which serve no purpose, and had better have been omitted! What is the use of that long story about the cactus with a flower that is unique in all the world? Why trouble us with that dahlia-root, which M. Caussade's neighbour has thrown over the garden wall? Was it necessary to inflict on us all that talk about the fox that plays havoc in the garden? . . . All this stuff only retards the action."
> "On the contrary," I replied, "all this is just what is going to

and two articles by P. Gillespie, "Plays: Well-Constructed and Well-Made," *Quart. Jr. Speech* 58 (1972) 313–321, and "Plays: Well-Complicated," *Speech Monographs* 42 (1975) 20–28. A collection of representative plays is S. S. Stanton, ed., *Camille and Other Plays* (New York 1957), which also includes an excellent introductory essay.

[6] Francisque Sarcey was drama critic of *Le Temps* from 1867 to 1899. The review is quoted with amusement by W. Archer, *Play-Making, A Manual of Craftsmanship* (Boston 1912) 214–215.

interest you. . . . That cactus-flower will play its part, you may be sure; that dahlia-root is not there for nothing; that fox to which you object, and of which you will hear more talk during two more acts, will bring about the solution of one of the most entertaining situations in all drama."

Melodramas of this type dominated the nineteenth-century stage. Scribe wrote or coauthored some five hundred plays between 1815 and his death in 1861. The death scene of *Adrienne Lecouvreur* made Sarah Bernhardt famous, and she later toured the world playing the title roles in such plays of Sardou as *Fédora*, *Théodora*, and *La Tosca*. Nearly half the plays Ibsen directed as a young man at Christiania and Bergen between 1850 and 1857 were by Scribe and his associates, and "adapted from the French" was a frequent note on the playbills of Victorian London.[7] Dramas like Pinero's *The Second Mrs. Tanqueray* and Wilde's *Lady Windermere's Fan* were essentially plays of the same sort. Bernard Shaw was a relentless foe of this style and mocked what he called "Sardoodledum" and the "clumsy booby traps" it produced, but *Arms and the Man* nevertheless takes its plot from Scribe's *Bataille des dames*. Though Scribe and his successors told silly stories, they told them well and developed techniques put to good use by better dramatists as diverse as Wilde and Ibsen. Beneath the symbolic value of Hedda Gabler's pistol and Hedwig Ekdal's wild duck lie the structural techniques of the *pièce bien faite*.

"The well-made play" is thus a critical catch phrase rooted in this nineteenth-century style of plot construction, but both the

[7] The English well-made tradition is discussed by J. R. Taylor, *The Rise and Fall of the Well-Made Play* (London 1967), with representative plays in G. R. Rowe, ed., *Nineteenth Century Plays* (London 1953). Cf. Shaw's review of Sardou's *Delia Harding* in *Our Theatre in the Nineties* (London 1932) 97–99. The lists of plays produced by Ibsen at Christiania and Bergen are reproduced in J. W. McFarlane and G. Orton, ed., *The Oxford Ibsen*, vol. 1 (London 1970) 595–599 and 647–648.

phrase and the concept continue to color scholarly opinions of Greco-Roman Comedy. "Terence found in the Attic comedies such a completely formed tradition of the well-made play," writes one modern critic, "that he knew his own attempts could not, as a rule, compete with it."[8] Such emphasis on the well-made aspect of Greek drama, often linked as here to a perceived Roman inability to match it, is the inevitable consequence of combining nineteenth-century dramatic taste with Schlegel's scholarly legacy. Yet we now possess genuine New Comedy unknown to Schlegel, and our concept of dramatic structure is not limited to that of his younger contemporary Scribe. We can read Menander for ourselves. We have learned to appreciate the willful illogic of Aristophanic comedy. Those sudden and expedient changes of character that make Shakespeare's happy endings possible do not irritate us. How deeply, then, should we continue to allow the concept of the well-made play to influence our opinion of Terence?

I

Real care in plot construction is apparent in Menander's *Dyskolos*, the one play that has survived complete.[9] The comedy deals with the love of the rich city boy Sostratos for the daughter of Knemon, the rustic misanthrope of the title. While hunting in the country, Sostratos was made lovesick by Pan. He eventually wins the girl with the help of Knemon's stepson Gorgias, and the play ends with the double betrothal of Sostratos to the girl and

---

[8] W. Ludwig, "The Originality of Terence and His Greek Models," *GRBS* 9 (1968) 180–181.

[9] Menander was famous in antiquity for such care; thus the comment reported by Plutarch, *Mor.* 347e: ᾠκονόμηται γὰρ ἡ διάθεσις, δεῖ δ' αὐτῇ τὰ στιχίδια ἐπᾷσαι. N. C. Arvin, *Eugène Scribe and the French Theatre* (Cambridge, MA 1924) 41, attributes a similar remark to Scribe. A memoir by Scribe's collaborator E. Legouvé, *Eugène Scribe* (Paris 1874) 17, quotes Racine, "quand mon plan est achevé, ma pièce est faite."

THE WELL-MADE PLAY   67

Gorgias to Sostratos' sister. Choral interludes divide this story into five acts, and these act divisions mark distinct and deliberate stages in the action. The first act presents the exposition and development of Sostratos' dilemma as he tries to approach Knemon. In the second act Sostratos secures Gorgias' help. The appearance of Sostratos' mother, leading a party of sacrificers to the neighboring shrine of Pan, keeps Knemon at home in Act III. Because he stays at home, Knemon falls down his well in Act IV, is rescued, and must recant his behavior. The fifth act presents the double betrothal and Knemon's final punishment for his misanthropy. Because Menander is thinking of his play in these logical sections, he manipulates the act breaks to create a certain rhythm for the action. He introduces the slave Daos to fetch Gorgias home at the end of Act I, and Act II begins with the foreshadowed conversation between them. At the end of Act II we meet Sikon the cook, and the third act begins with the arrival of the sacrificers who have hired him. Such control of the act divisions is also a hallmark of the well-made play. "A good first act should never end in a blank wall," observed William Archer in his practical manual *Play-Making*. "There should always be a window in it, with at least a glimpse of something attractive beyond."[10] Each act of *Lady Windermere's Fan*, for example, ends with an impend-

[10] Archer (above, n. 6) 186, cf. 136, where the act is called "no mere convention, but a valuable means for marking the rhythm of the story." Menander's similar manipulation of act breaks is discussed by E. W. Handley, "The Conventions of the Comic Stage and Their Exploitation by Menander," *Fondation Hardt Entretiens XVI: Ménandre* (Vandoeuvres-Geneva 1970) 11–13 and 27–29. The Latin adaptations were written for continuous performance, which inevitably affected the pace of the action and the audience's ability to think about it. The difference is readily apparent in Plautus' adaptation of Menander's *Dis Exapaton*, for which see E. W. Handley, *Menander and Plautus: A Study in Comparison* (London 1968), and more generally C. Questa, "Alcune strutture sceniche di Plauto e di Menandro," in the Fondation Hardt volume, pp. 181–228, and J.C.B. Lowe, "Terentian Originality in the *Phormio* and *Hecyra*," *Hermes* 111 (1983) 442–451.

ing crisis, and the action of Sardou's *A Scrap of Paper (Les Pattes de mouche)* does not really begin until just before the first curtain.

Even more striking in the construction of *Dyskolos* is the use of stage properties and related devices to develop the plot. We learn at line 190 that a pot has been lost down the well, at 576 that a mattock has been lost retrieving the pot, and at 625 that Knemon himself has fallen down the well while recovering pot and mattock. The whole plot turns on this carefully arranged accident, for Knemon's rescue by Gorgias convinces him to permit the marriage of his daughter. The sacrifice to Pan plays an equally important part in the play's structure. Sostratos' mother has come to Phyle because of a dream in which Pan had shackled her son and made him a farmer (407ff.). This dream echoes the prologue, in which Pan himself had taken responsibility for Sostratos' lovesickness (39–44). The crowd of sacrificers then prevents Knemon from working in the field, thus frustrating Sostratos' plan to meet him there but making possible the catastrophe at the well. The sacrifice also brings Sostratos' father and sister to Phyle, which sets up the betrothal of Gorgias, and it motivates some necessary farce. The sacrificers lack a cauldron, which leads first to amusing attempts by slave and cook to borrow one from Knemon (456ff.). His refusal later leads Sikon to remark that the accident down the well is Knemon's punishment for insulting a cook (639), and the motif of asking at the door resurfaces in the finale, where slave and cook torment Knemon with outrageous requests and drag him off to the wedding feast (911ff.).

This use of objects and recurrent motifs to develop the action brings to mind the nineteenth-century reliance on stage properties reflected in such titles as *A Glass of Water (Le Verre d'eau)*, *A Pair of Spectacles*, and *Lady Windermere's Fan*. Yet, at least to judge by the standards of the well-made play, there are some disquieting loose ends in the construction of *Dyskolos*. The disappearance of the clearly delineated characters Chaireas, Pyrrhias, and Daos is neither motivated nor explained. Knemon's daughter has no name and little character, and Sostratos' sister materializes at the end solely to reward Gorgias. This is not the kind of tight, economical structure often attributed to New Comedy. Even more disquieting are the loose ends of *Samia*, a better play which survives nearly complete. A contrast between old Demeas' wealth and Nikeratos' poverty is never developed, and Chrysis, the Samian woman of the title, receives cavalier treatment. She is the *pallake* of Demeas, Moschion's father by adoption. Her willingness to pass off Moschion's baby as her own by Demeas initiates the action and imperils her relationship with Demeas. He eventually throws her out of his house when he suspects the child is hers by Moschion, though he takes her in again when he learns otherwise. Then she vanishes. Menander is interested in the relationship between Demeas and Moschion. The dilemma of Chrysis is a momentary consequence of that relationship that is not expanded for its own sake. He uses the woman and child only to enrich the main action; they assume no independent existence. Both *Samia* and *Dyskolos* are carefully constructed without being well made in any technical sense. The sacrifice party and the well of *Dyskolos* and the baby moved from house to house in *Samia* are economizing, not complicating, devices of plot, nor are they intentionally exotic like Sardou's cactus-flower and dahlia-root. Menander keeps his action straightforward, even at the expense of loose ends and the late introduction of new characters.

An even greater tolerance of loose ends and internal inconsistencies characterizes Roman comedy and has been the bane of Plautine criticism for over a century. Earlier readers like Lessing, attracted by the sheer brilliance of Plautus, were relatively untroubled by his diffuseness, but the nineteenth-century insistence on structural coherence found a critical problem in plays that ignored logic and probability. "It is absolutely impossible," declared the Plautine editor Karl Hermann Weise in 1836, "that a good poet could say anything foolish and not to the point." We can expect complications and false leads, but the impossibility of outright contradictions in character and action must be "a firm principle and like an unassailable pillar" of criticism.[11] Weise is reflecting the dramatic structure eventually canonized in Gustav Freytag's *Die Technik des Drama* of 1863:

> It is the business of the action to represent to us the inner consistency of the event. . . . Whatever in the crude material does not serve this purpose, the poet is in duty bound to throw away. And it is desirable that he hold strictly to this principle, to give only what is indispensable to unity.[12]

Weise blamed textual corruption and interpolation for the notorious Plautine inconsistencies, citing as an example the great *canticum* of *Bacchides* 925–978 where Chrysalus likens himself to the Atridae: "This entire song should be completely passed over by a discerning reader, for its bad taste can only bring shame to the poetry and the plot."[13] His tone is deliberately polemic. The "latest corrector" of the pamphlet's title is Ritschl, whose revolutionary work on the text of Plautus was just beginning to bear fruit and was revealing a dramatic poet with quite different standards. Fear that Ritschl would establish dramatic texts that were authoritative but not well made eventually induced Weise to put his principles to work. In 1866 he produced an edition whose excisions and rewritings aimed to show how "the careful master Plautus could produce only the harmonious, only the refined, only the logical, and only the relatively respectable."[14] By

---

[11] K. H. Weise, *Plautus und seine neuesten Diorthoten* (Quedlinberg and Leipzig 1836) 16.

[12] I quote the English version of E. J. MacEwan, *Freytag's Technique of Drama* (Chicago 1900) 46. This was the standard handbook of dramatic art until the appearance of Archer's *Play-Making*.

[13] Weise (above, n. 11) 18–19. This attitude is not dead. See H. D. Jocelyn, "Chrysalus and the Fall of Troy," *HSCP* 73 (1969) 135–152.

[14] K. H. Weise, *Die Komödien des Plautus, Kritisch nach Inhalt und Form belechtet, zur Bestimmung des Echten und Unechten in den einzelnen Dichtungen* (Quedlinburg 1866) 79.

then, however, Weise's standard was an anachronism. Ritschl's strictly philological approach prevailed, and in his *Plautinische Studien* of 1886 Peter Langen demonstrated conclusively that inconsistencies of detail—and he devoted a long chapter to pointing them out play by play—are characteristic of Plautus' style. Langen drew no conclusions, but his analytic method provided the model for later work that went back to Schlegel for its perspective.

Whereas Weise had sought to impose his own standards on Plautus directly, later scholars projected similar aesthetic standards, not onto Plautus, whose text could no longer be so blithely amended, but onto his lost originals. Leo's superb *Plautinische Forschungen*, first published in 1895, showed the way by dealing at least as much with Greek as with Latin drama. "Leo loved Plautus," observed his student Eduard Fraenkel, "but he loved Attic comedy still more, and when through the work of the Roman poet he came to perceive Greek artistic forms, he was deeply satisfied and in some cases sought no further."[15] Fraenkel's own identification of the Plautine in Plautus used philological techniques to distinguish Greek from Latin elements, and Fraenkel's friend Gunther Jachmann went even further. In his *Plautinisches und Attisches* of 1931, Jachmann interpreted such inconsistencies as Langen had identified as clear signs of Plautus' tinkering with his originals, and he set out to compare the Latin texts with the underlying Greek plays he reconstructed from such clues. The result is an impressive but artificial web of hypotheses that reveals with sometimes embarrassing clarity the fusion of New Comedy as Schlegel had envisioned it and the nineteenth-century standard for making plays. "In the original," Jachmann writes at one point, "as always in such cases, everything was better ordered, collected, and to the point, and the model was ac-

---

[15] Fraenkel, *EPP* 3. The original German edition appeared in 1922.

cordingly more firmly joined, tight, and straightforward."[16] Whether this is true or false of New Comedy, one thing is certainly true of Plautus: he himself did not write well-made plays.

Terence, writing plays at Rome in the generation after Plautus, thus had two models for construction available to him, a Greek tradition that took a certain care in the making of plots and a Roman form that leaned toward fantasy and more readily sacrificed internal logic for comic effect. Plautus had generally chosen not to construct plays in the style of Menander. Terence also had to make a choice, but he did not have to choose the same standard for each play. Nor was his choice simply between tight structure and loose structure. A play's form has something to do with its meaning. Closely related to the structural integrity of the well-made play, for example, is its deliberate triviality. "You go to the theatre," Scribe told the French Academy in 1836, "not for instruction or correction, but to relax and amuse yourselves. Now what amuses you best is not truth but fiction. To relate what passes before your eyes each day is not the way to give pleasure, but what rarely occurs in everyday life—the extraordinary, the fabulous—that is what charms you and that is what we strive to offer."[17] This is the justification for those poisoned bouquets, dahlia-roots, and cactus-flowers unique in all the world. Menandrean comedy was not extraordinary and fabulous in this way. *Dyskolos* is perhaps trivial but neither complex nor exotic, and Menander at his most sophisticated did not simply entertain by telling a story well. Carefully constructed plays like *Epitrepontes*, *Perikeiromene*, and *Misoumenos* present their characters with real dilemmas, and the anguish of those characters is genuine and affecting. Action is generated by the characters

---

[16] G. Jachmann, *Plautinisches und Attisches* (Berlin 1931) 185. Cf. the pointed attack of G. Duckworth, "The Structure of the *Miles Gloriosus*," *CP* 30 (1935) 228–246.

[17] E. Scribe, "Discours de réception à l'Académie Française" in *Oeuvres complètes*, vol. 1., ed. E. Dentu (Paris 1874) xxiv–xxv.

THE WELL-MADE PLAY 73

themselves, not by stage properties or external circumstances. Plot and character combine to create truly thoughtful comedy.

When Terence adapts a play by Menander, he may choose a similar emphasis on character. What his characters represent is then more important than what they do, and the relationships among characters will be of greater interest than the plot itself. Consider the scene where Demea, the strict brother of *Adelphoe*, taxes the lenient Micio for his blithe acceptance of Aeschinus' illicit relationship with Pamphila.

>   DE. si non ipsa re tibi istuc dolet,
> simulare certe est hominis. MI. quin iam virginem
> despondi; res compositast; fiunt nuptiae;
> dempsi metum omnem: haec mage sunt hominis.
>
>   DE. If the thing itself doesn't bother you,
> a decent person would at least pretend it did. MI. Why, I've got
> the girl engaged, the business settled, a wedding party set.
> I've ended all anxiety. That's more like what a decent person
>   does.
>   (*Ad.* 733–736)

The characters of the two men are clearly drawn. Though harsh and inflexible, Demea is an idealist at heart, and the failure of his values leaves him clutching desperately at the appearance of values. Micio is pragmatic and smooth, quick to contradict Demea's standards and callous enough to turn Demea's language against him. Their disagreement reflects different personalities and different values and determines the course of the play's action. Yet the underlying substance of their argument has an importance that transcends the requirements of this particular plot. Beneath their comic attitudes and comic problems are real attitudes and real problems of social behavior and obligation. We move easily from the specific, rather fantastic dilemma posed by Aeschinus to the general and genuine kind of family dilemma we know from our own experience. The plot of *Adelphoe* is the vehicle for exploring and developing these characters and the kind of problems their attitudes create.

Compare the old men Demipho and Chremes of *Phormio*, based upon the *Epidikazomenos* of Apollodorus of Carystus. When the slave Geta launches an intrigue by reporting to them a conversation he pretends to have had with the parasite Phormio, Demipho and Chremes also react very much in character.

>   DE. quis te istaec iussit loqui?
> CH. immo non potuit melius pervenirier
>   eo quo nos volumus.

>   DE. Who ordered you to say such a thing?
> CH. No, no! There couldn't be a better way to get
>   where we want.
>   (*Ph.* 639–641)

Demipho, astute and anxious not to be swindled, is instinctively suspicious. His intelligence makes him a formidable opponent, and the intriguers must fight for every inch gained against him. His brother Chremes is a guilty man with a secret that he is eager to preserve at any cost. He is thus the perfect victim for the kind of intrigue Geta and Phormio have begun. As in *Adelphoe*, a few short lines display the characters of the two old men, and the plots of both plays turn upon those characters. In *Phormio*, however, the characters revealed and the problems faced have no life outside the dramatic context. Whereas *Adelphoe* approaches a serious issue in a comic way, *Phormio* avoids seriousness, using its characters simply to facilitate a story of intrigue, punishment, and reward. It still uses character to motivate action, but its appeal lies less in the values those characters represent than in the entertainment their actions provide. *Phormio* is the closest that Terence comes to presenting a play simply to tell an amusing

THE WELL-MADE PLAY   75

story. How closely does his effort approach the canons of the well-made play?

II

Phormio accepted thirty minae from Demipho and Chremes to annul the marriage he has contrived between the orphan Phanium and Demipho's son Antipho. He was supposed to marry the girl himself but has used the money instead to secure a music-girl for Phaedria, the son of Chremes. Now he learns that Phanium is actually Chremes' daughter by a bigamous marriage and thus the bride intended for Antipho all along. Their marriage need not be annulled. The young people are in the clear, and Phormio sees a new way to avoid trouble over the thirty swindled minae.

> Tantam fortunam de inproviso esse his datam!
> summa eludendi occasiost mihi nunc senes
> et Phaedriae curam adimere argentariam,
> ne quoiquam suorum aequalium supplex siet.
> nam idem hoc argentum, ita ut datumst, ingratiis
> ei datum erit: hoc qui cogam re ipsa repperi.
> nunc gestus mihi voltusque est capiundus novos.
> sed hinc concedam in angiportum hoc proxumum,
> inde hisce ostendam me, ubi erunt egressi foras.
> quo me adsimularam ire ad mercatum, non eo.

> *What good luck has come their way so unexpectedly!*
> *Now I've got a great chance to bilk the old men and*
> *remove Phaedria's money troubles so he won't have to*
> *beg from friends. That money that was paid him will*
> *stay paid, no matter what the old men say. I've found*
> *a way to make them. Now I need a new front and a new*
> *face. I'll just slip back here between the houses and*
> *confront them when they come out. As for that business*

trip I pretended I was taking, I'm not going.
(884–893)

With this monologue Phormio slips deftly from one scheme to another, announcing his control of the situation with a frank declaration to the audience. He is truly a parasite of many faces, and by frequent asides during the final confrontation with the old men he will maintain this close relationship with the audience and demonstrate complete control over his victims. We expect such control from Phormio, for Terence told us in the prologue that the play belongs to him.

> adporto novam
> Epidicazomenon quam vocant comoediam
> Graeci, Latini Phormionem nominant
> quia primas partis qui aget is erit Phormio
> parasitus, per quem res geretur maxume.

> I bring you
> a new comedy that Greeks call
> *The Litigant*. Latins call it *Phormio*
> because the parasite Phormio plays the
> leading role and calls the shots.
> (26–28)

Terence's change of title, the only such change among the six plays, deliberately associates his clever parasite with the Plautine parasite Curculio and the clever slaves Epidicus and Pseudolus.

Like *Epidicus*, the play emphasizes the skill of its title figure by beginning with a serious challenge to an earlier, apparently successful, intrigue. Phormio had secured the marriage of Antipho and Phanium through a court suit based upon the Athenian law regarding heiresses. He had claimed that Antipho was the orphan's nearest kin and was thus obliged to marry her. Demipho's return from abroad threatens this marriage. By denying kinship with Phanium, he may challenge the court order.[18] Phormio accepts with aplomb his responsibility for meeting Demipho's threat.

> ad te summa solum, Phormio, rerum redit:
> tute hoc intristi: tibi omnest exedendum: accingere.
>
> It's all up to you alone, Phormio.
> You've made this stew. You have to eat it. Brace up!
> (317–318)

His figurative language, so *apta parasito*, as Donatus remarks, and his willingness to take charge are characteristic of other comic contrivers (cf. *Ep.* 81ff., *Eun.* 1060).[19] Phormio then proceeds to talk circles around Demipho, who appears with three friends to test the possibility of reopening the case (348ff.). The old man loses the first round to Phormio, and we can hardly doubt that he will lose the last one as well. Yet there is something curious about Phormio's role as intriguer. He may seem to dominate the action, but someone else actually runs the machinery of the plot.

The play opens with discussion between the protatic Davos and Geta, the family slave to whose guardianship Antipho and Phaedria have been entrusted while the old men are abroad.[20]

---

[18] *Ph.* 125–126 summarizes the law for the benefit of the Roman audience: "lex est ut orbae, qui sint genere proxumi, / is nubant, et illos ducere eadem haec lex iubet." See E. Lefèvre, *Der Phormio des Terenz und der Epidikazomenos des Apollodor von Karystos*, Zetemata 74 (Munich 1978) 5–7.

[19] For the importance of language to the success of *Phormio* see W. G. Arnott, "*Phormio parasitus*. A Study in Dramatic Methods of Characterization," *G&R* 17 (1970) 32–57.

[20] R. K. Bohm, "Money Matters in *Phormio*," *CW* 70 (1976) 267–269, sees thematic significance in their conversation. The expository technique of this scene shares important features with *Hecyra*, also based on a play by Apollodorus. For the similarities, see D. Sewart, "Exposition in the *Hekyra* of Apollodorus," *Hermes* 102 (1974) 251–252.

CHAPTER III

Geta has been party to Phormio's machinations, and the problem posed by Demipho's return is first presented as Geta's dilemma.

> o Geta,
> quid te futurumst? :: nescio hercle; unum hoc scio,
> quod fors feret feremus aequo animo. :: placet:
> em istuc virist officium. :: in me omnis spes mihist.
>
> O Geta,
> what will happen to you? :: God, I don't know. I only know this:
> we must bear what Fortune brings with bravery. :: That's right.
> That's what a man must do. :: I am my only hope.
> (136-139)

Their language is comically grandiloquent. "Hae graves sententiae," says Donatus, "ex persona servorum cum dicuntur, ridiculae sunt et eo consilio interponuntur" (*ad* 138). Geta is the instrument for many of the play's traditional comic effects. He is twice a *servus currens* (179ff., 841ff.). He is also given important asides that shape the comedy of the first two confrontations between Phormio and Demipho.

Roman comedy often allows one character to eavesdrop on another and comment aside on what he hears.[21] Such eavesdropping rarely advances the plot, but it often suggests for the audience's benefit which of two characters in confrontation will eventually triumph. Early in *Andria*, for example, when we are still unsure whether Simo or the seemingly clever Davos will control events, Terence introduces their first scene together with parallel monologues. Simo speaks first, overhears Davos talking about him, and comments aside.

DA. numquam quoiquam nostrum verbum fecit neque id aegre tulit.

---

[21] V. E. Hiatt, *Eavesdropping in Roman Comedy* (Chicago 1946) 70-72, and D. Bain, *Actors and Audience* (Oxford 1977) 105-117, give examples from Roman comedy and Menander.

SI. at nunc faciet neque, ut opinor, sine tuo magno malo.
DA. He never answered any of us, nor took it badly.
SI. But now he will, and not without trouble for you, I think.
(*And.* 128–129)

Davos is about to be taken unawares: "erus est, neque provideram," he will say (183). The structure of the scene gives Simo an advantage over Davos that he will continue to exploit as the plot develops. In *Phormio* Geta is the character whose asides signal control of things. When we first meet Demipho at 231ff., his anger at the news of Antipho's marriage is made comic by Geta's comments aside to Phaedria. After Phaedria steps forward to greet his uncle, Geta's continued asides undercut the tension of their meeting. Similarly at 348ff., the threat posed by Demipho and his *advocati* is undercut first by the mock argument of Geta and Phormio and then by Geta's comments on the confrontation of Demipho and Phormio. The obvious humor of this device conceals an important dramatic function. Terence has interposed Geta between the audience and the action. Geta's license to comment on events signals not just that Demipho is being outmaneuvered, but that the dramatic balance of the play favors the intriguers.

Geta also does a good deal of running around. His first running scene announces the arrival of Demipho (179ff.). His second resolves Antipho's dilemma with the news of Phanium's true parentage (841ff.). Both pieces of information are crucial to the plot, but Geta is something more than a sideline observer and messenger. He is introduced as a *servus callidus*. "Quin tu quid faciam impera," Phaedria tells him (223). "Nunc prior adito tu," Geta will reply, "ego in insidiis hic ero succenturiatus, siquid deficias" (229–230). The military language so typical of the Plautine *callidus* continues to surround Geta (cf. 321, 346–347).[22] He recog-

---

[22] Geta's other contribution to the plot, the news of Chremes' bigamy, is also accompanied by heightened language. See Arnott (above, n. 19) 46–48.

nizes his own need to scheme (179–180, 235), and he does do service as an intriguer. He is the one who undertakes to get the thirty minae for Phaedria (557–559). The scheme will require Phormio's help, but Geta does the legwork. Even when he voices admiration for Phormio's cleverness, he still thinks of the intrigue as his own: "an quia quos fallam pro uno duo sunt mihi dati?" (602) Phormio himself takes complete control of the play's intrigue only after Geta announces the truth about Chremes and Phanium. From the monologue at 884 to the finale, the play is indeed his, but until that point the forward motion of the plot is controlled by Geta. Gilbert Norwood, who admired the sheer craftsmanship of the play, observed of Phormio that "all the action hangs upon him without his needing to shoulder his way into every scene."[23] The main reason this is so, the main reason that Terence can hold Phormio back so that each appearance becomes a dramatic highpoint, is because Geta is there to see to the mechanics of the plot.

Not every comic intriguer will, like Tranio of *Mostellaria*, exert personal control over all his schemes. Pseudolus works through a surrogate, and Phormio's need for Geta does not diminish his own domination of the action. Yet keeping the central character at a distance as Terence does inevitably affects the complexity of that action. When Molière turned *Phormio* into *Les fourberies de Scapin*, for example, he compressed the roles of Geta and Phormio into the single character Scapin and altered the plot in the process.[24] Scapin, the valet of Léandre (Phaedria), is recruited to advise Octave (Antipho). He is both intriguer and pedagogue. Like Phormio, he must protect the marriage of Octave and Hyacinte from Octave's father Argante and also secure money so

[23] Norwood, *AT* 77.

[24] K. E. Wheatley, *Molière and Terence* (Austin 1931) 10–43, provides a detailed comparison of the two plots. For general discussion, see H. Levin, "From Terence to Tabarin: A Note on *Les fourberies de Scapin*," *Yale Fr. Stud.* 38 (1967) 128–137, and B. Stambler, "Terence and Molière," in R. Johnson et al., *Molière and the Commonwealth of Letters* (Jackson, MS 1975) 417–429.

that Léandre may rescue his beloved Zerbinette from gypsies. In back-to-back scenes Scapin blackmails Argante and swindles Léandre's father Géronte. The scene with Argante corresponds to offstage action after *Phormio* 727 when Demipho leaves for the forum to pay Phormio. The scene with Géronte, probably borrowed from Cyrano de Bergerac's *Le pedant joué*, has no equivalent in Terence. These scenes not only enliven the play with farce but also complicate the stage action.

All Scapin's intrigues occur in the course of the play. Unlike the marriage of Antipho and Phanium, the marriage of Octave and Hyacinte was accomplished without intrigue, though Scapin protects it with a more theatrical version of the same ploy Geta and Phormio use against Demipho. An imaginary brother of Hyacinte, played by Octave's valet Silvestre, appears willing to annul the marriage if given enough money. Argante is first enraged by the suggestion but then intimidated by the threatening appearance of the "brother" himself. There is much stage business in the scene, and Scapin's use of Silvestre as his agent contrasts with the shared responsibility of Geta and Phormio in Terence's equivalent scheme. The swindling of Géronte uses a different device, the story of Léandre's abduction by a genteel Turk on a galley. Géronte must pay to rescue his son. The romantic dilemmas of Octave and Léandre thus have separate solutions, and the intrigues surrounding them are further complicated and enriched by farcical punishments meted out later to each father for his miserliness. The play is held together first by the single figure of Scapin carrying out both sets of intrigue and then by the artificial but appropriate discovery that Hyacinte is Géronte's daughter and Zerbinette the long-lost daughter of Argante. The play ends with a last trick by means of which Scapin escapes punishment for his trickery.

The complexity of *Les fourberies de Scapin* reveals the comparative simplicity of Terence's plot. There is the semblance of double intrigue in *Phormio*, but its two parts are not of equal weight. The story of Antipho's marriage that figured so prominently in the exposition creates our respect for Phormio's skill as an intriguer. Yet that marriage is a *fait accompli*, and Phormio protects it on stage simply by besting Demipho in debate. Only the intrigue over Phaedria's *citharistria* is both conceived and enacted in the course of the play. The basis for that scheme is indeed Demipho's hostility toward Antipho's marriage, but this is a mark more of economy than of complexity in plot construction. This economy of action is confirmed by the single resolution of the young men's problems. The recognition of Phanium as Chremes' daughter means that Antipho has the right girl, and the disclosure of Chremes' bigamy to his wife Nausistrata secures Phaedria's possession of the music-girl. How can Chremes object to Phaedria's *amica*, she will ask, when he himself had two wives? The elegant simplicity of this resolution is made possible by pairing Demipho and Chremes. Whereas Molière keeps Argante and Géronte distinct so that Scapin can trick them in succession, Terence pairs Demipho and Chremes just as he had paired Geta and Phormio. Chremes does not actually arrive from Lemnos until 567, but, once he does, the two old men are linked for the duration. Thus when Geta and Phormio contrive to get the thirty minae, Chremes provides the money, but Demipho goes off to pay it (713ff.). The roles of trickster and dupe are divided among four characters to yield the semblance of a double deception. There are two intriguers and two victims, but only one trick.

This trick, of course, never really has to succeed or fail. As so often in Roman comedy, it is simply subsumed by a new piece of information. A genuinely well-made plot reaches its conclusion by its own momentum, but *Phormio* does not resolve its dilemma through the intrigue Phormio and Geta have woven. New impetus comes from the sudden discovery of Phanium's parentage. This discovery is not really a complete surprise. It is foreshadowed and its results engineered by devices as obvious and as effective as the water to be drawn from Knemon's well and the gift of Lady Windermere's fan. The first involves the name Stilpo, and the second is the personality created for Chremes' wife Nausistrata.

When Phormio and Geta stage their little argument for the benefit of Demipho and his *advocati*, they mention the name of Phanium's father, the alleged cousin of Demipho.

> PH. nec Stilponem ipsum scire qui fuerit? GE. negat.
>
> PH. Nor does he know who Stilpo was? GE. No.
> (356)

We do not yet know if this name is correct or even if the detail is significant. A little later in the same scene, however, the name surfaces again in a curious way. Demipho approaches Phormio and demands the name of his "relative."

> PH. eho, tu, sobrinum tuom non noras? DE. enicas.
>   dic nomen. PH. nomen? maxume. DE. quid nunc taces?
> PH. perii hercle, nomen perdidi. DE. [hem] quid ais?
>   PH. (Geta,
>   si meministi id quod olim dictumst, subice.) hem,
>   non dico: quasi non nosses, temptatum advenis.
> DE. ego autem tempto? GE. (Stilpo.) PH. atque adeo quid mea?
>   Stilpost. DE. quem dixti? PH. Stilponem inquam noveras.
>
> PH. Hah! You don't know your own cousin? DE. You're killing
>   me.
>   Name him. PH. His name? Certainly. DE. Well?
> PH. I'm done for. I've forgotten the name. DE. What's that?
>   PH. (Geta,
>   if you remember what we just said, help.) Hmm.
>   I won't say. You're fishing, as if you didn't know.
> DE. Fishing? Me? GE. (Stilpo.) PH. Well, what's it to me?
>   The name is Stilpo. DE. Whom did you say? PH. I say you
>   know Stilpo.
> (384–390)

Why does Phormio suffer this sudden lapse of memory? Though the whispered asides make for good comedy and Phormio's presence of mind in adversity is impressive in any case, the triple repetition of the name in two lines signals an important technical function. The name is not completely strange to us—that was the purpose of its mention in line 356—and it is emphasized now by the repetition and comic byplay surrounding it. The comedy makes this a memorable scene, and "Stilpo" thus becomes a memorable name.[25] The reason to remember it becomes evident a little later.

We learned at Chremes' first appearance that he has had a daughter by his second wife on Lemnos (567ff.). When he went there to fetch her, he found she had gone to Athens in search of him. Now he suddenly encounters her nurse Sophrona near his own front door.

                                        CH. east ipsa:
conloquar. SO. quis hic loquitur? CH. Sophrona. SO. et meum nomen nominat?
CH. respice ad me. SO. di obsecro vos, estne hic Stilpo? CH. non. SO. negas?
CH. concede hinc a foribus paullum istorum sodes, Sophrona. ne me istoc posthac nomine appellassis. SO. quid? non obsecro es
quem semper te esse dictitasti? CH. st.

                                        CH. It's she.
I'll speak to her. SO. Who's speaking here? CH. Sophrona. SO. And uses my name.

---

[25] Both Lefèvre (above, n. 18) 27–31 and Arnott (above, n. 19) 39–40 recognize the comic and structural values of this lapse but underrate the latter. If the Greek original had an expository prologue, such emphasis in the body of the play might have been less necessary. Richard Bentley thought line 356 out of place, but it was well defended by G. Howe, "A Note on *Phormio*," *SP* 11 (1913) 61–63.

CH. Look at me. SO. Good God, isn't this Stilpo? CH. No.
SO. No?
CH. Come away from this door a little bit, please, Sophrona.
Don't call me by that name anymore. SO. What? Do you mean
you're not who you always said you were? CH. Sh!

(738–743)

The real purpose of Phormio's lapse was to make this scene so effective. Sophrona is Phanium's nurse, and her use of the name Stilpo identifies Phanium as the missing daughter. This discovery joins two pieces of the plot and resolves at a stroke the problem posed by Antipho's marriage. Like the humor that surrounds Phormio's earlier forgetfulness, the unexpected abruptness of Chremes' denial—after all, he both is and is not Stilpo—and the explanation that follows prolong the moment of recognition to impress its significance upon us. Chremes' own failure to perceive the ramifications of the discovery again uses humor to emphasize something important. When he learns that Sophrona's charge is actually married to Antipho, he remarks,

CH. quid? duasne uxores habet? SO. au obsecro, unam ille-
quidem hanc solam.
CH. quid illam alteram quae dicitur cognata? SO. haec ergost.

CH. What? Has he got two wives? SO. No, he at any rate has
just this one.
CH. What of that other one said to be a cousin? SO. She's
the one.

(754–755)

Bigamy is naturally on Chremes' mind, and *duae uxores* is a phrase with an important echo later (1041). His comic obtuseness here is skillfully placed to forestall our own confusion while prefiguring a later development. The careful placing of the Stilpo device, which needs the personalities established for Phormio, Demipho, and Chremes to make it work, is a deft variant on such common devices as birth tokens and sudden encounters to prepare the audience for a recognition and then to bring it about.

Chremes was so anxious to move Sophrona from his house door because of the wife he has inside: "conclusam hic habeo uxorem saevam" (744). This is scarcely an exaggeration. In accordance with the plan to separate Antipho and Phanium by bribing Phormio to marry the girl himself, Demipho recruited Chremes' wife, Nausistrata, to break the news to her. We first see Nausistrata as Demipho escorts her to his house to perform this task (784ff.). She is willing, but she does not go quietly. The thirty minae paid to Phormio came from her property on Lemnos, and she complains of how poorly Chremes manages her affairs. Her father used to get two silver talents from the property in less favorable times, but Chremes brings back only a fraction of that. This leads to her second source of frustration.

> NA. virum me natam vellem:
> ego ostenderem. DE. certe scio. NA. quo pacto . . .
> DE. parce, sodes,
> ut possis cum illa, ne te adulescens mulier defetiget.

> NA. I wish I'd been born a man:
> I would show him. DE. I'm sure. NA. The way . . .
> DE. Please,
> save yourself for her, so the young woman won't tire
> you out.
>
> (792–794)

Nausistrata's father, of course, was not supporting a second family on those revenues, but the vehemence and drift of her complaint explain Chremes' epithet *saeva*. Demipho can handle Nausistrata in this scene, but it is not easy.

This brief exchange sets up the comedy of the following scene. Chremes enters from Demipho's house, anxious to tell his brother that he has found his missing daughter and can cancel the arrangement with Phormio. He nearly says too much before catching sight of Nausistrata (795ff.). The resulting exchange, where Demipho demands an explanation that Chremes dares not give before his wife, is a kind of comedy set up by the situation but made effective because of the personalities involved. The slow-witted Chremes finds oblique explanations difficult, Nausistrata threatens untimely interference, and Demipho struggles to understand what is going on. There is a similar kind of scene at *Samia* 464ff., where Demeas thinks he knows everything, Nikeratos is trying to figure things out, and Moschion realizes that to correct Demeas requires him to admit that Nikeratos' daughter is the mother of his child. Demeas' mistaken self-assurance, Nikeratos' blustering foolishness, and Moschion's pusillanimity create the comedy of that scene just as the personalities of Demipho, Nausistrata, and Chremes are essential to Terence's effect here, but the two scenes function a little differently. Menander's scene signals the beginning of the play's climax, for Demeas and Nikeratos soon learn the truth and Moschion's marriage is then assured. Terence's scene is a transition between two sections of this plot. Antipho's marriage is already secure. The introduction and development of Nausistrata's character look ahead to a resolution of the play's second problem, Phaedria's relationship with the music-girl. Nausistrata is finally coaxed inside. Chremes' secret is momentarily saved, but when she reappears the force of her personality will shape the play's climax.

Phormio's new scheme to save the thirty minae for Phaedria really amounts only to fast talk and blackmail. When the old men refuse to let Phormio keep the money as recompense for his trouble, the parasite threatens to reveal Chremes' bigamy to his wife (894ff.). We recognize the power of Phormio's threat because we have seen Nausistrata. By keeping her on stage as long as he did, Terence whetted expectations for the confrontation that Phormio now threatens. Demipho does everything he can to prevent it, but he is outmaneuvered.[26] The old men must resort to force, and amid the resulting slapstick Phormio summons Nausistrata from her house (982ff.). The story she then hears brings exclamations of pain from her, but also answers the longstanding questions that had surfaced during her first appearance.

> haecin erant itiones crebrae et mansiones diutinae
> Lemni? haecin erat ea quae nostros minuit fructus vilitas?
>
> Is that why there were frequent trips and such long stays
> on Lemnos? Is that the "slump" that kept our income down?
> (1012–1013)

Nausistrata is very practical, even in adversity. She will of course forgive Chremes eventually, and Phormio knows the reason why: "She's got something to chew his ear with for as long as he lives" (1030). Chremes will certainly pay for his bigamy. Will he also pay for Phaedria's music-girl? Phormio himself raises the question of the thirty minae and what he has done with them. Nausistrata crushes Chremes' protest almost before he makes it:

> adeo hoc indignum tibi videtur, filius
> homo adulescens si habet unam amicam, tu uxores duas?
> nil pudere! quo ore illum obiurgabis?
>
> Does it seem so wrong to you that your young
> son has a girl friend, while you have had two wives?
> What nerve! How will you dare scold him?
> (1040–1042)

She caps his punishment by appointing Phaedria his judge and by inviting the parasite to dinner. A weaker character might still have maintained her dignity but could scarcely support so many converging threads of the action. Because Nausistrata is so strong, the punishment of Chremes, the happy ending of Phae-

---

[26] This final struggle of wits between Demipho and Phormio is analyzed in detail by Arnott (above, n. 19) 48–52.

dria's romance, and the parasite's reward are all hers to bestow. The play ends as Nausistrata commands.

Like the growing crisis at Knemon's well and the presence of the sacrificers to Pan, the name Stilpo and the personality of Nausistrata assume increasing importance as the play progresses. They are devices of quite deliberate plot construction and result in a play carefully built to keep its end in line with its beginning. The foundations for later developments are all deftly laid, events are kept consistent with character, and little can be called extraneous or incoherent. This may well reflect the dramatic skill of Apollodorus of Carystus, but a still more interesting point lies in Terence's decision to present so taut a play to his Roman audience.[27] Its success depends on its narrative technique, and Terence demonstrates that he can tell a story very effectively indeed. A few structural tricks help him. Though the threads of the story are carefully laid, they are neither numerous nor complex in their pattern. By pairing Phormio and Geta and Demipho and Chremes, and by keeping Antipho and Phaedria in the background, Terence gives the impression of complexity because a large number of characters figure in the action. Yet each character actually contributes just a little, and the action itself is straightforward. There are no loose ends because there are precious few ends to leave loose. To what extent is *Phormio* then "well made"?

Artful convergence of a bewildering variety of characters and details was both the hallmark and the affectation of the nineteenth-century well-made play, a tradition that reaches an appropriate culmination in the farces of Feydeau. The clockwork precision of *A Flea in Her Ear*, for example, is the essence of the

---

[27] Büchner, *TT* 307, believes we can speak without hesitation of *Phormio* as a play by Apollodorus, and Arnott (above, n. 19) seems to agree. In the introduction to his edition (London 1959), R. H. Martin reviews the alterations Terence seems to have made and calls them few and minor. Lefèvre (above, n. 18) now offers a quite different view: see the review by E. Fantham, *CP* 77 (1982) 365–370, and Lowe (above, n. 10) 431–437.

play's appeal, and we justly admire Feydeau's skill in setting the members of a large cast at cross-purposes before bringing them together again at the same time and place to meet initial embarrassment and eventual enlightenment. Deliberate complexity of this sort was generally avoided in ancient drama either by keeping the plot simple or by eliminating characters and devices when their retention threatened undue complication. Aristophanes never hesitated to drop a Xanthias or Euelpides who had served his purpose. Menander reduced Chrysis to a mute role when her immediate crisis was resolved, and Plautus could be deliberately and delightfully capricious. Intriguers like Tranio, Epidicus, and Pseudolus weave and abandon schemes at will, and their eventual success owes more to chance than to wit. Plautine plots may twist and turn, but the dramatic knot is more likely to be cut than unraveled. A play sufficiently exuberant did not have to make much sense. In *Phormio* Terence avoids such fantastic and willful confusion, offering instead a logical construction more closely paralleled in Menander and, presumably, found also in Apollodorus. The play is very well organized, but it lacks the complexity and exoticism that Scribe and his successors valued so highly. To call it "well made" is thus inexact and unhelpful. Nor was its kind of structural integrity the only technique for organizing a play available to Terence. In fact, one of his most notorious practices in composition yielded plays that are not even this well made, but are not therefore simply disorganized. They are, as we will now see, just different.

[IV]

Contaminatio

In the prologue to *Menaechmi*, Plautus jokes with evident affection about the artificiality of the comic scene and its stock characters.

> haec urbs Epidamnus est dum haec agitur fabula:
> quando alia agetur aliud fiet oppidum;
> sicut familiae quoque solent mutarier:
> modo hic habitat leno, modo adulescens, modo senex,
> pauper, mendicus, rex, parasitus, hariolus.

> This city is Epidamnus while this play is performed:
> when another one's performed, it becomes another town;
> just as households too are often swapped:
> sometimes a pimp lives there, sometimes an old man or a boy,
> a poor man, beggar, rich man, parasite, seer.
>
> (*Men.* 72–76)

In looking beyond the confines of *Menaechmi*, Plautus is acknowledging that his characters and situations are the common possession of the tradition itself, not the unique creations of any one play. The conventions have a transience and fluidity that make the Roman process of adaptation a matter more of recombination than invention. Yet when Terence sought to capitalize on the commonality of comic motifs by grafting specific elements of one Greek play onto the structure of another, his action brought howls of protest from rival dramatists. In his first play he had added material from Menander's *Perinthia* to a Latin version of *Andria*, and the interpolation did not go unnoticed.

> quae convenere in Andriam ex Perinthia
> fatetur transtulisse atque usum pro suis.

> id isti vituperant factum atque in eo disputant
> contaminari non decere fabulas.

> Our poet grants he transferred from Perinthia
> what suited Andria and used it as his own.
> They pick on this and argue that
> plays must not be contaminated.
>
> (*And.* 13–16)

Complaints were still being heard by the time *Heauton timorumenos* was produced.

> nam quod rumores distulerunt malevoli
> multas contaminasse Graecas, dum facit
> paucas Latinas: factum id esse hic non negat
> neque se pigere et deinde facturum autumat.

> As for the rumors the malevolent spread that
> he has ruined many Greek plays while making
> few in Latin: he won't deny that this is so.
> He's not ashamed. He'll even dare do it again.
>
> (*HT* 16–19)

Terence in fact continued the practice of interpolation in *Eunuchus* and *Adelphoe*, though now adding material to his versions from Greek plays that had previously appeared in Latin forms. This evidently struck his opponents as plagiarism.

> quam nunc acturi sumus
> Menandri Eunuchum, postquam aediles emerunt,
> perfecit sibi ut inspiciundi esset copia.
> magistratus quom ibi adesset occeptast agi.
> exclamat furem, non poetam fabulam
> dedisse et nil dedisse verborum tamen . . .

> We're about to perform
> Menander's Eunuch. After the aediles commissioned it,
> he got himself a chance to check it out.

The magistrate sat down and the show began.
He cried that not a poet but a thief had sold
this play and didn't write it . . .
                    (*Eun*. 19–24, cf. *Ad*. 9–14)

There thus seem to be two charges, one of theft and one of contamination, that involve Terence's addition of extraneous material to three plays, *Andria, Eunuchus*, and *Adelphoe*. This practice has long presented a scholarly puzzle.[1]

The charge of theft is the easier to understand. Terence added to his *Eunuchus* the soldier and parasite of Menander's *Kolax*, a play that both Naevius and Plautus had previously turned into Latin (*Eun*. 25–34). He had thus unwittingly borrowed from Roman predecessors instead of sticking to Greek sources. This he admits is wrong. Ignorance is his only excuse (*peccatum inprudentiast*, 27), though he bolsters his case with the useful, though not entirely relevant, argument that nothing in the tradition is ever entirely new ("nullumst iam dictum quod non dictum sit prius," 41). As for the use of Diphilus' *Synapothnescontes* in *Adelphoe*, Terence acquits himself on a technicality. Although Plautus did in fact use Diphilus' play, he had left out the one scene Terence has borrowed (*locum integrum*, 9–10). The audience should judge for itself whether this really constitutes plagiarism.

>   pernoscite
> furtumne factum existumetis an locum
> reprehensum qui praeteritus neglegentiast.
>
>   Discover
> if you think this was a theft or just a scene

---

[1] The debate is summarized by Duckworth, *NRC* 202–208, and Marti, *Lustrum* 8 (1963) 23–27, to which should be added O. Kujore, "A Note on *Contaminatio* in Terence," *CP* 69 (1974) 39–42. The following discussion owes most to W. Beare, "Contaminatio," *CR* 9 (1959) 7–11, and M. Simon, "*Contaminatio* und *Furtum* bei Terenz," *Helikon* 1 (1961) 487–492.

our predecessor skipped through carelessness.
(*Ad.* 12–14)

Most significant about this charge is its strictly practical character. Terence is accused not of making bad plays, but of threatening the integrity of the Roman stage. His plagiarism turns the *palliata* tradition inward by borrowing so quickly from itself. The charge must have been serious, since Terence takes great care to excuse himself.

The more perplexing charge of "contamination" must be understood against this background of concern with theatrical practice. Donatus' comments on the term survive in somewhat garbled form, but his drift is clear.

> (1) *Contaminari* "contaminare" proprie est manibus luto plenis aliquid attingere et— (2) Contaminare contingere est—polluere. Vergilius (*Aen.* 3.61) "linqui pollutum h." (3) *Contaminari* "contaminari" tangi et relinqui polluta manu ac per hoc velut foedari aut maculari, ut ipse ait (*Eun.* 552) "ne hoc gaudium contaminet vita aegritudine aliqua." (4) *Contaminari non decere* id est: ex multis unam non decere facere.

> (1) *Contaminari* "to contaminate" is, properly speaking, to touch something with soiled hands— (2) To contaminate is to defile—to pollute. Vergil (*Aen.* 3.61) "friendship left polluted." (3) *Contaminari* "to be contaminated" to be touched and abandoned by polluted hand and thus as if spoiled and stained, as he himself says (*Eun.* 552) "lest life's trouble spoil this happiness." (4) *Contaminari non decere* that is: not right to make one play from many.
>
> (*ad And.* 16)

The fourth entry explains the entire line, which surely does mean that it is wrong to make one play out of many. If we then ask *why* it is wrong, we come to the meaning of *contaminari* itself, which Donatus clearly defines as "to be spoiled." For whom are the plays spoiled? The related charge of *furtum* suggests the answer. Terence is spoiling plays for other dramatists. By making many into few (*HT* 17–18), he is unfairly reducing the store of Greek plays available for adoption. Whether there really was a shortage of suitable Greek plays circulating in Terence's Rome is impossible to know, but a persistent story preserved in the Suetonian *vita* may be relevant: Terence was said to have died at sea while bringing a trunk full of Menandrean plays to Italy.[2] Once again, though, the argument is practical. Terence is accused of violating operational, not aesthetic, rules. Only among modern critics has the charge of contamination become an aesthetic issue.

Friedrich Leo was the first to project the statements in Terence's prologues onto the larger corpus of Roman comedy and to seek in a developing practice of "contamination" the answer to the perplexing question of originality on the Roman stage. Since the *Andria* prologue claimed illustrious predecessors for Terence's practice of interpolation, Leo hoped to uncover the process by which these Roman dramatists turned Greek works of art into Latin ones.[3] Though subsequent efforts to find contamination in Plautus have not been particularly successful and the Terentian

---

[2] Suetonius cites versions of Terence's death by Volcacius, Cosconius (a predecessor of Varro), and anonymous *ceteri*, who all agree that he perished on a return trip from the east with either 108 plays "conversis a Menandro" (Cosconius) or—that number is clearly suspect—at least quite a few in his luggage (*ceteri*). See A. Rostagni, ed., Suetonio, *de Poetis* (Turin 1944) 39–40. By Terence's day, dramatists may well have replaced Plautine *neglegentia* with a firmer notion of presenting versions of specific Greek originals. See H. Oppermann, "Zur Entwicklung der Fabula Palliata," *Hermes* 74 (1939) 113–129, and Garton, *PA* 66–72.

[3] Leo, *PlF* 170: "Die Entwicklung die hier von Plautus zu Terenz vorliegt, ist so wichtig für die Geschichte des römischen Dramas, dass es gut ist, an den sicheren Beispielen der Art des Plautus näher nachzugehen." *Contaminatio* does not appear as a Latin noun until the third century A.D., when it means simply pollution, e.g., "locum lustrari . . . ab omni contaminatione," *Act. lud. saec. Sept. Sev.* 3.24. Neither Donatus nor any other ancient commentator uses the term.

sense of *contaminari* has never been entirely forgotten, a modern, technical concept of *Kontamination* has nevertheless arisen that centers on the question of adaptation from the Greek.[4] By concentrating on the derivative nature of the *comoedia palliata*, Leo's descendants can ignore the practical thrust of the ancient argument. If Terence is essentially a translator and a Latin play was "normally not an essentially new creation," it makes little difference if the borrowing was directly from Greek or Roman predecessors.[5] These scholars focus instead on the structural effects of the interpolations, hoping to reveal the relationship between each play and its Greek model and thereby to measure the extent of the Roman dramatist's creativity. Much good has come of this approach. Its necessarily close analysis of Latin texts has yielded, for example, a detailed study of how and when Terence gets necessary information to his audience and a book-length discussion of *Adelphoe* that makes important discoveries about Terence's use of his original.[6] Yet this analytic approach is also fraught with difficulties. Most obvious of these are its basis in speculation and the danger of circularity in a method that compares an extant Latin text to a Greek one reconstructed from it by internal analysis. As a sympathetic reviewer observed of the *Adelphoe* book,

[4] Fraenkel and Jachmann both sought to find "contaminatio" in Plautus, but see Fraenkel's *retractatio* at *EPP* 431–433 and the excellent survey by K. Gaiser, "Zur Eigenart der römischen Komödie," *ANRW* 1.2 (1972) 1058–1063. The issue has since been reopened by L. Schaaf, *Der Miles Gloriosus des Plautus und sein griechisches Original* (Munich 1977). The goals of *Kontaminationsforschung* are stated most cogently by W. Ludwig, *Gnomon* 36 (1964) 152–160.

[5] The quotation is from W. Ludwig, "The Originality of Terence and His Greek Models," *GRBS* 9 (1968) 181. Cf. Jachmann, *RE* 5A (1934) 625, s.v. P. Terentius Afer: "Literarische Reproduktion dieser Art ist im Grunde Übersetzung."

[6] E. Lefèvre, *Die Expositionstechnik in den Komödien des Terenz* (Darmstadt 1969); O. Rieth, *Die Kunst Menanders in den Adelphen des Terenz* (Hildesheim 1964).

"It is easy to forget that the theory for all that remains a speculative hypothesis in the absence of the Greek original. It may therefore be completely wrong. . . ." In fact, few of an analyst's conclusions ever escape modification or even contradiction.[7] A second difficulty, the inevitable consequence of the first, is that textual analysis of this sort does not equip its practitioners to make aesthetic judgments. Although the *where* of Terence's interpolations can be debated with some success, *why* Terence interpolated is an aesthetic question where progress has been only superficial. Vague comments about enriching and coarsening stage action are ultimately unhelpful.[8] Nevertheless, the question of "why" lies at the heart of the modern issue of *contaminatio*. How does the interpolated material affect the meaning of the play? This chapter will deal directly with that aesthetic question by examining the two clearest cases of Terence's "contamination" and by asking what his interpolations aimed to accomplish.[9]

I

The interpolation easiest to identify has proved most difficult to interpret. Terence is explicit about the addition to his Menandrean *Adelphoe*.

[7] The observation about Rieth is by W. G. Arnott, *Gnomon* 37 (1965) 261. Rieth's findings have since been vigorously contested by, *inter alios*, E. Fantham, "*Heautontimorumenos* and *Adelphoe*. A Study of Fatherhood in Terence and Menander," *Latomus* 30 (1971) 970–998, esp. 990–996, and C. Lord, "Aristotle, Menander, and the *Adelphoe* of Terence," *TAPA* 107 (1977) 183–202. The same analytic skills that produced the excellent *Expositionstechnik* have since led Lefèvre to contradict his own findings, at least for *Heauton timorumenos* in his *Die römische Komödie* (Darmstadt 1973) 443–462, and *Phormio* in *Der Phormio des Terenz und der Epidikazomenos des Apollodor von Karystos* (Munich 1978).

[8] Thus Ludwig (above, n. 5) 174–175, though not all such vagueness is restricted to the German analytic school. See *CW* 75 (1981) 81–86.

[9] Terence's alterations in *Andria* present special problems, for he provides

> Synapothnescontes Diphili comoediast:
> eam Commorientis Plautus fecit fabulam.
> in Graeca adulescens est qui lenoni eripit
> meretricem in prima fabula: eum Plautus locum
> reliquit integrum, eum hic locum sumpsit sibi
> in Adelphoe, verbum de verbo expressum extulit.
>
> Synapothnescontes is a play by Diphilus.
> Plautus turned it into Partners in Death.
> Early in the Greek, a boy steals a whore
> from a pimp. Plautus left that scene
> untouched. Our poet took it for his
> Brothers, fitting it in word for word.
>
> (*Ad.* 8–11)

The opening of Act II from lines 155 to at least line 196, in which young Aeschinus insults the pimp Sannio and has him beaten, has therefore been taken not only from a different play but from a different Greek author. Why has Terence incorporated this lively, amusing, and rather nasty scene?

Discussing *Adelphoe* has become less a matter of original thought than of defending a side. For the better part of two centuries controversy has raged over the play's characters and philosophies, its ending, and of course the form of its Greek original. Lessing was the first modern reader to wrestle seriously with its difficulties, and subsequent generations have been similarly fascinated and irritated.[10] Micio, often seen as the personification of

---

no sure guide to them. See G. Calboli, "Terenzio, *Andria* 481–488," *Philologus* 124 (1980) 33–67, and for some of the specific changes, Chapter 5 below.

[10] For Lessing's reading of *Adelphoe* see J. G. Robertson, *Lessing's Dramatic Theory* (New York 1965) 318–321 and 327–330. Two recent discussions in English, both with full bibliography, are J. N. Grant, "The Ending of Terence's *Adelphoe* and the Menandrian Original," *AJP* 96 (1975) 42–60, and N. A. Greenberg, "Success and Failure in the *Adelphoe*," *CW* 73 (1979/80) 221–236.

enlightened childrearing, is eventually routed when his rustic, severe brother Demea turns his philosophy against him. Having won our sympathy by his wit, charm, and generosity, Micio is suddenly compelled to free slaves, part with money and a small estate, and marry against his will. Is this the price of enlightenment? Does the play's ending confirm or deny all that has gone before? Does Micio get what he deserves? These are difficult questions, and in answering them we must not forget that the play is essentially about people, not philosophies. Benedetto Croce, though a little flowery, perhaps puts it best: ". . . the contrast in the educational methods of the two fathers in the *Adelphoe* is not, as some moralizing critics would have it, designed to inculcate the lesson of avoidance of extremes, but serves to illustrate and to express wonderment at the variety of human conduct and its unforeseeable consequences. . . . There is no question, then, of a 'problem' or an educational programme, but simply of a clash of temperaments and feelings, and a tangle of chances, eluding all educational theory."[11] The action is built upon faults of character, and while Demea's faults are not far to seek, the error of Micio's ways is perhaps harder for us to recognize. Yet we must try to see Micio as Terence intended and to put the actions of his son in the context of the unique relationship between them.

Terence begins the play, as Menander probably began his own *Adelphoi*, with a monologue by the lenient Micio. Its closest parallel is Moschion's speech at the beginning of *Samia*, and that Menandrean example can help put Micio's speech in the necessary perspective. Moschion is an adopted son, just as Micio is an adoptive father, and he has been raised with just the kind of sympathetic indulgence that Micio advocates. The ties of adoption

---

[11] B. Croce, "Terence" in *Philosophy, Poetry, History*, tr. C. Sprigge (Oxford 1966) 797–798. Konrad Gaiser, in an Afterword to Rieth (above, n. 6) 145–151, nevertheless maintains that a philosophical concern was indeed at the heart of Menander's play: Menander representing an ideal in Micio, Terence seeking a mean. Contrast Lord (above, n. 7).

are fragile, and in each case they have been strengthened by good will. Moschion has never lacked anything. His father's money has financed his service as *choregos* and *phylarchos*. He has owned horses and hunting dogs. His speech is filled with the sophisticated catchwords of his time and class: ἄνθρωπος, ἀνθρώπινον, φιλανθρώπως φιλοτιμία, κόσμιος, ἀστεῖα χάρις. It seems a genial picture, but as Moschion proceeds to describe the domestic arrangements of his father's household, our opinion of the boy begins to change. His self-confidence sounds increasingly like egotism, and by the time he reaches the key point of his speech—that he has gotten the neighbor's daughter pregnant—we have realized that this elegant young man is also a rather pampered and pretentious prig.[12] This is an important and carefully orchestrated realization, for the plot of *Samia* will turn on Moschion's repeated failure to confess his misdeeds and accept their consequences. Menander has sowed beneath the glibly expository surface of Moschion's speech those seeds of doubt about his character that develop the intellectual tension of the play. Though we may still like Moschion, his inner weakness has been revealed, and we will not be surprised when the play ends with his final, embarrassed surrender to his father's better sense.

Terence's play opens with the same device. Micio enters from his house to express concern over the whereabouts of his son Aeschinus. He explains that Aeschinus is actually his brother Demea's natural son, and this leads him to describe the differences of character and outlook between himself and his brother. Demea has attempted to raise his second son Ctesipho with the rough standards of the country. Micio's philosophy of life is quite different.

[12] For the cultural elements in Moschion's speech see A. W. Gomme and F. H. Sandbach, *Menander, A Commentary* (Oxford 1973) 544-551, and for the revelation of his own character, Goldberg, *MMC* 92-95.

> ego hanc clementem vitam urbanam atque otium
> secutus sum . . .
>
> I've pursued an easy life in town,
> enjoyed my leisure . . .
>
> (42–43)

This too seems a genial picture, but just as Menander soon led us to doubt the rightness of Moschion's declarations, so Terence has orchestrated false harmonies to strike the ear of his Roman audience. Though the Greek word *asteios*, for example, is frequently a term of general praise in Menander, *urbanus* in the time of Terence had less positive connotations. The word first appears in Plautus associated with the *scurra* or "city slicker" (*Most.* 15, *Trin.* 202).[13] Strabax, the country boy of *Truculentus*, refers contemptuously to "urbanos istos mundulos amasios" (658), and in *Miles Gloriosus* Periplectomenus, like the parasite of Menander's *Dyskolos*, defines for himself a refined sophistication that consists largely of a talent for egregious remarks and the playing of parts (635ff., cf. *Dys.* 57ff.). *Otium* in itself is not equally pejorative. The Romans saw a proper place for *otium* in life's rhythm of work and leisure, of public and private service. Thus Cato's *Origines* promised a record of private as well as public achievement: "clarorum hominum atque magnorum non minus otii quam negotii rationem extare oportere" (fr. 2P).[14] Deliberate pursuit of *otium*, however, is another matter, for that makes leisure an end in itself. *Otium sequi* has the negative connotation of "doing nothing" (cf. C., *Pro. Mur.* 27.55, Nep., *Pelop.* 2.1); in the Terentian pro-

---

[13] E. S. Ramage, *Urbanitas* (Cincinnati 1973) 30–31; P. B. Corbett, "The *Scurra* in Plautus," *Eranos* 66 (1968) 118–131.

[14] Cf. Cicero's statement at *Off.* 3.1.1: "P. Scipionem . . . dicere solitum scripsit Cato, qui fuit eius fere aequalis, numquam se minus otiosum esse, quam cum otiosus." For the role of *otium* in Roman life, see J.-M. André, *L'Otium dans la vie morale et intellectuelle romaine* (Paris 1966) 17–65.

logues *transdere in otium* and *ut in otio esset* mean, in effect, to harm the poet by depriving him of work (*Ph.* 2, *Hec.* 26). This social context puts Micio's declaration in a different light. Suave Micio in his *pallium* advocating the pursuit of an urbane, leisurely life conjures up the indolence of that *otium graecum* Romans so often ridiculed. A century later, Cicero was to use a similar picture to ridicule Gellius, a prosecutor of Sestius, because "ex impuro adulescente et petulante . . . Graeculum se atque otiosum putari voluit" (*Pro Sest.* 51.110). When Demea repeats Micio's words near the end of the play, the irony of his echo comes from the abrupt return to the moral color commonly attached to them.

> ille suam semper egit vitam in otio, in conviviis,
> clemens placidus, nulli laedere os, adridere omnibus.
>
> He's always spent his life in leisure, parties,
> easy, relaxed, with scowls for none, laughs for all.
> (863–864)

Equally striking, and equally suspicious to the Roman ear, are the terms Micio uses to describe the relationship between himself and his son.

> do, praetermitto, non necesse habeo omnia
> pro meo iure agere
>
> I pay. I let things pass. I don't think all
> must go my way.
> (51–52)

> et errat longe mea quidem sententia
> qui imperium credat gravius esse aut stabilius
> vi quod fit quam illud quod amicitia adiungitur.
>
> I, at any rate, believe a man goes far afield
> who thinks authority imposed by force is stronger

and more stable than what's linked with friendship.
(65–67)

Ius and *imperium* normally describe relations in comedy between a father and child. Dutiful Mnesilochus of *Bacchides*, for example, is "obsequens oboediensque . . . mori atque imperiis patris" (459). As Phidippus tells his daughter in *Hecyra*, "scio ego, Philumena, meum ius esse ut te cogam quae ego imperem facere" (243). Fathers frequently forgo this right—Phidippus will do so in the very next line—but they do not forfeit it entirely. Children in comedy may subvert the *patria potestas*, but it remains an omnipresent obstacle to them. The *amicitia* that Micio prefers depends upon shared values and opinions; it is values and opinions in conflict that generate the intrigue plots of the *palliata*.[15] Micio's monologue presents a philosophy that, by the Roman moral vocabulary and by the very conventions of Roman comedy, is doomed to failure. An audience sympathetic to these signs will hardly be surprised to see such principles lead Micio to disaster.

Terence has captured the subtlety of Menander's device in *Samia*. He has built into an engaging monologue the cultural overtones necessary to awaken both the audience's interest in his character and their suspicion of him. Whether Menander also used the device in his own *Adelphoi* is immaterial; Terence has certainly used it to tune Micio's speech for the Roman ear. His success perhaps explains the curious statement in the Suetonian *vita* that Varro preferred this beginning to the opening of the Greek original. Unhappiness with the ending of *Adelphoe* nevertheless comes largely from a feeling that Micio's discomfiture is undeserved. As one critic writes, ". . . nothing that is said or

---

[15] Cf. Sal., *Cat.* 20.4 (Catiline addressing his supporters): "nam idem velle atque idem nolle, ea demum firma amicitia est." The philosophical basis of the concept is discussed by J. Hellegouarc'h, *Le Vocabulaire latin des relations et des parties politiques sous la république* (Paris 1963) 41–48.

done by Micio or his son in the first four acts of *Adelphoe* suggests that his concept of fatherhood is anything but successful."[16] This is why the scene introduced from Diphilus is so important to Terence's design. Micio's first speech was in fact intended to sow the seeds of doubt. Those doubts grow as Aeschinus' first appearance reveals either Micio's failure to reproduce his own grace and refinement in his son or, perhaps, that Micio's grace does not actually run very deep.

What we call Act II of *Adelphoe* introduces Aeschinus in hot debate with the *leno* from whom he has just stolen a slave girl. We thus meet this product of Micio's enlightened views for the first time in a scene of harsh language and hard blows as he sets his slave Parmeno on the obstreperous pimp. We should perhaps recall here that in this play Aeschinus, having gotten a free-born girl pregnant, hesitates to seek permission to marry her, and he has responded to his brother Ctesipho's infatuation with the slave girl by stealing her and cheating her pimp out of a fair price. Both actions certainly figured in Menander's play, though we cannot know what dramatic value he assigned them. Terence has chosen to emphasize the brutality of these actions by devoting stage time to the bullying. Aeschinus is arrogant and rude to Sannio as Parmeno stands by to deliver the blows.

> SA. o facinus indignus! AE. geminabit nisi caves. SA. ei,
>   miseriam!
> AE. non innueram; verum in istam partem potius peccato
>   tamen.
>   i nunciam. SA. quid hoc reist? regnumne, Aeschine, hic
>   tu possides?
> AE. si possiderem, ornatus esses ex tuis virtutibus.
>
> SA. Oh, outrage! AE. He'll double it if you don't watch out.
>   SA. Yeow!

[16] Fantham (above, n. 7) 984.

AE. I didn't give the signal, but better to err on that side.
In you go. SA. What's this? Have you got a kingdom here, Aeschinus?
AE. If I had, you'd be decked out as you deserve.

(173-176)

The young man's manner here reflects badly both on himself and on the father whose educational principles he embodies. He is overbearing only when his rival is weak. Though he boldly routs this pimp, he will later become immobilized with fear when called upon to face the consequences of his actions (61-2). This first appearance works, like Micio's introductory monologue, to establish his character and the way we are to see his subsequent activities.

The actions of the son reflect the attitudes of the father. Aeschinus' fastidious arrogance toward Sannio is a cruder form of the patronizing smugness with which Micio continually irritates Demea.[17] The scene from Diphilus is meant both to dramatize the character of Aeschinus and to reinforce our earlier doubts about Micio. Terence uses the interpolation in a limited way here to heighten the drama and strengthen its significance. The scene is integrated into the action and meaning, its function determined and circumscribed by the basic structure of the *Adelphoe*. Yet the effect of a Terentian interpolation need not be so limited, as a more detailed study of *Eunuchus* will demonstrate.

II

In *Eunuchus* young Chaerea falls in love with Pamphila, the gift of a soldier named Thraso to the *meretrix* Thais. To gain access to his love, Chaerea disguises himself as this eunuch and eventually rapes Pamphila. She proves to be a citizen. Chaerea is

[17] W. R. Johnson, "Micio and the Perils of Perfection," *CSCA* 1 (1968) 171-186; Grant (above, n. 10) 47-48.

happy to marry her, and Phaedria, at the urging of Thraso's parasite Gnatho, agrees to share Thais with the soldier.

Modern discussions of this play fluctuate between cool dissection and acute discomfort. The play was an immense success in Terence's day—returned for two encores by popular demand, says Donatus—but some critics no longer care for its morals, and others seem to care only about its structure. It is based upon a lost *Eunouchos* of Menander, but Terence is fairly explicit about certain interpolations.

> Colax Menandrist: in east parasitus Colax
> et miles gloriosus: eas se non negat
> personas transtulisse in Eunuchum suam
> ex Graeca . . .
>
> Menander wrote The Fawner. In it is a fawner parasite
> and a braggart soldier. Our poet won't deny
> he moved those figures to his Eunuch from
> the Greek . . .
>
> (30–33)

Unfortunately, the hundred odd lines of Menander's *Kolax* that survive reveal very little about its plot. There was a young man in love named Pheidias and a soldier named Bias. Whether the soldier's parasite was a Gnathon or a Strouthias, or whether there were perhaps *two* parasites is uncertain, and while Bias and Pheidias probably both loved the same girl owned by a pimp, the action that developed from their rivalry is unknown. How much the interpolations from *Kolax* have altered the action of Terence's *Eunuchus* is thus impossible to determine.[18] We can assume with

---

[18] Recent discussions of this problem include W. Ludwig, "Von Terenz zu Menander," *Philologus* 103 (1959) 1–38 (reprinted with an important *addendum* in E. Lefèvre, ed., *Die römische Komödie* [Darmstadt 1973]) 354–408; W. Steidle, "Menander bei Terenz," *RhM* 116 (1973) 326–347; and J.C.B. Lowe, "The *Eunuchus*: Terence and Menander," *CQ* 33 (1983) 428–444. For

confidence only that all the appearances of Thraso and Gnatho are at least to some extent Terence's additions to that play. These characters have four prominent scenes: Gnatho's entrance at 232, which prefigures the appearance of Thraso at 391, Thraso's assault on Thais' house at 771, and the finale, in which Phaedria agrees to share Thais with Thraso (1025ff.). What do these scenes contribute to the dramatic effect and the meaning of Terence's play? The most obvious point is still worth exploring. Soldier and parasite introduce an element of broad comedy and lively action, first with Gnatho's entrance monologue and especially in the fourth act with the assault on Thais' house.

Eduard Fraenkel has compared Gnatho's entrance monologue to a fragment of Eupolis' *Kolakes* in which the chorus of fawners explains its technique.[19] The agora is its hunting ground.

ἐκεῖ δ' ἐπειδὰν κατίδω τιν' ἄνδρα
ἠλίθιον, πλουτοῦντα δ', εὐθὺς περὶ τοῦτον εἰμί.
κἄν τι τύχῃ λέγων ὁ πλούταξ, πάνυ τοῦτ' ἐπαινῶ,
καὶ καταπλήττομαι δοκῶν τοῖσι λόγοισι χαίρειν.
εἶτ' ἐπὶ δεῖπνον ἐρχόμεσθ' ἄλλυδις ἄλλος ἡμῶν
μᾶζαν ἐπ' ἀλλόφυλον, οὗ δεῖ χαρίεντα πολλὰ
τὸν κόλακ' εὐθέως λέγειν, ἢ 'κφέρεται θύραζε.

There, when I spy a mark,
a fool, but rich, at once I'm all about him.
Anything my gilded sap should say I praise,

---

the Greek text, see Gomme-Sandbach (above, n. 12) 420ff., and for attempted reconstructions of Menander's *Eunouchos* and *Kolax*, T.B.L. Webster, *Studies in Menander*[2] (Manchester 1960) 67–76. Certainly nothing Terence did to the structure of his model made the Latin play less stageworthy. Both Don., *Praef.* 266 w, and Suet., *Vit. Ter.* 40 (Rostagni), comment on its encore performance and the extraordinary fee of 8,000 sesterces it earned.

[19] E. Fraenkel, *De media et nova comoedia quaestiones selectae* (Diss. Göttingen 1912) 74ff.; for the parasite as a comic type, see W. G. Arnott, "Alexis and the Parasite's Name," *GRBS* 9 (1968) 161–168, and Duckworth, *NRC* 265–268.

108　　　　　　　　　　CHAPTER IV

>   and stand amazed as if delighting in his words.
>   When we go our separate ways to dinner
>   on a stranger's cake, there the fawner needs
>   a string of pleasantries, or else he's out the door.
>   (fr. 159.7–13K)

The fragment is from a *parabasis*, that part of Old Comedy where dramatic time and action stand still, and Fraenkel sees in it the germ of those monologues of self-description so common in fourth-century comedy. The parallel is suggestive, and many critics have seen Gnatho's monologue, too, as a kind of interlude, a halting of the action for a traditional comic effect.[20] It is certainly a set piece. Gnatho begins with a high-flown question of some philosophic import.

>   Di inmortales, homini homo quid praestat? stulto intellegens quid inter est?

>   Immortal Gods, what sets a man apart from men? What
>   separates the smart one from the fool?
>   (232–233)

He at once proceeds to the mundane occurrence that led to this meditation, a chance meeting with a down-at-the-heels acquaintance. Gnatho explains his practice of the parasite's art in the form of a conversation with this poor fellow, who in the end becomes Gnatho's disciple.

>   ibi homo coepit me obsecrare
>   ut sibi liceret discere id de me: sectari iussi,
>   si potis est, tamquam philosophorum habent disciplinae
>   ex ipsis
>   vocabula, parasiti ita ut Gnathonici vocentur.

>   Then the man began to beg that
>   I should take him as a pupil. I ordered him to follow.

[20] Denzler, *Monolog* 65–69, and Büchner, *TT* 245–248.

It just may be that as philosophers give their names to
schools, so parasites will be called Gnathonists.
(261–264)

The monologue that began with a philosophic question ends with the founding of a philosophic school.[21] This monologue, no doubt accompanied by the appropriate gestures and verbal mimicry, gives Gnatho ample opportunity to attract the audience to his point of view. Donatus suggests one way to envision the essential stage business: ". . . in hac scaena non stans sed quasi ambulans persona inducitur; constitit tamen aliquantam intuens spectatores, dum secum loquitur" (*ad* 232). We must also remember that Gnatho has Pamphila in tow, a girl so beautiful that a single look has already left Chaerea hopelessly in love with her (cf. 293). They are being watched from one side of the stage by Phaedria's slave Parmeno with an Aethiopian girl and the homely eunuch he is bringing for Thais. The contrast between Pamphila and Parmeno's motley pair is devastating, as Parmeno himself knows (230–231). The visual and verbal effects make for a very funny scene. Gnatho's slow progress across the stage, his animated speech, and Parmeno's caustic asides while holding his own charges in the background highlight the parasite, while the rivalry between Parmeno and Gnatho reflects the developing rivalry between Thraso and Phaedria. Dramatic time may indeed stand still during Gnatho's entrance monologue, but the play's shape and meaning do not cease to develop. The scene is both an expository statement and a promise.

The comic part of that promise is soon fulfilled. Thraso's entrance dramatizes at once both the soldier's stupidity and the technique of fawning that Gnatho has just described.

TH. magnas vero agere gratias Thais mihi?
GN. ingentis. TH. ain tu, laetast? GN. non tam ipso quidem

---

[21] K. Büchner, "Epikur bei Menander," *SIFC* 14 (1937) 151ff., discusses the philosophical overtones of Gnatho's monologue.

dono quam abs te datam esse: id vero serio
triumphat.

TH. Does Thais really send great thanks to me?
GN. Immense. TH. Tell me, was she pleased? GN. Not as much
by the gift itself as by the giver: that was
the crowning touch.

(391–394)

Each of Thraso's questions receives an inflated reply. "Magnas" becomes "ingentis"; "laeta" turns into "triumphat." As Cicero remarks of this passage, "semper auget assentator id quod is, cuius ad voluntatem dicitur, vult esse magnum" (*de Am.* 26). The fawning culminates with Thraso's claim of an old Roman stage joke as an original witticism.[22]

"quid ais" inquam homini "inpudens?
lepus tute's, pulpamentum quaeris?" GN. hahahae.
TH. quid est? GN. facete lepide laute nil supra.
tuomne, obsecro te, hoc dictum erat? vetus credidi.
TH. audieras? GN. saepe, et fertur in primis. TH. meumst.

"What do you say, you rogue," I say to him.
"You're a hare and seek for game?" GN. Ha! Ha! Ha!
TH. What is it? GN. Cleverly, gracefully, finely done.
Superb.
Tell me, was that joke your own? I thought it's old.
TH. You've heard it? GN. Often. One of the best. TH. It's
mine.

(425–429)

---

[22] The same joke is ascribed to Livius Andronicus. Fraenkel, *EPP* 402, came to doubt this attribution, but Terence's joke certainly implies a tired witticism. Wright, *DiC* 24–27, points to a similar Greek proverb, though Menander's *Kolax*, fr. 3, suggests a different remark in Terence's original. See Gomme-Sandbach (above, n. 12) 432.

Contaminatio

Gnatho flatters Thraso even as he reminds us of the joke's antiquity, thus setting up a *sotto voce* gibe at Thraso's expense.

The didactic streak of Gnatho's entrance monologue also surfaces in this scene. In addition to being a fawner, Gnatho is a kind of *praeceptor amoris*.[23] Thraso is uneasy about his standing with Thais and fears that his gift of Pamphila will not overcome Thais' inclination toward Phaedria. Gnatho, quick of tongue himself, advises Thraso to win her with words.

> ubi nominabit Phaedriam, tu Pamphilam
> continuo; siquando illa dicet "Phaedriam
> intro mittamus comissatum," Pamphilam
> cantatum provocemus; si laudabit haec
> illius formam, tu huius contra.

> When she mentions Phaedria, you at once
> bring up Pamphila. If she says, "Let's invite
> Phaedria to a party," we'll call on
> Pamphila to sing; if she praises his
> looks, you mention hers.

(440–444)

This is all broad and traditional, but Thraso's comment on the advice is a little short of comic: "If she loved me, then it would help, Gnatho" (446). Gnatho replies with a bit of sophistry that wins Thraso's agreement without actually easing his mind. As Donatus observes, Thraso is not a complete fool. He sees the difference between himself and Phaedria, and this self-awareness saves him from being entirely ridiculous. Part of Donatus' long and interesting note on line 446 observes: "There are four kinds of foolishness: not to think of what is necessary, to think of it but

---

[23] As in Antiphanes, fr. 195 K, where the parasite is an advisor of young men. A similar role earns Chaireas the label "parasite" in *Dyskolos*. The Roman parasites Curculio and Phormio extend the role by assuming the function of the *servus callidus* as well.

not do it, not to take good advice, to take bad advice." Thraso shows only the foolishness of the dupe. He and Gnatho are not villains but, as Croce remarks, simply "poor devils who get on as best they can."[24] They are essentially ineffectual and harmless, as the aborted assault on Thais' house demonstrates.

When Thraso finds Thais insufficiently grateful for the gift of Pamphila he decides to take the girl back by force. He marches on the stage with a motley group of followers while Gnatho buzzes around him like a gnat around a bull.

> TH. Simalio, Donax, Syrisce, sequimini.
> primum aedis expugnabo. GN. recte. TH. virginem
>   eripiam. GN. probe.
> TH. male mulcabo ipsam. GN. pulchre.

> TH. Simalio, Donax, Syriscus, follow me!
> First I'll storm the house. GN. Right! TH. I'll snatch
>   the girl. GN. Great!
> TH. Thais I'll maul. GN. Splendid!
>   (772–774)

Thraso then carefully arranges his forces in military fashion reserving a place for himself at the rear. Thais, and a young man named Chremes, meet them. Thais knows that Pamphila is freeborn and has arranged for Chremes, who is the girl's brother, to appear and declare her freedom. Chremes does so, and Thraso's assault is halted before it can really begin. Frustrated in the only kind of action he understands, Thraso surrenders his troops to Gnatho and forfeits his one claim to Thais' attention.

Terence has emphasized the comic quality of this scene. Soldier and parasite appear in their most typical forms: Thraso loud but cowardly, Gnatho a flattering but dubious ally. Thraso's military language as he deploys his troops is echoed by his follower Sanga, who remarks with straightfaced hyperbole, "this

[24] Croce (above, n. 11) 799.

can't be done without bloodshed" (799). When it becomes clear that force must yield to argument, Thraso yields place to Gnatho, who then apes his swagger in a battle of words. Yet the scene ends quietly as Chremes cows them with a simple declaration of the truth. When the Tudor schoolmaster Nicholas Udall wrote this encounter into the fourth act of his own *Ralph Roister Doister*, he let the action progress from verbal play between soldier and parasite to slapstick as the opposing sides come to blows. Terence has avoided that temptation. Much frenzied motion and wild gesticulation no doubt accompany his action, but he keeps Thraso's opponents colorless and lets a victory of words make the soldier's retreat pathetic as well as ridiculous.

The humor that Thraso and Gnatho provide is extremely effective, but it can hardly be their sole function. The four scenes that feature this bumbling soldier and parasite comprise over a quarter of the entire play. More stage time is devoted to them than to anyone else in *Eunuchus*. The simple mathematics of their parts is even more striking when we remember that they figure in two of the most brilliant scenes in the entire play, Gnatho's entrance and the assault, and they share in the finale. Only Chaerea's monologue describing the rape of Pamphila equals their scenes in dramatic prominence. Why does Terence devote so much attention to his interpolated soldier and parasite?

We cannot claim the requirements of plot. Gilbert Norwood, for whom "Plautine" was a term of considerable opprobrium, points out how inorganic the roles of Thraso and Gnatho actually are. To introduce Pamphila, to get Phaedria off the scene, and to bring the lovers together at the end do not require a soldier and parasite.[25] Norwood condemns this "Plautine underplot" for being both vulgar and useless, but recent dramatic criticism has shown that an essential contribution to the action is not the only possible justification for a character's presence in a play, nor

[25] Norwood, *AT* 64–67.

must comic relief be the only alternative. Plautus' *Captivi* offers a useful example. Like Thraso and Gnatho, the parasite Ergasilus is sometimes thought to have been added or his part at least expanded by Plautus to enliven the stage action. He certainly does so, but a brilliant article by Eleanor Leach reveals how much more than comic relief is involved in his scenes. "As a stock character whose personality does not alter with circumstances," she writes, "he serves as a measure for the more fragile, unpredictable persons in the foreground."[26] Ergasilus' anguish at the loss of his patron parodies Hegio's anguish at the loss of his son, and the parasite's scenes take on thematic as well as comic value in a play about separation and dependency. This possibility of thematic significance in stock figures suggests that we look beneath the surface in assessing the contribution of Terence's soldier and parasite.

Thraso and Gnatho are subservience personified. Gnatho's entire creed, which he has been permitted to develop at some length, is to get one's way by fawning. Thraso, despite his bluster, invariably consents to be led by the nose. He is always putting himself in the power of others, seeking guidance and inevitably yielding control. We expect such servility in a soldier and parasite. It is funny in them. It is less amusing in other characters, but consider their conduct. Philippe Fabia claimed with much truth that the play is in essence about Chaerea's love for Pamphila. Everything else, including Phaedria's love for Thais, Thraso's gift of Pamphila, and Chremes' appearance, are all designed to initiate, consummate, and legitimize this love.[27] How

---

[26] E. W. Leach, "Ergasilus and the Ironies of the *Captivi, C&M* 30 (1969) 263–296. Interpolation and expansion of the role are argued by, respectively, J. N. Hough, "The Structure of the *Captivi*," *AJP* 63 (1942) 26–37, and G. van N. Viljoen, "The Plot of the *Captivi* of Plautus," *A Class* 6 (1963) 38–63.

[27] P. Fabia, ed., *Eunuchus* (Paris 1895) 1 ff., an edition of enduring value. More recent criticism tends to put Thais at the center of the action, but a

is it accomplished? The play's action as well as its title originate in a sordid masquerade as a eunuch. The ruse receives considerable attention. The real eunuch, a singularly wretched creature, was on the stage throughout the second act (i.e., 207–390). His distinctive costume does not spoil Chaerea's own good looks—*Thraso* at least will find him attractive (479)—but it eventually becomes a liability to him. There is much comic play over his later difficulty in finding a place to discard it, as well as in the inevitable confrontation with Thais (840 ff.). Putting the rape of Pamphila in the play is, as Fabia also notes, extremely unusual. Childbirth is not unknown in the course of a play, and sexual overtures of various kinds are fairly frequent, but the actual rape of a girl later proved free is a commonplace of *Vorgeschichte*, not of dramatic action. In assuming the guise of a eunuch, Chaerea abandons the decorum of the Terentian *adulescens*. His costume symbolizes the degradation he so willingly assumes. Phaedria is not much better. He begins the play by complaining that Thais has reduced him to servility, and his inability to keep away for even the two days she asks is proof of it. Parmeno's continuous presence onstage for the first half of the play unifies its succession of expository scenes, but he is a witness to the action, not a controller of it. He proposes the eunuch scheme only in jest and is frightened at the very idea of being involved in a trick: "vide ne nimium calidum hoc sit modo" (380). He later denies all responsibility for what Chaerea has done and is reduced to terror by the indignant Pythias (923ff.). The willing subservience so explicit in Gnatho and Thraso thus lies just beneath the surface in the other characters until it surfaces in the finale.

---

theatre audience would probably not see things this way, nor is Terence likely to feature a romance that does not end in marriage. *Adelphoe* is not a partial exception, for there Aeschinus, who does marry, is only acting for his brother, and neither romance is as important as the clash of Micio and Demea. Büchner, *TT* 301–302, discusses this problem of emphasis in *Eunuchus*.

This finale begins with the reappearance of Thraso and Gnatho (1025ff.). Thraso, still hopelessly in love with Thais, is now willing to serve her "as Hercules served Omphale." His appeal for Gnatho's help reflects the self-awareness of their earlier scene (1054ff., cf. 446). Thraso has no illusions, and is perhaps the only character who does not. He is certainly the only character who has learned humility and the only one prepared to make a sacrifice. Gnatho extorts a meal ticket from him and agrees to help. Chaerea and Phaedria have appeared by this time, and Gnatho approaches them. He words his appeal with consummate skill: "militem rivalem ego recipiundum censeo" (1072). As Donatus notes, Gnatho recommends the soldier as *rivalis*, not *socius*, because Thraso is an opponent easily beaten and says *recipio*, rather than some vague expression such as *non excludo*, to suggest that something positive can be got from him. Gnatho also speaks as advisor, not petitioner: *censeo*, not *peto* or *rogo*. He casts himself on the side of the young men—he has already pushed Thraso out of hearing (1068)—and he earns the promise of another meal (1084-1085). Gnatho's argument derives from the economic facts of life with Thais: "quod des paullumst et necessest multum accipere Thaidem" (1075). Thraso's stupidity and newly found humility will make his presence tolerable; his substantial purse makes it highly desirable. Phaedria and Chaerea see the point, and the reconciliation is made.

No one knows where this ending comes from, but everyone seems uncomfortable with it. Karl Büchner thinks so deft a resolution of the play's loose ends can come neither from Menander's *Eunouchos* nor *Kolax*, but his praise is hardly enthusiastic. To appreciate the humor of this ending, says Büchner, we must forget most of what has gone before.[28] The source of this disquiet is not far to seek; no modern scholar has liked the idea of the shared mistress. Pasquali perhaps puts the ethical question best:

[28] Büchner, *TT* 303-305.

". . . perhaps this final scene, so unworthy of this refined creature, would not have offended the greater part of the spectators, but it would surely have offended Terence's more cultured readers: to us moderns, it is intolerable." Walther Ludwig tried to be more objective, condemning the scene on structural rather than moral grounds. He reconstructed a Menandrean *Eunouchos* focused on a *bona meretrix*. Terence, either misunderstanding Menander's intention or suffering a lapse of taste, substituted the coarser ending of the *Kolax* and thus, thinks Ludwig, created the anomaly that is the Latin play.[29] With neither Menander's *Eunouchos* nor *Kolax* before us, we cannot test the validity of Ludwig's hypothesis, but one thing is clear from the play Terence wrote. To call Thais a *creatura gentile* or even a *bona meretrix* is to read more into her character than Terence troubled to put there.[30]

Vanity, greed, and perfidy are rampant among the whores of Roman comedy. Phronesium of *Truculentus*, who pits three lovers against each other and ends by living happily with two of them, may be the greatest of these *malae*, but she does not lack rivals, and both *Asinaria* and *Bacchides* end with a comparable sharing of favors. Throughout *Eunuchus* Terence plays off his own characterization of Thais against this expected character. Like *Curculio* and *Pseudolus*, the play begins with a young man telling his troubles to his slave, and Phaedria's complaint about the "meretricum contumelias" he has endured suggests the traditional figure. The scene is a masterful version of a common comic type, and both Horace and Persius eventually echoed it to

[29] G. Pasquali, "Studi terenziani III: un personaggio e due scene dell' Eunuco," *SFIC* 13 (1936) 117–129; Ludwig (above, n. 18) 36–38. P. W. Harsh, "Certain Features of Technique Found Both in Greek and Roman Drama," *AJP* 58 (1937) 285–287, offers Greek parallels for such "crudity."

[30] D. Gilula, "The Concept of the *Bona Meretrix*," *RFIC* 108 (1980) 142–165, esp. 161–164, puts Thais' good qualities in perspective. We must not press too far such (non-Terentian) labels as *bona* and *mala*.

ridicule the young man who has surrendered reason to love.³¹ Thais here sounds typically greedy, vain, and capricious, but her appearance in the next scene immediately modifies this view. She declares genuine affection for Phaedria and a desire to do good for the girl Pamphila, once almost a sister to her. She is conscious of and explicit about the difference between her own character and the character Phaedria has assigned her.

> me miseram, forsitan hic mihi parvam habeat fidem
> atque ex aliarum ingeniis nunc me iudicet.
>
> Alas, perhaps he has little faith in me
> and judges me by other women's characters.
>
> (197–198)

Terence uses the contrast between individual and stereotype to create sympathy for Thais. We do not expect a *meretrix* to act this way, and so we are particularly intrigued and charmed by one who does. Though her character may depart from the stereotype, however, her motives still originate in her station. She is not entirely *mala*, but she is certainly a *meretrix*. Pragmatism, not idealism moves her. She is explicit about this, too.

> sola sum; habeo hic neminem
> neque amicum neque cognatum: quam ob rem, Phaedria,
> cupio aliquos parere amicos beneficio meo.
>
> I'm alone. I've no one here,
> not friend or family. That's why, Phaedria,

---

³¹ Hor., *Sat.* 2.3.259–271; Pers. 5.161–174. Persius seems to be thinking of the Menandrean original. See E. Fantham, "Roman Experience of Menander in the Late Republic and Early Empire," *TAPA* 114 (1984) 299–309, esp. 303. There is detailed discussion of these echoes in Fabia (above, n. 27) 50–54, Büchner, *TT* 232–233, and Lowe (above, n. 18) 432–433. Other allusions to the *meretrix* of stereotype are Parmeno's "meretrix avara" (927) and "audacia meretricum" (994), each calculated to contrast what we find with what we might expect. For the lovers' competition with gifts, so crucial to the action, cf. Pl., *Men.* 192ff.

I want to cultivate friends for my protection.
(147–149)

When she eventually learns of Pamphila's rape, she thinks first of herself, and she makes her anger and disappointment clear to Chaerea.

> ita conturbasti mihi
> rationes omnis, ut eam non possim suis
> ita ut aequom fuerat atque ut studui tradere
> ut solidum parerem hoc mi beneficium, Chaerea.

> You've ruined
> all my plans, so now I can't return her
> to her people as she was and as I hoped.
> I wanted sure protection for myself, Chaerea.
> (868–871, cf. 827)

Chaerea's willingness to marry Pamphila solves her problem. Thais leaves the stage for good at 909, though the play still has nearly a hundred lines to run. She has played her part.

Like Bacchis of *Hecyra*, Thais' good nature motivates a crucial action without making her the play's central figure. When the final resolution comes, Terence keeps her in the background. Chremes confirms Pamphila's identity offstage, and we see Parmeno abused on it for failing to curb Phaedria's passion (910–1024). The eunuch scheme is over, and the reappearance of Thraso and Gnatho signals the final wrapping up. The structure of this finale reflects the requirements and the priorities of the plot. Chaerea comes first. He proclaims his own happiness and only then turns to the second love interest of the play.

> tum autem Phaedriae
> meo fratri gaudeo esse amorem omnem in tranquillo:
>   unast domus;
> Thais patri se commendavit in clientelam et fidem,
> nobis dedit se.

> As for my brother
> Phaedria, I'm glad his affair is in the clear.
> We're one family.
> Thais has entrusted herself to father's patronage.
> She's one of us.
>
> (1037–1040)

Thais has found in their father the protector she had sought in Chremes, and so she is free to devote herself to Phaedria.[32] Chaerea and Phaedria are lavish with praise of her, but a comic undercurrent saves their grandiose remarks from seriousness. "Ista nostrae omnist fautrix familiae," says Chaerea, by which he really means only Phaedria and himself, and his label echoes without correcting Parmeno's earlier, less favorable, phrase, "nostri fundi calamitas" (1052, 89). Thais' threat to their fortune remains. The comedy is further strengthened by the parallel conversation of Gnatho and Thraso. Love of Pamphila cast Chaerea in the role of eunuch. Love of Thais reduces each of her loves to a caricature of the other. Thraso's servility and complete dependence on Gnatho here in the finale parodies the opening scene between Phaedria and Parmeno. Now Phaedria and Chaerea fall victim to the parasite's tongue. They yield to his wishes and end by promising him a meal. Gnatho brings Thraso and Phaedria together by satisfying what has become the idealism of the soldier and the materialism of the young man. Thraso is willing to share; Phaedria realizes that he must. Thais is by no means a loser in all this. She has already found the patron she needed; now she is assured of lover and income. If the continued presence of Thraso seems a high price to pay for security and pleasure, the judgment is ours, not hers. Terence keeps Thais offstage so that

---

[32] OCT and most editors since Bentley punctuate after *commendavit*, but Fabia (above, n. 27) 245, rightly points out that the father, not the boys, is the patron. "In clientelam et fidem" has a legal ring, as in Cic., *S. Rosc.* 33.93: "esse in fide et clientela."

her tacit agreement will not distract us from the sight of Thraso and Phaedria reaching an accord.

The moral is spelled out by Gnatho: "me huius quidquid facio id facere maxume causa mea" (1070). Parasites are expected to look out for themselves, but their creed is no less true in this play for *miles*, *meretrix*, and *adulescentes*.[33] Self-interest requires a subservience that each character embraces without hesitation. Terence has made the stock relationship between soldier and parasite a grotesque paradigm for relationships to which the other characters aspire. Chaerea stoops to deceit and violence, winning for himself by subterfuge what Thraso's frontal assault failed to win. Phaedria takes on a parasite. Thais, like Gnatho, sacrifices independence for security. Each seeks and receives his heart's desire, and each is diminished by the process of getting it.

Terence dramatizes with wit and skill the price of selfish desires. His play hangs together less through the artful structure of its narrative than through the unity of its theme as each character points in his own way to the same lesson. If Menander's *Eunouchos* showed something similar, its message must have come in different guise. The soldier and parasite taken from *Kolax* not only make Terence's play funny, but make the Latin *Eunuchus* what it is. Where *Phormio* sacrificed depth of character and broadness of interest for the sake of telling a story deftly, *Eunuchus* assumes a less even pace in order to develop its basic theme through the antics of its characters. It is not well made, but neither is it made without point. The practice of "contamination" reveals an alternative to simple structural coherence in a play. In *Adelphoe*, the circumscribed interpolation serves to develop character, and that development is more important to Terence's design than the consistency of Aeschinus' negotiations with San-

---

[33] A point well made by Douglass S. Parker, whose introduction to *Eunuchus* in P. Bovie, ed., *Five Roman Comedies* (New York 1970) 3–7, is among the most perceptive of modern discussions.

nio, the pimp. The more extensive additions to *Eunuchus* obscure the steady progress of Chaerea's love affair but develop the real significance of the play's action. What Terence has sought to do in each case must determine our choice of critical standard for judging the result. Plays that make us uncomfortable are not *ipso facto* bad plays, and both *Adelphoe* and *Eunuchus*, though they lack well-made plots, lack neither the power nor the brilliance of comic masterpieces.

[V]
THE *duplex comoedia*

> These are plots built after the Italian Mode of Houses, you see thorow them all at once; the Characters are indeed the Imitations of Nature, but so narrow as if they had imitated onely an Eye or an Hand, and did not dare to venture on the lines of a Face, or the Proportion of a Body.
>
> —JOHN DRYDEN,
> *Of Dramatick Poesie* (1668)

Roman comedy, as Dryden fairly observes, features a limited range of stage actions and the outline, rather than a full portrait, of its characters. Nor is it exotic. Plays in the tradition of New Comedy contain fewer novelties in plot and character than their Aristophanic ancestors. Yet the tradition Terence inherited was by no means impoverished. Changing conditions brought more than just the end of Old Comedy's social criticism and the fantastic humor that had made it palatable. New formulae emerged in the fourth century B.C. that reflected the development of new interests and a new relationship between character and plot. Aristotle reflected this new interest in the *Poetics* when he put plot construction at the center of the dramatist's art. By the fourth century A.D., the grammarian Diomedes was repeating a conventional view when he says that Menander and his contemporaries had replaced the trenchant wit of Old Comedy with complexity of plot, and this change of values is also implicit in the famous remark Plutarch ascribes to Menander, that once he had finished his plot he needed only set the lines to it.[1] The new interest in

---

[1] Diomed., *A.G.* (XXIV.2.52–55 Koster): "secunda aetate fuerunt Aris-

plot construction, however, was not as simple a matter as it sounds. For Menander, it did not mean that a play took its appeal from the telling of a convoluted story. Dryden is right. The plots of New Comedy are too predictable and the dramatic roles too uniform to be interesting in themselves. The appeal of a Menandrean play comes instead from the interplay of the two as the dramatist uses the twists of plot to challenge his characters in unexpected ways and forces them to grow before our eyes. The suspicions that arise in *Samia*, for example, over Moschion's treatment of Chrysis and her baby become central to the action in an unexpected way when they jeopardize the relationship between Moschion and his father. In *Dyskolos*, Sostratos' love for Knemon's daughter is significant not for itself—Sostratos is an insipid lover and the girl a nonentity—but because it creates the turmoil that eventually forces the old recluse to face his social obligations. The dramatic interest of such comedies is always a little different from the romantic thrust of their plots.[2] We may indeed "see thorow them all at once," but we are invariably surprised by their implications.

The Roman comic tradition took a different tack. Plautine plots, too, are hardly unique, but Plautus did not use them in Menandrean fashion to pose significant challenges to basically sympathetic characters. A satiric play like *Truculentus* makes its

---

tophanes, Eupolis et Cratinus, qui et principum vitia sectati acerbissimas comoedias composuerunt. tertia aetas fuit Menandri, Diphili et Philemonis, qui omnen acerbitatem comoediae mitigaverunt atque argumenta multiplicia †graecis† erroribus secuti sunt." Evanthius, *de Fab.* (xxv.1.71 Koster) calls New Comedy *concinna argumento*. Menander's comment is at Plut., *Mor.* 347f: νὴ τοὺς θεοὺς ἔγωγε πεποίκα τὴν κωμῳδίαν· ᾠκονόμηται γὰρ ἡ διάθεσις· δεῖ δ' αὐτῇ τὰ στιχίδια ἐπᾷσαι. W. Görler, "Über die Illusion in der antiken Komödie," *A&A* 18 (1973) 41–57, discusses the effect of this new emphasis on plot.

[2] The same is true of Terence, as we have already seen in *Phormio* and *Eunuchus*. Thus even so intelligent a study as P. Flury, *Liebe und Liebessprache bei Menander, Plautus und Terenz* (Heidelberg 1968), inevitably seems a little beside the point. Love is never as central a theme as we might expect.

trenchant statements about human values without the help of a coherent plot.³ Episodic plays like *Amphitruo* and *Menaechmi* are essentially series of scenes orchestrated simply to create or avoid the confrontations that generate the humor of mistaken identities. Intrigue plots, too, are intended to make only superficial sense. They deliberately leave us breathless and slightly in awe of the Epidicus or Pseudolus who can emerge unscathed from the resulting chaos. Plautus' cavalier attitude toward story telling is nicely illustrated in *Casina*, where he jettisons a familiar romantic plot and frames the stage action with jokes about its absence. The play has room for a romantic story of a young man and a slave girl of mysterious parentage, but the girl never appears and, as the prologue claims, Plautus breaks a bridge to keep the boy from appearing as well (64–66). The play can then deal instead with the father Lysidamus' effort to secure the girl Casina for himself by marrying her off to his compliant bailiff. Lysidamus' wife, recognizing his motive for what it is, combats the plan by proposing an alternative marriage to her son's slave. The old man is eventually beaten, and an epilogue suffices to tie up the loose ends.

> spectatores, quod futurumst intus, id memorabimus.
> haec Casina huius reperietur filia esse ex proxumo,
> eaque nubet Euthynico nostro erili filio.
>
> Spectators, I'll tell you what will happen inside.
> This Casina will turn out to be our neighbor's daughter,
> and she will marry our young master Euthynicus.
> (1012–1014)

Plot here has become simply the demonstration of Lysidamus' lust and its consequences. No progress is made. The old man's final humiliation leaves him abashed, but not educated, and his domestic situation remains unchanged. The arch references to Euthynicus and Casina—the progress of true love relegated to an

³ C. S. Dessen, "Plautus' Satiric Comedy: the *Truculentus*," *PQ* 56 (1977) 145–168.

epilogue—stand in wry contrast to the staged spectacle of Lysidamus' muddled goals and thwarted desires. Plautus has derailed the conventions of plot in the interests of comedy.[4]

Terence put plot back on the track. His use of stage action to challenge and develop his characters returns to the tradition of his Greek predecessors. When he tells a story of cleverness, as in *Phormio*, he organizes his plot to create the semblance of complexity without the actual diffuseness of a Plautine intrigue play. When he enriches stage action through that process of borrowing we call *contaminatio*, the additions contribute in true Menandrean fashion to the play's significance either by developing its theme (*Eunuchus*) or by revealing an important dimension of its characters (*Adelphoe*). Each play we have examined so far is organized around a single, coherent, and easily identified challenge: the challenge to Phormio's wit posed by Demipho's return, the challenge of dealing with Thais' mercenary household, the challenge to Micio's complacency created by Aeschinus' conduct. Each play may double its love interest, but only to embellish that central challenge.[5] Yet there remain two plays where a doubled love interest is not so easily explained. Why did Terence add the second lover Charinus to his *Andria*, and why does he call the structure of *Heauton timorumenos duplex*?

I

Charinus and his slave Byrria were not in the Menandrean original of *Andria*. They are either Terence's own invention or bor-

[4] The role (if any) of Euthynicus and Casina in Plautus' Greek original unfortunately remains uncertain. See W. T. MacCary, "The Comic Tradition and Comic Structure in Diphilos' *Kleroumenoi*," *Hermes* 101 (1973) 194–208, and M. Waltenberger, "Plautus' *Casina* und die Methode der Analyse," *Hermes* 109 (1981) 440–447.

[5] The juxtaposition of a "marriage-plot" with a "liaison-plot," as suggested by R. Levin, "The Double Plots of Terence," *CJ* 62 (1967) 301–305, is too simplistic an explanation of Terence's purpose. See W. Görler, "Doppelhandlung, Intrige und Anagnorismos bei Terenz," *Poetica* 5 (1972) 164–182.

rowed from Menander's *Perinthia*, and they serve the obvious purpose of providing a second lover. As Donatus says, ". . . et audacter et artificiosissime binos amores duorum adulescentium et binas nuptias in una fabula machinatus est, et id extra praescriptum Menandri, cuius comoediam transferebat" (*ad* 977).[6] Charinus loves Philumena, a girl old Simo is attempting to foist upon his son Pamphilus. Charinus' hopes thus depend on Pamphilus, who really loves only the poor Andrian girl Glycerium. Charinus and Byrria make four appearances. They are introduced together at 301, where Charinus declares his love for Philumena in highly stylized terms: he calls himself sick (309), he prefers death to life without her (311), he threatens disappearance if Pamphilus marries her instead (322).[7] When Pamphilus' slave Davus announces that the proposed marriage is only a sham intended to test Pamphilus' loyalty to his father, Charinus' spirits are restored (370). At 412, however, Byrria comes onstage and overhears a conversation that leads him to suspect Pamphilus of double-dealing. He exits at 431 to find Charinus and will not reappear. Charinus returns alone at 625 to voice his indignation, and he confronts Pamphilus with his suspicions. Pamphilus reassures him of his good will, and the two put their trust in Davus to prevent the unwanted marriage. Schemes, however, prove unnecessary. Glycerium turns out to be a citizen, and Pamphilus may now marry her. In the last scene (957ff.), Charinus has learned of Pamphilus' good fortune and secures his help in win-

---

[6] Probability favors an origin in *Perinthia*, but scholarly opinion is divided. See the summary by K. Gaiser, "Zur Eigenart der römischen Komödie," *ANRW* 1.2 (1972) 1063–1064, to which add W. Steidle, "Menander bei Terenz," *RhM* 116 (1973) 303–325, and G. Calboli, "Terenzio, *Andria* 481–488," *Philologus* 124 (1980) 33–67. The putative difficulties of the *contaminatio* are reviewed by H.-J. Glücklich, *Aussparung und Antithese. Studien zur terenzischen Komödie* (Diss. Heidelberg 1966) 108–111.

[7] Terence's claim for himself at *Ph.* 6 that "nusquam insanum scripsit adulescentulum" is only true in the strictest sense. The desperate Charinus comes very close to the comic stereotype. For Terence's erotic vocabulary, see E. Fantham, *Comp. Stud. in Rep. Latin Imagery* (Toronto 1972) 82–91.

ning Philumena for himself. The two leave together to find the girl's father. As Davus says, "ne expectetis dum exeant huc: intus despondebitur" (980).

Yet to describe *Andria* in these terms is like summarizing the action of *Hamlet* through Laertes' eyes. These four appearances do not amount to a major part for Charinus and Byrria. Pamphilus' love for Glycerium and his resulting conflict with Simo are unquestionably the play's true focus. What do Charinus and Byrria contribute, then? A structural point has some obvious validity. Thus Donatus observes that Charinus has been added to furnish a husband for the spurned Philumena: "Has personas [Charinum et Byrriam] Terentius addidit fabulae—nam non sunt apud Menandrum—ne παθητικόν fieret Philumenam spretam relinquere sine sponso, Pamphilo aliam ducente" (*ad* 301). This kind of reasoning, especially with Donatus' authority behind it, had great appeal in the Renaissance. The poet Battista Guarini, for example, in his *Compendio della poesia tragicomica* of 1599 defended the Terentian "sub-plot" in just these terms.

> Now that girl who was going to be that day a wife and who had been announced as such in the house of her father, was she then to remain disappointed because of the marriage of Glycerium? Was she to be all that day in the belief and hope of being a wife and then to be left high and dry? It would be very unwise and unfitted to a comic poem that, whenever there is introduced a person so necessary to tying the knot and to such an extent an accessory to untying it, no account should be made of her at the end of the story and she should not share in the common rejoicing. Hence it was necessary to prepare her a husband. . . .[8]

[8] The translation is that of A. H. Gilbert, *Literary Criticism: Plato to Dryden* (New York 1940) 528–529. For the context of Guarini's essay see M. H. Herrick, *Comic Theory in the Sixteenth Century* (Urbana 1950) 89–129.

Unfortunately, Guarini's noble sentiments are inaccurate and even a little beside the point. Though Philumena's betrothal to Pamphilus was reported in the play's prologue (99–102), in the play itself, her father Chremes seeks periodically to break off that engagement. As he tells Simo,

> perpulisti me ut homini
> in alio occupato amore, abhorrenti ab re uxoria,
> filiam ut darem in seditionem atque in incertas nuptias,
> eius labore atque eius dolore gnato ut medicarer tuo.

> You've pushed me to give
> my daughter over to discord and a dubious union
> with a man looking elsewhere and shirking marriage,
> so I can reform your son through her trouble and pain.
> (828–831)

As so often in New Comedy, the girl's opinion is never considered, for she is not a character in her own right. Philumena exists solely as an object of male negotiation, and there is no scene of general rejoicing at the end for her to share. Menander presumably ignored her entirely in his *Andria*, just as he ignored the heiress of *Aspis* and Nikeratos' daughter in *Samia*. Terence did not do quite the same, but neither did he stage any part of her dilemma or its solution. Guarini's sentimental concern for Philumena's feelings was probably encouraged by an alternate ending for *Andria* that did stage Charinus' final negotiations with Chremes for Philumena's hand. Donatus knew of this ending and rejected it as spurious, but it survives in some manuscripts. The problem with the ending is precisely that it makes too much of Charinus. Its colorless repetition of the betrothal formula already used for Pamphilus is anticlimactic, and it makes little sense to move from the high drama of Pamphilus to the banality of Charinus.[9] The fifth act of *Dyskolos*, where Gorgias is betrothed to

---

[9] Don. *ad* 977 perceives the wisdom of Terence's economy, "ne vel longior

Sostratos' sister, makes an instructive contrast. This sister is hardly a greater presence in *Dyskolos* than Philumena is in *Andria*, but Gorgias is far more integral a character than Charinus. Gorgias masterminds Sostratos' courtship and wins for him Knemon's consent to the marriage with his daughter. There is thus deep satisfaction in seeing Sostratos return the favor by securing this second engagement, which is done against token resistance from both Sostratos' rich father and the poor but proud Gorgias himself. Even so, Menander does not end his play with marriages. He returns to Knemon, whose final humiliation reminds us of the misanthropy that is the play's central concern. Charinus is not so central a character, and his ability to provide for Philumena is more a pretext than a justification for his appearance.

Nor is the simple enrichment of stage action a significant part of his role. This is frequently an important element in Terence's *contaminatio*, but Charinus and Byrria are not very lively characters. Byrria is not a doublet of Davus. He is not a schemer. He initiates no actions, makes only one (wrong) deduction, and then vanishes for good. His appearance at 412ff., where he overhears Simo and Pamphilus, is a brilliant stroke by Terence to tie this character to the main action, but Byrria succeeds only in causing needless pain to his master.[10] He remains an essentially passive character. Charinus too is always responding to actions rather than initiating them. Only once does he try to take the initiative by asking Davus for help, and then he is curtly rebuffed.

                        CH. quid me fiet?
DA. eho tu inpudens, non satis habes quod tibi dieculam addo,

---

fieret vel in eandem propter rerum similitudinem cogerentur." See Büchner, *TT* 116–118.

[10] Görler (above, n. 5) 171 calls Terence's addition of Byrria to this scene "a masterstroke." It is certainly a deft way to weave Charinus and Byrria into the plot. For the technical difficulty of their integration, see Denzler, *Monolog* 58–60.

quantum huic promoveo nuptias? CH. Dave, at tamen . . .
  DA. quid ergo?
CH. ut ducam. DA. ridiculum. CH. huc face ad me [ut] venias,
  si quid poteris.
DA. quid veniam? nil habeo. CH. at tamen, siquid. DA. age
  veniam.

                                      CH. What about me?
DA. The nerve! Isn't it enough I've won you a little time
  and delayed his wedding? CH. But Davus . . . DA. What
  is it?
CH. I want to marry. DA. Ridiculous. CH. Promise to come
  to me if you can arrange it.
DA. I can't. Why come? CH. But if you can . . . DA. All right,
  I'd come.

                                                (709–713)

Charinus gets no direct reward for his persistence, and Davus has no intention of coming to his aid. Charinus and Byrria are to be spectators, not participants. They do not influence the outcome of Pamphilus' difficulties, and Charinus' own happy ending is purely a byproduct of his.

The song Charinus sings at 625ff., however, suggests a more meaningful reason for his presence. It is a short *canticum* primarily in cretics, a common enough meter for voicing complaint or distress in Plautus, but lyrics of any kind are extremely rare in Terence. Only *Adelphoe* 610–617, where Aeschinus sings a complex *canticum* to voice his inner turmoil, is at all comparable. The form of Charinus' declaration is thus itself significant, and so is its content.[11] The passage warrants quotation in full.

[11] For the use of cretics in comedy, see W. M. Lindsay, *Early Latin Verse* (Oxford 1922) 291–296. The only other lyric passages in Terence are, beside *Ad.* 610–617, *And.* 481–484 (in bacchiacs), and perhaps *Eun.* 560, where the scansion is unclear. For Plautine parallels to the content, see Denzler, *Monolog* 56–58.

> Hoccinest credibile aut memorabile,
> tanta vecordia innata quoiquam ut siet
> ut malis gaudeant atque ex incommodis
> alterius sua ut comparent commoda? ah
> idnest verum? immo id est genus hominum pessumum in
> denegando modo quis pudor paullum adest;
> post ubi tempus promissa iam perfici,
> tum coacti necessario se aperiunt,
> et timent et tamen res premit denegare;
> ibi tum eorum inpudentissuma oratiost
> "quis tu es? quis mihi es? quor meam tibi? heus
>   proxumus sum egomet mihi."
> at tamen "ubi fides?" si roges,
> nil pudet hic, ubi opus [est]; illi ubi
>   nil opust, ibi verentur.

> Can you believe it? Have you heard of such a thing?
> Can someone be so heartless that he revels
> in another's ills and counts as gains
> another's loss? Can it be true?
> There is indeed that wretched type of man
> who's always too ashamed to turn you down,
> but when the time has come to keep his word
> he then is forced to show himself.
> He trembles but at last says no.
> Then you get that crowning impudence:
> "Who are you? What are you to me? Why give up
>   my girl to you? I see to myself."
> And if you ask, "What of your word?"
> he's not ashamed just when there's need and feels
>   that shame when there's no need.
>   (625–638a)

When we last saw Charinus, he was dying of love, but love is not his subject here. Neither is it mental anguish of the kind that besets Aeschinus, Terence's other lyric lover. Charinus is indignant. He sings of broken promises. Pamphilus had set a high moral tone much earlier when he denied claim to Charinus' thanks for seeking a way out of marriage with Philumena.

> ego, Charine, ne utiquam officium liberi esse hominis puto,
> quom is nil mereat, postulare id gratiae adponi sibi,
> nuptias effugere ego istas malo quam tu adipiscier.
>
> I don't think it right, Charinus, for an honest man
> to pass off as a favor what he gladly does.
> I'm as keen to flee that marriage as you are to seek it out.
>
> (330–332)

Now, when he thinks his hopes have again been dashed, Charinus' thoughts turn not to Philumena nor even to his own misery, but to Pamphilus' conduct. His role as friend, not as lover, is being emphasized, and that emphasis in turn suggests his primary function in the play.

Following this *canticum*, Charinus taxes Pamphilus for betraying him (639–683). His suspicions are ill-founded, as Pamphilus eventually makes clear to him, but the challenge to their friendship is as real as the marriage Simo is planning. If Pamphilus is not free to choose his own wife, he is not free to honor his pledge to Charinus. This scene of confrontation, with its inexorable revelation of Pamphilus' divided loyalties, will be echoed and expanded later when Simo taxes him for having betrayed his responsibilities to his family (872–903). Simo's suspicions are *not* ill-founded, and *his* accusations will bring the play to its crisis. The plot of *Andria* is designed to entangle Pamphilus in a web of conflicting obligations, tearing him between responsibility for the girl he loves and duty to his father. Only the chance revelation of Glycerium's true parentage will save him from making a painful choice. The addition of Charinus heightens the dilemma by entangling him in further obligations to a friend. As in *Eunu-*

chus, where the addition of Thraso and Gnatho dramatizes the underlying theme of subservience, Charinus' presence brings with it the additional burden of a social context. Pamphilus runs the full gamut of responsibilities toward self, family, and friend. Once again, the enrichment serves an essentially thematic rather than strictly structural purpose.

Nevertheless, the passivity of Charinus and Byrria remains curious. Terence could easily have made them active contributors to the play's action. Early on, Pamphilus urges them to be just that.

>nunc siquid potes aut tu aut hic Byrria,
>facite fingite invenite efficite qui detur tibi;
>ego id agam mihi qui ne detur.
>
>>Now if you or Byrria here is able,
>>arrange, think up, invent, effect a way to get her;
>>I'll see to it that I don't.
>>
>>>(333–335)

Davus is there to take steps on Pamphilus' behalf, but neither Charinus nor Byrria does anything comparable. Alternatively, they might have been involved directly in the scheming that does go on. Instead, Charinus is, as we have seen, rebuffed in his own bid for such inclusion (709–713). The two can only stand aside as the action develops around them. Terence handles these minor characters much as Menander handled the subordinate characters in a play like *Samia*. No true sub-plot develops around them; they contribute only to developing the main action.[12] To have done otherwise would have altered the balance of the play and obscured its basic design. *Andria* is dominated by Simo, who created the conflict that engulfs Pamphilus and who controls the

---

[12] Goldberg, *MMC* 106–108.

course of the plot through his negotiations with Chremes.[13] A greater role for Charinus and Byrria would either have intensified the play's romantic element at the expense of its social one or strengthened the character of Pamphilus at the expense of Simo. Terence prefers a simple structure, using Charinus to heighten his theme while keeping him on the fringe of the action. Despite the addition of this second lover and slave, the plot of *Andria* is hardly *duplex*. What kind of Terentian plot warrants that label?

II

The prologue to *Heauton timorumenos* contains a famous and difficult statement.

> ex integra Graeca integram comoediam
> hodie sum acturus H[e]auton timorumenon,   5
> duplex quae ex argumento facta est simplici.
>   simplici] duplici A (corr. Iov.)

A longstanding philological problem with these lines is no longer quite so pressing. The sentence is not really contradictory, and we need doubt neither Jovialis' correction to *simplici* nor the authenticity of line 6 itself.[14] Terence is not making a statement about what he has or has not done to his Greek original, which was a play by Menander. *Integra* means "untouched" in the sense "untouched by a previous translator," i.e., new to the Roman stage. That almost technical sense is also found in the *Adelphoe* prologue where he defends the scene interpolated from Diphilus' *Synapothnescontes* with a remark that Plautus, when

---

[13] S. M. Goldberg, "The Dramatic Balance of Terence's *Andria*," *C&M* 33 (1981/82) 135–143. Calboli (above, n. 6) 66–67, thinks Simo's prominence to be the deliberate result of Terence's restructuring of Menander's play.

[14] A. J. Brothers, "The Construction of Terence's *Heauton timorumenos*," *CQ* 30 (1980) 94–119, esp. 95–108, discusses the philological problem in detail. To that discussion add A. Primmer, "Zum Prolog des *Heauton-timorumenos*," *WS* 77 (1964) 61–75, esp. 62–66.

turning the play into his *Commorientes*, had left that one scene out (*locum integrum*, 9–11). A metrical argument resolves the question of *simplici*. In early Latin verse, a short vowel before a mute and liquid remains short, and *dŭplici* does not scan. As for the authenticity of line 6, the following line confirms both its position and the sense of *integra* because Terence has his prologue-speaker summarize what he has just said.

> novam esse ostendi et quae esset.

> I've shown the play is new and what it's like.

The passage, then, means something like this:

> Today I'm about to perform *Heauton timorumenos*,
> a fresh comedy from a fresh Greek source,
> a double one made from a single plot.

Philology takes us this far, but a second, literary problem remains. What does Terence mean by the terms *duplex comoedia* and an *argumentum simplex*? What is double and what is single about *Heauton*? The question involves not so much the meaning of the words in isolation as the structure of the play they are meant to describe and the integration of its various elements.[15]

The play opens with the sight of old Menedemus staggering under the weight of a heavy mattock as he tills his field. When accosted by his neighbor Chremes, Menedemus explains that he has sold his property in town, purchased this farm, and works it himself as punishment for having quarreled with a lovesick son. The boy Clinia has since gone off to Asia as a mercenary soldier, and so Menedemus chooses physical discomfort for himself, too.

> nam usque dum ille vitam illam colet
> inopem carens patria ob meas iniurias,
> interea usque illi de me supplicium dabo
> laborans parcens quaerens, illi serviens.

---

[15] Yet see Brothers (above, n. 14) 105–108.

> So long as he leads such a life
> poor and far from home because of my injustice,
> for just as long will I make recompense to him,
> working, saving, seeking, serving him.
> (136–139)

The character of each old man is carefully drawn. Menedemus, though well off, works hard and keeps to himself. He barely knows his neighbor Chremes, speaks simply, and refuses an invitation to dinner, a refusal with important consequences for the plot. Chremes is perplexed by such unsociability. His long-winded opening speech reveals the gossip's observant eye and insatiable curiosity. Like most busybodies, he is also a slick talker, as Menedemus soon discovers.

> ME. Chreme, tantumne ab re tuast oti tibi
> aliena ut cures ea quae nil ad te attinent?
> CH. homo sum: humani nil a me alienum puto.
>
> ME. Chremes, do your affairs leave you such leisure
> that you can see to business not your own?
> CH. I'm human. No human business isn't mine.
> (75–77)

Chremes' famous line is, of course, ironic, but it is also as true as he can make it.[16] He knows everyone: a neighbor Phania who will soon be a dinner guest (169–170), two others named Simus and Crito who seek his help as an arbiter (498–500). Given a suitable opportunity, he will readily claim true acquaintance with Menedemus, too (180). Noble sentiments and prompt advice come easily to him. When, in the next scene, his son Clitipho tells him that Clinia has returned from Asia and is now at their house, the stage seems set for a reunion of Menedemus and his son as arranged by the officious Chremes.

---

[16] H. D. Jocelyn, "Homo sum: humani nil a me alienum puto," *Antichthon* 7 (1973) 14–46, argues rightly that a Roman audience would not approve of Chremes' sophistry.

But things are not to be this simple. Clitipho remains on the stage and begins a rather surprising monologue.

> Quam iniqui sunt patres in omnis adulescentis iudices!
> qui aequom esse censent nos a pueris ilico nasci senes
> neque illarum adfinis esse rerum quas fert adulescentia.
> ex sua lubidine moderantur nunc quae est, non quae
>   olim fuit.
>
> What unfair judges fathers are of sons!
> They think it right for us to be like old men from our youth
> and not enjoy those things that youth deserves.
> They govern by desires they have now and not by those
>   they had.
>
> (213–216)

This is a true enough comment about Menedemus before his misfortune and reform, but the father in question turns out to be Chremes. Clitipho has been ensnared by a particularly expensive *meretrix* named Bacchis. He makes an explicit contrast between her and Antiphila, the girl Clinia loves.

> nam hic Clinia, etsi is quoque suarum rerum satagit, attamen
> habet bene et pudice eductam, ignaram artis meretriciae.
> meast potens procax magnifica sumptuosa nobilis.
>
> Clinia here, though stuck up to his neck, at least
> has found a nice and modest girl, no whore.
> Mine is bold, expensive, impudent, and proud.
>
> (225–227)

Though his allowance is insufficient to support this secret affair, Clitipho both fears to approach his father for help and refuses to give up Bacchis. His monologue completes the exposition by revealing this second problem parallel to Clinia's difficulty, and in doing so it takes on structural significance.

Clitipho's monologue brings sudden but necessary complexity

to the play. After all, there is hardly a drama in Clinia's situation. Menedemus would take him back in any case, even with a mistress, though such extreme indulgence proves unnecessary. When Antiphila turns out to be a daughter of Chremes who had been exposed in infancy, a marriage with Clinia is arranged almost immediately. The action reaches an easy and conventionally satisfactory conclusion as Menedemus is rewarded for his change of heart and Clinia for his loyalty to Antiphila.[17] Clitipho's problem is not so easily resolved. His slave Syrus will have to weave an elaborate scheme to swindle money from Chremes to support Bacchis. They pass her off as Clinia's mistress and seek money to "buy" Antiphila from her, but the plan hits a snag. The truth comes out, and Clitipho is compelled not only to give up Bacchis but to choose a proper wife for himself. By bringing Antiphila and Bacchis together to Chremes' house, Terence manages to intertwine the fates of the two young men and bring them both to respectable unions. Yet they do not receive equal dramatic treatment. The easy romance of Clinia and Antiphila moves to the background as Syrus' scheme on Clitipho's behalf occupies an increasing share of the stage time. The play that starts out centered on Menedemus and Clinia directs most of its attention to Chremes and Clitipho.

The *duplex* idea of *Heauton timorumenos* is thus easy to see. The play uses what is often called a dual plot in Terence, "the method of employing two problems or complications to solve each other."[18] Antiphila is restored to both family and lover because

[17] Görler (above, n. 5) 172 is nevertheless correct: "Das Ziel der Clinia-Antiphila-Handlung ist nicht nur das ungestörte Zusammenleben der beiden Liebenden, sondern ihre Verehelichung, der jedoch die vermeintliche Unebenbürtigkeit der Antiphila entgegensteht." There is certainly movement in Clinia's situation, but that movement is not as dramatically interesting as Clitipho's.

[18] The definition is Norwood's, *AT* 146. Sometimes, of course, one problem first complicates the other, as in *Eunuchus*. O. Bianco, *Terenzio* (Rome

Clitipho has offered shelter to his friend. Menedemus regains his son and will see him happily married. Clinia, by aiding his friend's intrigue, inadvertently leads him to respectability. And Chremes, for all his self-declared sagacity, comes dangerously close to repeating Menedemus' original error. Given such richly parallel action, what is *simplex* about the play?

Some critics have suspected *contaminatio* or at least such extreme reworking of a Menandrean *simplex argumentum* that the play is truly double.[19] Nevertheless, a simple design lies just below the surface. The very nature of the play's parallelism helps us see it. Clinia and Clitipho make essentially the same progress from illicit love to respectable marriage. Their affairs are so easy to intertwine precisely because they are so similar. Both young men have entered into unsuitable relationships and paid the social price. The difference comes from the different characters of their lovers. Clinia has had the good sense to choose another Lucretia, a girl who sticks to her spinning and is faithful to her love. She *deserves* to be a citizen, and her eventual recognition as one is hardly a surprise.[20] Clitipho chooses only the greedy Bacchis.

1962) 121, defines the *duplex comoedia* as a play with two actions, one of which picks up where the other leaves off. He is thinking specifically of *HT*. Also see Görler (above, n. 5) 166–167 and Glücklich (above, n. 6) 122–125.

[19] Thus, in different ways, W. Steidle, "Menander bei Terenz," *RhM* 117 (1974) 247–276, who subjects its structure to the same kind of analysis he lavishes on *Andria* and *Eunuchus*, and E. Lefèvre, "Der *Heautontimorumenos* des Terenz" in his *Die römischen Komödie: Plautus und Terenz* (Darmstadt 1973) 443–462, who believes that Terence has doubled the action himself by turning Menander's Chremes, a *homo humanus*, into a *homo curiosus*. Primmer (above, n. 14) 63–66 defends the easier view that both the Latin play and its model were developed from a *simplex argumentum*.

[20] The story of Dromo's visit to fetch Antiphila (274–291) sounds much like the visit of Collatinus and his friends to Lucretia as told in Liv. 1.57.6–9, no doubt a traditional story. Antiphila's good character is, given the conventions of New Comedy, tantamount to a guarantee that she will prove marriageable. The industrious maiden of this type is not uniquely Roman:

Yet the point of the contrast is not to tell us about Clinia and Clitipho. These young men are not very interesting in themselves. They have no depth and show no growth. The dilemmas they face are too typical of the comic genre and resolved too conventionally to arouse deep interest. Their significance lies in the challenge they pose to the two fathers and in what the sons reveal about them. Clinia's choice of the modest and faithful Antiphila is designed to reflect well on his upbringing. Menedemus was obviously wrong to drive off such a son, and so both his self-punishment and his eventual reunion are earned. Clitipho's choice, so frankly and selfishly confessed in that first monologue, reveals something the matter with Chremes' style of fatherhood, and the revelation of that something is the play's real center of interest.

The initial, careful contrast between Menedemus and Chremes is neither misplaced nor unimportant.[21] The problems the young men face find their interest and their function in bringing about the reversal of the old men's roles. Terence is explicit about this reversal. When Chremes finally learns the truth about Clitipho and Bacchis, his outrage receives only limited sympathy from Menedemus.

> CH. derides merito. mihi nunc ego suscenseo:
> quot res dedere ubi possem persentiscere,
> ni essem lapis! quae vidi! vae misero mihi!
> at ne illud haud inultum, si vivo, ferent!
> non iam . . . ME. non tu te cohibes? non te respicis?
> non tibi ego exempli satis sum? CH. prae iracundia,
> Menedeme, non sum apud me. ME. tene istuc loqui!

---

cf. Eubulus, fr. 42, and the comments of R. L. Hunter, *Eubulus, The Fragments* (Cambridge 1983) 134–135.

[21] E. Fantham, "*Heautontimorumenos* and *Adelphoe*. A Study of Fatherhood in Terence and Menander," *Latomus* 30 (1971) 970–998, esp. 978–983, is very good on this contrast. As she says, "The characters of the fathers . . . are far more complex and clearly the real focus of interest for playwright and audience" (978).

>   nonne id flagitiumst te aliis consilium dare,
>   foris sapere, tibi non posse te auxiliarier?
> CH. quid faciam? ME. id quod me fecisse aiebas parum.
>   fac te patrem esse sentiat . . .
>
> CH. You're right to laugh. I'm angry at myself.
>   How many clues there were to see the truth
>   if I hadn't been a fool! The things I saw! Idiot!
>   But they won't get off scot-free, not if I live!
>   Right now . . . ME. Won't you restrain yourself? Think
>   first.
>   Am I not good enough example? CH. Anger,
>   Menedemus, makes me not myself. ME. Stop such talk!
>   Isn't it wrong to give advice to others,
>   being wise in public, but helpless now to help yourself?
> CH. What should I do? ME. Exactly what you said I did too
>   little.
>   Let him know you are his father . . .
>   (915–925)

Chremes takes this advice, but in a particularly brutal way. He threatens to disinherit Clitipho and thus comes dangerously close to repeating Menedemus' error. Only the combination of his wife's appeal for mercy and Menedemus' gentle good sense forces a suitable compromise and, at the last moment, averts the creation of a second self-punisher.

The suave Chremes is brought to this pass because his complacency has been irretrievably shaken. The course of action that forces him to ask for advice also reveals his hypocrisy. Menedemus, as a father who has already paid for undue severity, remains consistently gentle and humble. Not even Chremes' fatuous pedantry ever shakes that humility. Their first encounter made this clear.

THE *duplex comoedia*

CH. tu illum numquam ostendisti quanti penderes
nec tibi illest credere ausus quae est aequom patri.
quod si esset factum, haec numquam evenissent tibi.
ME. ita res est, fateor: peccatum a me maxumest.

CH. You never showed how much you cared for him,
nor did he dare trust you as sons should.
Otherwise, this never would have happened.
ME. That's the case, I must confess. I am very much
to blame.

(155–158)

This is the remark to which Menedemus refers at 924. It was true enough when Chremes said it, but ill-timed and therefore offensive. Menedemus' timing of its repetition is much better. It has become true advice instead of criticism, but Chremes proves incapable of taking it to heart. His meddling has revealed a coarse egotism behind the polished facade. The didactic and censorious tone he adopted with Menedemus turns to simple abuse by the time he vents on his wife Sostrata the exasperation he feels with Clitipho.

convinces facile ex te natum; nam tui similest probe;
nam illi nil vitist relictum quin siet itidem tibi;
tum praeterea talem nisi tu nulla pareret filium.

You'll easily prove that he's your boy. He's just like you.
He hasn't got a fault that you don't have.
No other woman could have borne a son like that.

(1020–1022)

Menedemus did some growing before the play opened. Chremes has not grown, but he does seem to change before our eyes. The plot strips away his pretense and reveals at the end what he truly is.

This unmasking of Chremes creates the *argumentum simplex* of *Heauton timorumenos*. The play features a revelation of character made possible by the challenge of Clitipho's intrigue and made meaningful by the counter-example of Menedemus, whose condition provides the necessary perspective for judging him. The schemes of Syrus and the hopes of Menedemus are designed to serve this one central purpose. There is an obvious comparison with *Adelphoe*, which also uses the actions of sons to reveal the characters of their fathers. In that play, however, the issue between Micio and Demea is always in the foreground. Conflict has been continual between them; the sudden challenge posed by Aeschinus' actions simply precipitates the final round in a long-standing feud. Micio and Demea must be the constant focus of attention because the issues that divide them are complex and require careful development. Their self-righteous monologues and bickering dialogues always combine some measure of right on each side with an undercurrent of wrong. Terence is not so much arguing one side as observing the pitfalls that surround even the best intentions. The resulting moral ambiguity contrasts with the simplicity of *Heauton timorumenos*. The moral issue between Menedemus and Chremes is much clearer. Menedemus' character can remain static, while Chremes' fall is unambiguous. There is more time to spend elaborating and savoring the challenge posed by their sons. Unlike *Adelphoe*, the play must explore only a single character's weakness. Its complexity is thus, like that of *Phormio* and *Eunuchus*, a bit deceptive. The various interests and intrigues have not only a common denominator but a common purpose. They move toward the same conclusion, and a single process of action resolves them. Such uniformity of action reveals some important features of doubled action in Terence.

First, Terence shares with the entire tradition of New Comedy a tendency to represent the interests of only a single social class. Charinus and Pamphilus, Clinia and Clitipho, Antipho and Chaerea, though all lovers with different temperaments, are still young men facing the same kind of problem caused by the same kind of upbringing. Their fathers, perhaps because they face a wider variety of problems, are usually more interesting and more varied in their responses, but as members of the same social class they too share among themselves the same concerns and the same powers of action. In Terence, the class in question is always a monied one, but it need not be so. Part of the joke in Plautus' *Persa* is that the play acts out a standard comic plot among slaves, but the action stays on the level of slaves. The point of *Captivi*, where the perspectives of slave and free seem to intertwine, is that a mistake has been made. Philocrates and Tyndarus act nobly because they are noble. A second feature, unique to Terence, is a distinct uniformity of tone within each play. Plautus, like Menander before him, freely contrasts serious and light elements either for major effects as in *Amphitruo*, where Alcumena faces a real crisis and Sosia a comic one, or minor effects, as in *Poenulus*, where a comic intrigue ends at the last minute with the dignified pathos of Hanno's sudden arrival. Terentian plays do not mix serious and light in such generous proportions. Terence establishes a single tone for each play and maintains it. The didacticism of *Heauton timorumenos* and *Adelphoe*, the debased fawning of *Eunuchus*, the intellectual agility of *Phormio* become consistent, unifying forces in those plays. Terence cares neither to depict the diversity of human experience nor to demonstrate the universal application of what he does depict. He simply assumes the relevance of his characters and situations, confident that even within the comic conventions, the tensions between a Pamphilus and Simo or a Micio and Demea will touch responsive chords in an audience itself composed of parents and children. The point of doubling roles is not to widen the significance of a play's action but to concentrate it. The presence of Charinus heightens Pamphilus' dilemma. The paired sons of *Heauton timorumenos* and *Adelphoe* focus the contrast between their fathers. The complexity Terence creates by such doubling invariably meets the specific needs of a fundamentally simple design. To call the resulting pattern of action a "double plot" can mislead us. As with the notion of the well-made play, there is danger in applying a modern term uncritically to an ancient phenomenon.

That modern term has a uniquely modern pedigree. When Shakespeare turned Plautus' *Menaechmi* into *The Comedy of Errors*, for example, he created true sub-plots by using structural devices unparalleled in ancient comedy. The first of these involves the weaving of the material from Plautus' prologue into the fabric of the play. The Menaechmi's dead father becomes Egeon, the Syracusan merchant who wanders under sentence of death through Shakespeare's Ephesus seeking his lost sons and the thousand marks needed to ransom his life. His pathetic dilemma works in counterpoint to the broader humor of the confused twins until at last Egeon discovers not only them, but also his lost wife. Neither Plautus nor Terence approaches the complexity of Egeon's role. The old Carthaginian Hanno of *Poenulus* perhaps comes closest to Egeon's situation, but Plautus keeps Hanno at a distance. He figures only in the last third of the play and primarily, like the colorless Crito of *Andria*, to resolve a romantic problem through recognition of his nephews and his daughters. Neither the potential pathos of his scattered family nor the difficulty of his social position in Calydon receives more than joking notice. For Egeon's dilemma and the complexity of plot it creates, Shakespeare has gone to ancient romance rather than comedy. Egeon's Roman ancestor is not Hanno but Apollonius of Tyre.[22] The second alteration involves the doubling of the slave role. Where only Menaechmus of Sicily had a slave (Messenio), Shakespeare gives each Antipholus a Dromio, servants who are themselves twins and whose errors and escapades parallel those

---

[22] L. Salingar, *Shakespeare and the Traditions of Comedy* (Cambridge 1974) 59–67. Use of the Apollonius romance explains Shakespeare's shift of the scene from Epidamnus to Ephesus.

of their masters. Shakespeare's source for this doubling is generally taken to be *Amphitruo*, but the point of the doubling is quite different. In Plautus, the confusion is only on one side. Sosia meets his divine "double" in the very first scene and is never quite the same again. This is precisely the kind of confrontation that plays like *Menaechmi* and *The Comedy of Errors* must postpone until the end, since their humor comes from a sequence of inevitable mistakes and missed opportunities and ends when the twins at last come face to face. Mercury is a trickster, not a twin, and he makes *Amphitruo*, to borrow the Renaissance terms, a play of "supposes" rather than "errors."[23] Shakespeare's doubled servants are important not simply because they quadruple the play's opportunities for error, though that is no small contribution in itself, but because they extend the action into a second social sphere.

The Elizabethan double plot, which is rooted in medieval rather than ancient stagecraft, regularly serves to broaden rather than concentrate the significance of a play's action.[24] These structurally discrete processes of action complement the meaning even more than the mechanics of the plot. As William Empson observes,

> . . . a situation is repeated for quite different characters, and this puts the main interest in the situation, not the characters. Thus the effect of having two old men with ungrateful children, of different sorts, is to make us generalize the theme of Lear and feel that whole classes of children have become unfaithful. . . . The situation is made something valuable in it-

---

[23] The relevance of this distinction is nicely developed by H. Levin, "Two Comedies of Errors" in *Refractions* (New York 1966) 128–150.

[24] For the medieval roots and the thematic complexity of Shakespeare's double plots, see R. Weimann, *Shakespeare and the Popular Tradition in the Theater*, ed. R. Schwartz (Baltimore 1978) 151–160 and 237–246. Shakespeare's twin servants, even if they have an ancient source, are used in a typically Elizabethan way.

self, perhaps for reasons hardly realized; it can work on you like a myth.[25]

This is equally true in comedy. *As You Like It*, for example, juxtaposes the bookish love of Orlando for Rosalind, the pastoral love of Silvius for Phebe, and Touchstone's ironic courtship of Audrey to create a picture of love fuller than each quite separate act of wooing. Similarly, because each confused Antipholus has an equally confused Dromio, the schizophrenia latent in *The Comedy of Errors* embraces the whole world of Ephesus, not simply one merchant and his twin. Shakespeare's multiple plots add a richness to the significance of action that is unmatched in ancient drama.

Gilbert Norwood, in one of his best-honed barbs, once likened Plautus' skill as an adapter of Greek New Comedy to that of "a blacksmith mending a watch." Like any good polemicist, he is being wonderfully unfair. It has taken us the better part of a century to convince ourselves that Plautus' considerable skill was by no means inappropriate or unequal to his task. He was no blacksmith, but neither did the mechanism of New Comedy ever approach the complexity of a watch. Terence avoided many of the inconsistencies and loose ends that bedevil the analyzers of Plautine plots, not through special skill in intricate plotting, as if he were a Scribe or a Feydeau, but, like Menander before him, by sticking to a fundamentally simple design.[26] A play like *Heauton timorumenos* uses its doubled and intertwined characters to perform the single task of unmasking Chremes' hypocrisy. Even as we admire the play's *duplex* structure for what it is, we need to recall what it is not.

[25] W. Empson, *Some Versions of Pastoral* (New York 1935) 54.

[26] Leo, *PIF* 169–170, observes that we would not perceive Terence's tampering with his originals if his prologues and the ancient commentators did not point them out. For the contrast with Plautus, see his further comments at *GRL* 246–247.

[VI]

THE PRICE OF SIMPLICITY

The ending of *Heauton timorumenos* brings acute discomfort to Chremes' son, the rather foolish Clitipho. Faced with the imposed termination of his affair with Bacchis and fearful of being disinherited in favor of his newly recognized sister, he must choose a proper wife. Chremes threatens. His mother Sostrata cajoles. Clitipho must accept.

CL. faciam pater.
SO. gnate mi, ego pol tibi dabo illam lepidam, quam tu facile ames,
filiam Phanocratae nostri. CL. rufamne illam virginem,
caesiam, sparso ore, adunco naso? non possum pater.
CH. heia ut elegans est! credas animum ibi esse. SO. aliam dabo.
CL. immo, quandoquidem ducendast, egomet habeo propemodum
quam volo. CH. nunc laudo, gnate. CL. Archonidi huius filiam.
SO. perplacet.

CL. I will, father.
SO. Son, I'll get a pretty girl for you, a girl you'll easily love,
the daughter of Phanocrates our neighbor. CL. That red-haired,
grey-eyed, freckled, hook-nosed girl? I couldn't, father.
CH. How finicky he is! You'd think he had some feelings.
SO. I'll find another.
CL. Seeing that I have to marry, I know a girl at least

I like. CH. That's better, son. CL. I choose
   Archonides' daughter.
SO. A very good choice.

(1059–1066)

It does not matter, of course, that Clitipho chooses his bride by the color of her hair and the shape of her nose. We are not expected to ask what kind of husband he will make. Once the plot has brought him to this point, it need look no further. As Northrop Frye remarks of such comic endings, "we are simply given to understand that the newly married couple will live happily ever after, or that at any rate they will get alone in a relatively unhumorous and clear-sighted manner."[1] Yet in one play, probably the second that he sold to producers, Terence did look at the kind of marriage that the comic formulae so frequently generate. It is an odd play, too, not only because of this comparatively unusual theme, but because it combines a truly simple structure with an unusual perspective.

Hecyra, which is based on an original by Apollodorus of Carystus, examines a forced marriage that is, if not yet on the rocks, at least approaching the shoals. Like Clitipho, young Pamphilus was compelled to give up his own Bacchis in favor of marriage with Philumena. At first he continued to see Bacchis and refused to consummate the marriage, but Philumena's fine character eventually won his love. Yet this love may have come too late. While Pamphilus was abroad on business, Philumena abruptly left her mother-in-law Sostrata and now refuses even to see her. The play opens with Pamphilus' return and deals with the possible reasons for Philumena's retreat to her own family and Pamphilus' sudden refusal to take her back. Terence makes a mystery of their behavior, but we need not keep his secret. The situation has obvious affinities with Menander's *Epitrepontes*, in which a similarly estranged couple is reconciled when the untimely preg-

[1] N. Frye, *Anatomy of Criticism* (Princeton 1957) 169.

nancy that caused the rift proves to be the husband's doing. Both wives were raped before marriage, and both husbands are too priggish to forgive until they discover that they were themselves the culprits. This discovery makes for a powerful dramatic moment in *Epitrepontes*. In discovering that his wife's fault is no more than his own, Menander's Charisios experiences a revelation about his own attitudes and moral postures that is genuine, impressive, and moving. The action of *Epitrepontes* had been developed through surrogates, the slave-girl Habrotonon and the father Smikrines. Only at the end do the main characters appear to make their own discoveries.[2] The wife Pamphile displays a modest dignity, and, while watching her, Charisios learns an important lesson about himself.

ἐγώ τις ἀναμάρτητος, εἰς δόξαν βλέπων
καὶ τὸ καλὸν ὅ τι πότ' ἐστι καὶ ταἰσχρὸν σκοπῶν
ἀκέραιος, ἀνεπίπληκτος αὐτὸς τῷ βίῳ

I thought I was faultless, looking to my reputation
and judging right—whatever that is—and wrong as one
quite pure and blameless in his life.

(908–910)

The action culminates with this anguished admission and his acceptance of responsibility for his wife's dilemma.

The Pamphilus of *Hecyra* never makes this admission and avoids this responsibility. Having consistently hidden behind conflicting claims of *pietas* and *amor*, he is eventually entangled by his willingness to accept whatever sacrifices others are prepared to make for him.[3] The play ends conventionally enough

---

[2] Goldberg, *MMC* 61–71, and for the comparison with *Hecyra*, M. R. Posani, "Originalità artistica dell' *Hecyra* di Terenzio," *A&R* 8 (1940) 225–246. Posani's admiration for Terence's *meretrix* is tempered by D. Gilula, "The Concept of the *Bona Meretrix*," *RFIC* 108 (1980) 142–165.

[3] The chapter on *Hecyra* in D. Konstan, *Roman Comedy* (Ithaca 1983) 130–

with the imminent prospect of his reconciliation with Philumena, but not with any general revelation of the truth. Pamphilus prefers to hide the reason for his sudden change of heart.

> placet non fieri hoc itidem ut in comoediis
> omnia omnes ubi resciscunt. hic quos par fuerat resciscere
> sciunt; quos non autem aequomst scire neque resciscent neque
> scient.

> It's better not to have this end like comedies
> where everyone learns everything. Those who should find out,
> know. Those who have no need to know won't learn.
> (866–868)

More than a comic convention is being mocked here. In Menander, Charisios' knowledge brings him self-knowledge. Pamphilus is evading the self-revelation implicit in his discovery, and in the process he forfeits his last chance to win our compassion. Like so many Terentian *adulescentes*, he is a rather unappealing "hero." Though his estrangement from Philumena is the single issue of *Hecyra*, neither husband nor wife is actually the center of dramatic interest. The older generation, which is faced with the pending breakup and is eager to ascertain its cause and possible cure, proves far more interesting. The initial focus is on the two mothers-in-law and the dilemma that the estrangement from Philumena creates for them. These two women are the characters whose anguish is most fully portrayed, and they are the ones who move us.[4]

141, examines the demands of *pietas* and *amor*. Büchner, *TT* 170, notes the distinction between Pamphilus and Menander's Charisios.

[4] W. Schadewaldt, "Bemerkungen zur *Hecyra* des Terenz," *Hermes* 66 (1931) 1–29, nevertheless treats the play as Pamphilus' story. Among the few critics to appreciate the central role of the women is Norwood, *AT* 91: "It is a woman's play—not feminist—but with women as the chief sufferers, the chief actors, the bearers here of the Terentian *humanitas*." B. Croce, "Terence," *Philosophy, Poetry, History*, tr. C. Sprigge (London 1966) 776–

The play opens with the mystery of Philumena's flight from her mother-in-law. Sostrata's husband Laches, citing the *odium* often found between a young wife and her husband's mother, blames her for the girl's departure: "itaque adeo uno animo omnes socrus oderunt nurus" (201). Sostrata really has no idea what has come over Philumena and certainly does not hate her, but she is powerless to refute his charge. Terence ends her first appearance with a short monologue in which she affirms her innocence and expresses her helplessness.

> non facile est expurgatu: ita animum induxerunt socrus
> omnis esse iniquas: haud pol mequidem . . .
>
> It's not easy to clear myself. They're convinced all
> mothers-in-law are mean. Well, I'm not . . .
> (277–278)

In this scene of confrontation, Laches is a typical *senex iratus*; his bluster and the exaggeration of his complaint mark him as a comic figure. The categorical sweep of his opinion about mothers-in-law, a pointed senarius in a speech of octonarii, is as incongruous as it will prove incorrect. While Laches is a stock figure, however, Sostrata must refute the stereotyped character he attributes to her. Sostrata's monologue makes clear that the *odium*, *pertinacia*, and *malitia* of Laches' complaint have no place in her character. Her husband's error helps make his anger ridiculous even as it creates a real dilemma for Sostrata.[5] The truth of Philumena's condition, which is of course the actual reason for her

---

801, thinks *Hecyra* is Terence's best play largely because of his sensitive portrayal of the women.

[5] Donatus notes Terence's inversion and juxtaposition of the comic types. Thus *ad* 198: "senex enim est difficilis et iratus . . . conatur Terentius adversum famam socrum bonam reperire" and *ad* 774: "multa Terentius feliciter ausus est arte fretus, nam et socrus bonas et meretrices honesti cupidas praeter quam pervulgatum est facit." The hostile *socrus* may well have been a stock type, though the character is not found in extant comedy.

hasty departure, will not be revealed for another two hundred lines, when Pamphilus alone discovers it (376ff.). By creating mystery now Terence emphasizes Sostrata's bewilderment and confusion. The audience is meant to share her ignorance and her dilemma. She will eventually offer to leave for the country to make a reconciliation between the young people possible, and when she does so Pamphilus and the audience, who by then both know the truth, will be affected by the sincerity and goodness of the sacrifice she offers to make.

This scene of conflict between an abusive husband and an innocent wife has a parallel later in the play when Philumena's father Phidippus takes his own wife Myrrina to task for the fact of their daughter's pregnancy and the resulting threat to her marriage (516ff.). Laches had begun the first confrontation with two long exclamations to reveal his state of mind and to set the grounds for the argument. Terence initiates this parallel scene with a similar use of questions by Myrrina.[6]

> Perii, quid agam? quo me vortam? quid viro meo respondebo misera? nam audivisse vocem pueri visust vagientis . . .

> Alas, what shall I do? Where shall I turn? What shall I tell my husband? He must have heard the baby cry . . .
> (516–517)

Where Laches was bombastic and therefore comic, however, Myrrina's short, agitated questions are a signal for the audience to take her anxiety seriously. When her husband Phidippus enters, he proves to be another *senex iratus*, and he accuses Myrrina as unfairly as Laches had accused Sostrata of seeking to undermine the marriage from the start because she disapproved of Pamphilus' earlier affair with Bacchis (538–539). Myrrina, already in anguish over her daughter's difficulty, must add the re-

---

[6] For the equivalence of exclamation and rhetorical question in such contexts, see J. B. Hofmann, *Lateinische Umgangssprache*, 3 ed. (Heidelberg 1951) 66–69, and Denzler, *Monolog* 77–83.

proaches of an angry husband to her misery. Terence has her end the scene with a monologue that works on several levels (566–576). It is not simply an expression of anguish, but a genuine evaluation of the situation that threatens her.[7] Phidippus' adamant, tyrannical insistence that they must keep the child has only increased her burden. She voices concern for herself and her daughter, for the marriage, and for the family that faces the possible acceptance of a child whose paternity is uncertain. This progression of thought culminates with the revelation that the child is the result of a rape and that the attacker has taken a ring from Philumena, but Terence deliberately mutes the significance of this potential recognition token. He focuses instead on Myrrina's mental state, revealing her to be as innocent, sensitive, and perplexed as her counterpart Sostrata.

Terence had a talent for writing scenes of confrontation, and those two examples are particularly effective. The contrast between the stock figures of the angry old men and the more complex, sympathetic matrons is a very deft piece of theatre. The two husbands do most of the talking. Each is at least as angry at being thought a fool as at the threat to the young people's marriage.

> LA. tu inquam, mulier, quae me omnino lapidem, non
> hominem putas. (214)
> PH. tu virum me aut hominem deputas adeo esse? (524)
>
> LA. You, I say, woman. You must think me a dolt and not a man.
> PH. What kind of husband do you think I am? What kind of man?

Each assumes the situation to be his own wife's making.

---

[7] Büchner, *TT* 148, calls this monologue "a restless calculation and consideration of all the possibilities." Denzler, *Monolog* 134, observes that a central function of monologues throughout the play is to reveal states of mind.

LA. in te omnis haeret culpa sola, Sostrata. (229)
PH. non sic ludibrio tuis factis habitus essem. (526)

LA. All the blame's on you alone, Sostrata.
PH. Otherwise, your acts would not have made me such a fool.

Their misplaced emphasis cannot be taken seriously, and their similar speech and manner on the stage reinforce this comic coloring for the audience. The women show much greater individuality. Because the entire situation mystifies her, Sostrata is helpless to defend herself before Laches. Her only words are denials of guilt, responses to the charges he makes. Myrrina is less easily bullied. She understands the immediate situation all too well and aims to keep Phidippus from learning that Philumena's child was conceived out of wedlock. She too must deny a charge of *odium*, but she also takes an initiative.

> mitte adulescentem obsecro
> et quae me pecasse ais. abi, solus solum conveni,
> roga velitne uxorem an non: si est ut dicat velle se,
> redde; sin est autem ut nolit, recte ego consului meae.

> Please forget the boy
> and the wrong you say I've done. Go, get him alone,
> ask if he wants his wife or not. If he says he does,
> send her back; if not, then I've given good advice to her.
> (556–559)

She succeeds for the moment in turning aside Phidippus' rage, but—as her monologue then makes clear—real difficulties still face her. The rage of Laches and of Phidippus is of a familiar comic type, but Sostrata and Myrrina suffer their own anguish, each for her own reasons and in her own way.

The problems these women face are certainly the most significant and moving problems in the play, and to keep it focused on their anguish requires a reordering of the traditional comic priorities. After all, we might have expected the play to be about Pamphilus. He is the real source of the trouble, and he has a self-important slave named Parmeno who could easily have become the *servus callidus* so central to Plautine comedy. The plot itself turns, not on any psychological subtleties, but upon the all-too-mechanical discovery that the ring Philumena snatched from her attacker belongs to Pamphilus. In terms of plot, the young people are central to the play. Because the dramatic interest lies elsewhere, Terence must leave undeveloped those traditional comic elements that revolve around them, and he introduces instead a new element of suspense to disorient our expectations and turn our attention in a different direction.

Toning down the familiar stuff of comedy does not prove to be very difficult. First of all, the role of Parmeno is reduced and actually reverses the relationship expected between slave and young master. Parmeno figured prominently in the initial exposition, where he told the story of Pamphilus' marriage and earlier affair with Bacchis to two protatic characters. Yet later events and statements show that Parmeno actually misread the situation. He had told Philotis and Syra that Bacchis grew cool to Pamphilus after his marriage and that her increasing harshness brought him closer to his wife (157–170). Subsequent statements by Bacchis and her very willingness to help save his marriage reveal the injustice in Parmeno's portrait of her (750ff., cf. 855ff.). He is equaly wrong in his initial assurance to Pamphilus that the cause of Philumena's estrangement from Sostrata is "a trifle," as both Pamphilus and the audience will soon discover (306ff., 361ff.). These errors are signals that Parmeno lacks that true grasp of the situation we expect from a *servus callidus*. He is not as clever as he thinks.[8] As the action develops, Pamphilus comes to

---

[8] For such critics as Schadewaldt (above, n. 4) and E. Lefèvre, *Die Expositionstechnik in den Komödien des Terenz* (Darmstadt 1969) 60–80, these inconsistencies in Parmeno's account reveal Terence's reworking of his Greek model, which has resulted in contradictions and loose ends. See J.C.B.

fear his interference in this increasingly delicate situation and has little difficulty in keeping the slave at a distance. Pamphilus had ordered him out of the way at the first sign of trouble, and he then contrives a fool's errand to keep Parmeno harmlessly engaged (359, 430 ff.). The slave's eventual report of a fruitless search on the Acropolis for the nonexistent Callidemides provides comic relief at the crisis by bringing him on the stage in a reverse *currens* scene; he is exhausted by his errand but has no message to deliver (799ff.). Bacchis promptly orders him off again in search of Pamphilus, with a terse injunction to mind his own business (810). Rather than being a controller of events, Parmeno is reduced to the role of ignorant messenger always off the stage at the key moment. As Donatus remarks, "quanto magis Parmeno curiosus est, tanto magis nesciat illa quae cupit" (*ad* 851).

A second indication of Terence's deliberate muting of traditional comedy is the truncated recognition. In *Casina*, Plautus joked about omitting a recognition entirely, but comic recognitions tend to be elaborately foreshadowed and often, as in *Rudens*, brilliantly staged. In the *Epitrepontes*, where a ring also reunites the estranged couple, the entire action of the play involves the process of bringing home to Charisios and Pamphile the true import of its discovery. Terence pays comparatively little attention to this device. Myrrina tells us at line 574 that Philumena lost a ring to her attacker, but only at the play's climax do we learn that Pamphilus gave this same ring to Bacchis and that the *meretrix*

Lowe, "Terentian Originality in the *Phormio* and *Hecyra*," *Hermes* 111 (1983) 439–442. D. Sewart, "Exposition in the *Hekyra* of Apollodorus," *Hermes* 102 (1974) 247–260, argues instead that Terence omitted only an expository prologue that revealed Parmeno's unfounded self-importance for what it is. The conflict between Parmeno's story of Bacchis and her own later statements creates a special problem. Contrast the interpretations of Gilula (above, n. 2) 154–161 and T. McGarrity, "Reputation v. Reality in Terence's *Hecyra*," *CJ* 76 (1980/81) 149–156.

has made the necessary connection. Laches and Phidippus had asked her to see Myrrina and Philumena simply to assure them that her affair with Pamphilus was over. Myrrina's recognition of the ring she is wearing as Philumena's lost ring is unexpected, and its resolution of the play's crisis takes place off the stage. We learn of these events only from a short monologue by Bacchis (816–840). Donatus says that in the Greek original by Apollodorus, much more of this action was staged.[9] By compressing the actual recognition into a monologue and thereby reducing the amount of stage time devoted to it, Terence minimizes the importance of its contribution to the plot and willingly forfeits much of its traditional comic value.

Yet the most remarkable feature of *Hecyra* is Terence's introduction of genuine suspense in the modern sense of audience uncertainty and tension. Scenes of anguish are familiar in both Greek New Comedy and the *palliata*: Daos lamenting his dead master in Menander's *Aspis*, Plautus' Alcumena swearing in confusion and fright that no mortal has touched her except Amphitruo, Menedemus reproaching himself for the harshness he has shown his son in *Heauton timorumenos*. Such anguish is as genuine and as carefully portrayed as anguish in *Hecyra*, but it is also accompanied by an irony that comes from the audience's superior knowledge. Menander soon tells us in a delayed prologue that Daos' master is alive and will later appear. Plautus has Mercury make clear at the outset of *Amphitruo* that this is a "tragico-comoedia" in which he and Jupiter will themselves figure, and no sooner is Menedemus off the stage than Terence reveals that his son Clinia is no longer suffering abroad as a mercenary. Three-quarters of the way through *Hecyra*, when Pamphilus asks rhetorically if he should raise a child whose own father has abandoned it, neither he nor the audience yet knows that he himself

---

[9] Don. *ad* 825: "brevitati consulit Terentius, nam in Graeca haec aguntur, non narrantur."

is that father (670). There is no hint that the attacker whom Myrrina says has taken Philumena's ring is Pamphilus and no suggestion that his previous association with Bacchis will make possible this discovery. Terence holds all this back until the climax. The resulting suspense, which he probably created simply by omitting the expository prologue of his Greek original, is his prime method for putting a new face on a familiar dramatic pattern.[10] He wants to reveal facts slowly as they would be revealed in real life, and he wants us to share the confusion and pain of Sostrata and Myrrina. As Donatus remarks, the play's ending is meant to strike us, not like a comedy, but like the truth (*ad* 866).

Creating suspense of this kind was a very daring thing to do. Greco-Roman comedy generally provided the audience with fuller knowledge of the dramatic situation than the characters possess. This was a practice at least as old as Euripides, who had developed the expository prologue as a device for putting the audience in a position of superior knowledge and enabling it to watch the play with a set of expectations. Those expectations might or might not be fulfilled, but the audience would inevitably measure the actions and characters of the play against them.[11] By refusing to grant any superior knowledge, Terence seeks to

---

[10] The arguments of Sewart (above, n. 8) on this point are persuasive. He assumes the Greek prologue to have revealed the limits of Parmeno's knowledge, the true motives of Bacchis, and the truth about the child. Compare Tyche's prologue in Menander's *Aspis*, which reveals Smikrines' true character, the hopes of his brother Chairestratos, and the fact that Kleostratos is still alive without telling all that will happen in the play. Büchner, *TT* 484–497, claims that the Greek originals of *Hecyra*, *Andria*, and *Heauton timorumenos* also lacked prologues, but the newly discovered texts of Menander argue against this possibility.

[11] For this use of the prologue in Euripides, see D. C. Stuart, "Foreshadowing and Suspense in the Euripidean Prolog," *SP* 15 (1918) 295–306, and R. Hamilton, "Prologue, Prophecy and Plot in Four Plays of Euripides," *AJP* 99 (1978) 277–302. S. M. Goldberg, "The Style and Function of Menander's *Dyskolos* Prologue," *SO* 53 (1978) 57–68, discusses a parallel use of

put us on the same level as his characters. He wants them to seem no better or worse than ourselves, and so he tells us no more than they know. Once we learn why Philumena has returned to her mother, there is indeed irony for us in Sostrata's offer to retreat to the country and in the inability of Laches and Phidippus to grasp Pamphilus' reluctance to accept Philumena and the child (577ff., 622ff.). But we have no more understanding of the situation and can make no more sense of it than can either Pamphilus or Myrrina. Terence's careful rationing of knowledge is an ingenious and economical way to alter the play's focus. We share much of the ignorance that has caused the dilemma, and we ought therefore to share the emotional experience of the characters. Given the strong—some might say monotonous—pattern of action in Terence's tradition, this alteration of focus in *Hecyra* is a noteworthy innovation, but it does not necessarily make for a successful play. Though Sostrata and Myrrina are among the most finely drawn women in Roman comedy and though their difficulties are credible and dramatic, there is still something wrong with *Hecyra*.

Lack of practical experience in the theatre may make it easy to think that withholding the truth about Philumena's child creates such real suspense that the play's appeal can be built around resolving it. This is to reckon, however, without the considerable history of the *palliata* tradition and the effect of that tradition on an audience. The memory of only a few recognition plays quickly takes the edge off the suspense that Terence has been at such pains to create.[12] He may arouse curiosity in the first act, but how will he keep our interest if his hesitation to reveal the truth leads us to feel quicker of wit than both the poet and his

---

the prologue in New Comedy. For the relevant Roman material, see Duckworth, *NRC* 209–235.

[12] For the familiarity of the recognition motif, see P. W. Harsh, *Studies in Dramatic "Preparation" in Roman Comedy* (Chicago 1935) 34–51. Terence's

characters? Even if the audience does not guess the truth, it may well lose interest in the proceedings because it lacks the knowledge necessary for sufficient appreciation. There is a good modern example of precisely that problem. In *Lady Windermere's Fan*, Oscar Wilde intended to conceal until the climax that the mysterious Mrs. Erlynne, to whom Lord Windermere seems suspiciously accommodating, is actually the virtuous Lady Windermere's scandalous and now blackmailing mother. When the play was in rehearsal, Wilde's producer urged him to reveal this fact sooner, but "the chief merit of my last act," he replied, "is to me the fact that it does not contain, as most plays do, the explanation of what the audience knows already, but that it is the sudden explanation of what the audience desires to know. . . ."[13] After one performance Wilde altered the play as his more experienced advisor had urged. The play reaches its climax when Mrs. Erlynne sacrifices her prospects for returning to society in order to save Lady Windermere's good name, but, however dramatic the moment, it lacked sufficient point when the audience did not know that it was witnessing a mother's effort to save her daughter from repeating her own past indiscretion. Terence's audience, like that London audience of 1892, needed sufficient information to realize the significance of what they were seeing. Suspense was not an adequate substitute. By restricting his use of irony, Terence surrendered his most potent tool for bringing the play's meaning home to his audience.[14]

---

variation of the motif is known to us only from Menander and Apollodorus, but the cues to the audience remain traditional.

[13] Wilde to George Alexander, written in mid-February 1892 and published in *The Letters of Oscar Wilde*, Rupert Hart-Davis, ed. (London 1962) 308–309.

[14] Cf. J. L. Styan, *The Elements of Drama* (Cambridge 1960) 49: ". . . one joy in the play is to see our wisdom confirmed by events. This is the true irony of drama, through which the dramatist does most of his work; it is the steady and insistent communication to the privileged spectator of a meaning

One other possibility was open to him. A fast pace can absorb the audience even in the unraveling of a situation they do not fully understand. This is the standard technique in plays of intrigue, where complicated and shifting schemes deliberately enrich and confuse the action. An audience may be hard pressed to explain after the fact what a Pseudolus or an Epidicus was really up to, but because the plays move quickly, doubts and confusion do not affect attention and enjoyment.[15] *Hecyra* is a short play, but it is not a quick one. Terence's interest in mental states requires frequent monologues to reveal them, and these monologues have a retarding effect on the play's movement.

The norm in New Comedy is to reveal character through action. In the last act of Menander's *Samia*, for example, Moschion threatens to go abroad on the eve of his marriage simply to punish his father for doubting his good faith. There is a slapstick scene with his slave and much nervous pacing before the house door before Demeas discovers the scheme and shames Moschion into abandoning his pose. Moschion's foolish ruse reflects the egotism and shallow thinking he has exhibited throughout the play. Similarly in Terence's *Adelphoe*, Aeschinus' rough treatment of the pimp indicates a coarseness of character that gives the lie to the humanistic philosophy of childrearing his adopted father Micio extols. In both cases, stage action is the result and the reflection of character. We are impressed less by what Aeschinus and Moschion say than by what they actually do on the stage. In *Hecyra*, Terence reveals character primarily through talk. He can indeed

---

hidden from the characters." This is of course a favorite Menandrean technique.

[15] Harsh (above, n. 12) 56–75 reviews preparation and the lack of it in intrigues. One may perhaps be excused for remembering director Howard Hawks's confession that neither he nor his writers (who included William Faulkner) really understood how the clues fitted together in *The Big Sleep*. The chain, though long, had to be sound in Chandler's novel; in the fast-paced film it did not matter.

write taut, dramatic dialogue. Thus, to cite one simple example, Sostrata and Pamphilus discuss Philumena's "illness."

> so. quid tu igitur lacrumas? aut quid es tam tristis?
>   pa. recte, mater.
> so. quid fuit tumulti? dic mihi: an dolor repente invasit?
> pa. ita factumst. so. quid morbi est? pa. febris.
>   so. cotidiana? pa. ita aiunt.
>   i sodes, intro, consequar iam te, mea mater. so. fiat.
>
> so. Why are you crying, then? Why so sad? pa. It's nothing, mother.
> so. What was the noise? Tell me: is she suddenly sick?
> pa. That's it. so. What kind of sickness? pa. Fever.
>   so. Every day? pa. So they say.
>   Go inside, please, mother. I'll follow soon.
>   so. All right.
>
>   (355–358)

The parataxis, the single word replies, and the quickly paced questions and answers suggest the economy and rapidity of colloquial speech.[16] Sostrata's questions reveal genuine concern for Philumena, and thus her basic goodness. The brevity of Pamphilus' replies marks his extreme discomfort at the situation. His lie about the fever is one more missed opportunity to face the crisis squarely. The dialogue reflects the characters of the two speakers. Yet at key moments Terence time and again writes not true dialogue such as this but only juxtaposed speeches which make his characters' thoughts explicit. Pamphilus expresses his misery to Parmeno in a series of such speeches before the pace

---

[16] Such imitation of colloquial speech was one of Terence's major achievements and contrasts with the sprightly but more artificial dialogue of Plautus. See H. Haffter, *Untersuchungen zur altlateinischen Dichtersprache* (Berlin 1934) 135–143, and J. Straus, *Terenz und Menander, Beitrag zu einer Stilvergleichung* (Diss. Bern 1955) 38–54.

accelerates into true dialogue (281ff.), and Sostrata's offer to retreat to the country, an offer designed to increase sympathy for her and further demonstrate her good nature, is phrased in speeches delivered to Pamphilus (577ff.). Because action in *Hecyra* is largely offstage, Terence must resort to talk even when he wants to quicken the pace. Philumena's pregnancy is announced in a monologue by Pamphilus, and Bacchis narrates the results of the ring's discovery in another one. The precision and grace of Terence's style make such speeches extremely economical, but they bring stage action to a standstill. Nothing is happening while these monologues are delivered. For a theatre audience to feel their effect, it must feel for the characters who speak them, but in practice Terence's pace and structure work against creating that sympathy. *Hecyra* lacks the arresting action and lively tempo necessary to seize the audience's attention and to interest it in characters whose problems at first sight seem so typical. What intellectual satisfaction may come from unraveling the mystery of Philumena's action depends on overcoming the technical obstacles the play creates for itself.[17]

Problems of pace and perspective are noticeable at once. It takes well over two hundred lines, what modern editors call the first and second acts, just to complete the exposition. Terence first introduces two deftly drawn *meretrices* gossiping about Pamphilus and Bacchis (58–75). Parmeno joins them, tells the circumstances of Pamphilus' marriage, and speaks of the mystery surrounding Philumena's flight from her mother-in-law (76–197). As we have seen, his narrative is neither omniscient nor entirely correct, and we do not yet know what kind of dramatic action will develop from this situation. The following quarrel be-

[17] D. Gilula, "Terence's *Hecyra*: A Delicate Balance of Suspense and Dramatic Irony," *SCI* 5 (1979/80) 137–157, nevertheless finds dramatic tension and interest "created by the intellectual involvement of the spectators in the plot. Thanks to this active participation, the pleasure and satisfaction in the unravelling of the plot are much enhanced."

tween Laches and Sostrata finally locates the emphasis of the play. This emphasis is unexpected, and there is no hint of where it will lead. Pamphilus' first appearance, where he tells his troubles to Parmeno, hardly sharpens the focus. The audience does not know where it stands, does not know what kind of play it is seeing, and this is extremely dangerous for a dramatist working in a tradition that thrived on manipulating the expectations of its audience. Terence's innovations in structure and focus only bewilder the audience here at the beginning and create a similar problem at the end.

The play's action has stressed the dilemma of parents, but Terence ends only with the reconciliation of children. Such a conclusion fails to satisfy because, in the dramatic context he has created, it emphasizes the wrong thing. Though the intervention of Bacchis is deftly done and Pamphilus' final, happy scene is inevitable, we sorely miss the reappearance of his elders. Sostrata and Myrrina, whose anguish we have shared, are never openly rewarded for their fortitude, and Phidippus and Laches never discover how a selfish concern for *fama* brought their wives and children to the brink of disaster. Denying Pamphilus the self-revelation of Menander's Charisios is consistent with Terence's design, but denying vindication to the matrons and chastisement to the old men is not. We are happy to have the young couple reunited, but it was Sostrata and Myrrina who had really won our concern. *Hecyra* was their play, but they are missing from its conclusion. Terence instead returns to a more conventional focus on the resolution of Pamphilus' problem, and there is thus some irony in his final request not to have the play end *ut in comoediis* (866). Caught between a new perspective and a familiar action, Terence has suddenly reverted to the letter of his plot without treating the spirit he created for it. The settling of accounts that explains the ending of plays like *Phormio* and *Adelphoe* is disconcertingly absent. *Hecyra* withholds rewards and punishments, and so its real issues are never resolved.

There is a curious irony, if not a cause, in the fact that a play with such a dubious ending also had a notoriously dubious stage history. Its two prologues record our only definite examples of failed dramatic performances at Rome.[18] When first produced at the *ludi Megalenses* of 165, anticipation of a tightrope act distracted the audience and aborted the performance. Terence withdrew the play, and only after successes with *Heauton timorumenos*, *Eunuchus*, and *Phormio* did he offer it again, this time in tandem with *Adelphoe* at the funeral games of Aemilius Paullus in 160. At first all went well, but the rumor of a gladiatorial show again caused turmoil in the crowd and halted the production. Only later that year, at the *ludi Romani*, did an audience see the play through.[19] Such troubles suggest the kind of audience that Horace was to mock in the *Letter to Augustus*.

saepe etiam audacem fugat hoc terretque poetam,
quod numero plures, virtute et honore minores,
indocti stolidique, et depugnare parati
si discordet eques, media inter carmina poscunt
aut ursum aut pugiles; his nam plebecula gaudet.

Often this too drives off and frightens the daring poet:
a crowd full in number, in taste and status paltry,
unschooled and foolish, and prepared to fight it out
if a knight should disagree, in the middle of a play demands
a dancing bear or boxers. That's what the masses like.
(*Ep.* 2.1.182–186)

---

[18] In the second prologue to *Hecyra* 14–23 Ambivius Turpio implies that he had similar difficulties performing plays of Caecilius ("partim sum earum exactus, partim vix steti"). Whether this is true literary history or Terentian rhetoric is unknown. Caecilius was certainly a traditional dramatist, but contrast the interpretations of Leo, *GRL* 217–226, and Wright, *DiC* 87–126.

[19] This chronology, which is based on the evidence of didascalia and prologues, represents the modern *communis opinio*. There are difficulties with it, but no alternative scheme has gained acceptance. See Marti, *Lustrum* 8 (1963) 20–23. There is no reason to suppose that Terence revised the play significantly in these intervals.

Yet the problem Terence faced with *Hecyra* did not lie solely with the audience nor with the improvised Roman stage that inevitably mingled theatrical and gladiatorial crowds.[20] It is hard to believe that only an accident of scheduling at Paullus' funeral saved *Adelphoe* from a similar fate or that any such thing could ever have happened to *Pseudolus*, whatever the following attraction. *Hecyra* was itself not a play easy for a Roman audience to love.

Terence had tried to revitalize the fundamentally simple plot of *Hecyra* by presenting it from an unfamiliar perspective. He brings unexpected characters to the foreground. He keeps his audience in suspense, first about the dramatic problem itself and then about its solution, and he limits the function of such common devices as the ring and the clever slave that might point the way to the climax. He chose an odd play for his model—odd at least by the norms of the Roman stage—and he probably compounded its oddity by suppressing the expository prologue that would have explained it.[21] He perhaps forgot an important fact of theatrical life. The innovator in as conservative a tradition as the *comoedia palliata* must always know what boundaries he can transcend and which ones he must respect. Or, like Plautus in such plays as *Amphitruo* and *Persa*, he must know where to explain and where to apologize. An audience has to be won to a kind of play it does not know. "Like a modern opera audience," says John Wright, "they [the Roman audience] were conservative and knew what they wanted (as Terence found out to his cost),

---

[20] F. H. Sandbach, "How Terence's *Hecyra* Failed," *CQ* 32 (1982) 134–135. D. Gilula, "Who's Afraid of Rope-Walkers and Gladiators? (Terence, *Hec.* 1–57)," *Athenaeum* 59 (1981) 29–37, nevertheless thinks we should take Terence at his word in accounting for *Hecyra*'s two failures.

[21] The Greek original of *Hecyra* may well owe a deliberate debt to *Epitrepontes*; Apollodorus is thought to have been a particular admirer of Menander. There are no other Roman plays on this theme or with this degree of true suspense. Terence's play is apparently innovative by Roman standards whether or not he made appreciable changes in the structure of his model.

and their expectations would have been a major force in shaping the Roman comic tradition."[22] Terence's failure to take those expectations into account meant inevitable failure for *Hecyra*.

This particular innovation was not repeated. Terence never again told so simple a story or embraced so unusual a perspective. As we have already seen, he found other, often extremely effective, ways to put a new slant on an old story and to develop its significance. Yet there is an ironic propriety in ending our discussion of these six comedies with what is arguably the most daring and the least successful of the group. Terence never won really lasting popularity as a dramatist. Despite the record fee earned by *Eunuchus*, the traditional good fun of *Phormio*, and the sophistication of *Adelphoe*, his plays did not become true classics of the Roman stage. Thus, while Cicero liked Terence very much and quoted him often, it was the revival of Plautus that he enjoyed on the stage and that made the actor Roscius rich. Terence won his lasting fame as a stylist, not a playwright, and his dramatic tradition did not long survive so bookish an achievement. How and why this was so are the remaining questions before us.

[22] Wright, *DiC* 191.

[VII]

THE *purus sermo*

The inquisitive Chremes of *Heauton timorumenos* opens that play with a long speech beginning like this:

> Quamquam haec inter nos nuper notitia admodumst
> (inde adeo quod agrum in proxumo hic mercatus es)
> nec rei fere sane amplius quicquam fuit,
> tamen vel virtus tua me vel vicinitas,
> quod ego in propinqua parte amicitiae puto,
> facit ut te audacter moneam et familiariter
> quod mihi videre praeter aetatem tuam
> facere et praeter quam res te adhortatur tua.

> Although this acquaintance of ours is recent
> (You've only just bought the farm next door)
> and we've really had only minimal contact,
> nevertheless, your goodness and proximity,
> which I consider a first step to friendship,
> urge me to advise you frankly and familiarly,
> since you seem to be working beyond your years
> and surely beyond what your means require.
> (HT 53–60)

The sentence is a masterpiece of exposition. In just eight lines Terence establishes the setting, the characters of the two men on the stage, and the relationship between them. We learn at once that they are new neighbors who have rarely spoken together. Chremes' presumption is thus manifest. He rather officiously equates *vicinitas* with *amicitia* and does not hesitate to address a comparative stranger *audacter et familiariter*. His reclusive, hard-working neighbor must be well off, for though he has just bought his farm, he could still hire labor to work it if he chose. Yet even more remarkable than the economy of Terence's presentation is the ease with which he weaves its information into a single sentence. The correlation of *quamquam . . . tamen*, the casual interruption of the parenthesis, and the explanatory *quod*-clauses surround a simple predicate with the web of detail that develops its dramatic significance. This manipulation of clauses is comparable to the rhetorical skill we have already noticed in the prologues, and Terence uses some of the same stylistic devices: alliteration (*inter nos nuper notitia, vel virtus . . . vel vicinitas, in propinqua parte . . . puto*), parallelism (*praeter aetatem tuam . . . praeter quam res tua*), the same simple connectives. The result is the kind of precise and unobtrusive organization often found in good Latin writing, and a reader looking back to this sentence from Cicero or Caesar might well take its suppleness for granted. By classical standards, its elegance is neither contrived nor unusual.

Yet the prose of Terence's own day was hardly like this. Latin prose required another sixty years and the formalization of rhetorical training to achieve a comparable sophistication. The anonymous *Rhetorica ad Herennium*, for example, exhorts readers to seek a similarly disingenuous artfulness in the *exordium* of a speech.

> Exordienda causa servandum est ut lenis sit sermo et usitata verborum consuetudo, ut non apparata videatur oratio esse . . . vitiosum [exordium] est quod nimium apparatis verbis conpositum est, aut nimium longum est; et quod non ex ipsa causa natum videatur ut proprie cohaereat cum narratione.
>
> In beginning a case, take care that the style be smooth and the vocabulary familiar so that the speech seems extemporaneous . . . that [beginning] is faulty which is composed with too much labor or is too long; and that which does not seem born

from the case itself so that it is appropriate to the statement of facts.

(*Rhet. Her.* 1.11)

Terence's easy, but hardly unstudied, manner thus foreshadows the deliberately graceful prose of the next century, and the greatest architects of that stylistic advance were to recognize his contribution to their eventual achievement. What he had to teach them and why he became a stylistic model are crucial questions for understanding his place in the history of Latin literature.

In discussing the rambling style of early Latin, Eduard Norden follows a fragment of Cato's speech *De bello Carthageniensi* (fr. 193M)—"homines defoderunt in terram dimidiatos ignemque circumposuerunt: ita interfecerunt"—with the remark that Cicero would have written, "homines in terram defossos igni circumposito interfecerunt."[1] Norden is perhaps overconfident, but his hard-working participles indeed represent not only a familiar syntactic device of classical prose, but an important step in the development of prose writing. Cato's paratactic organization was superseded. Careful authors of later times thought out more complex relationships among their ideas and used such subordinating structures as participles to express those relationships succinctly and unambiguously. They made deliberate choices in the organization of their sentences, preserving parataxis as only one of many devices in their repertoire.[2] When it was not so fully an object of choice, however, parataxis often led to the stiffness characteristic of early Latin.

---

[1] E. Norden, *Antike Kunstprosa*, vol. 1 (Stuttgart 1958) 166. The early orators are cited from E. Malcovati, *Oratorum romanorum fragmenta*, 3 ed. (Turin 1967), the historians from H. Peter, *Historicorum romanorum reliquiae*, 2 ed., 2 vol. (Leipzig 1914).

[2] Contrast, for example, Caes., *Gal.* 4.15 (a German retreat narrated in periodic style) and *Gal.* 7.88 (a rout described in short, dramatic sentences).

In nonliterary prose such stiffness hardly mattered. It might even be a virtue. Cato's *De agricultura*, for example, preserves several religious formulae on the pattern: "Iane pater, te hac strue ommovenda bonas preces precor, uti sies volens propitius mihi liberisque meis domo familiaeque meae" (134). The *figura etymologica*, the nearly synonymous adjectives, the paired sequence *mihi liberis* and *domo familiaeque*, and the simple, linear structure give the prayer a stark and modest power. The same kind of structure lends precision, if not grace, to official documents. Here, for example, is an order of Aemilius Paullus issued in Spain in 189 B.C. Note the chiasm *decreivit utei . . . habere iousit* and the simple, sequential clauses of the second sentence.

L. Aimilius L. f. inpeirator decreivit, utei quei Hastensium servei in turri Lascutana habitarent, leiberei essent. agrum oppidumque, quod ea tempestate posedisent, item possidere habereque iousit, dum poplus senatusque Romanus vellet. act. in castreis a.d. XII K. Febr.

Lucius Aemilius, son of Lucius, commanding general, decreed that those who live in Turris Luscitana as slaves of the Hastenses should be free. The land and town which they possessed at that time, he ordered that they should likewise possess and keep as long as the Roman people and senate wish. Done in camp twelve days before the Kalends of February.

(CIL i² 614)

Paullus' decree is terse and clear, but only because his content is as simple as his syntax. More complex ideas could not be so easily expressed in this way. Pronoun referents too easily become confused, and repetitions become tedious. We have already seen such stylistic difficulties in Cato's oratory. In narrative prose, which often requires a complex sequence of ideas, the need for clarity and the difficulty of early prose to achieve it are even more pronounced.

Consider, for example, a passage from Cato's story in his *Origines* about the military tribune Quintus Caedicius, whose suicidal mission saved a Roman army during the First Punic War.

> Dii immortales tribuno militum fortunam ex virtute eius dedere. nam ita evenit: cum saucius multifariam ibi factus esset, tamen vulnus capiti nullum evenit, eumque inter mortuos defetigatum vulneribus atque quod sanguen defluxerat, cognovere. eum sustulere, isque convaluit saepeque postilla operam rei p. fortem atque strenuam perhibuit illoque facto, quod illos milites subduxit, exercitum ceterum servavit.

> The immortal gods gave the military tribune good fortune because of his courage. It came about this way: although he had received many wounds there, nevertheless he received no head wound, and they discovered him among the dead, worn out with wounds and because blood had flowed. They took him up, and he recovered, and often afterwards he did brave and vigorous service for the state, and by that deed, which rescued those soldiers, he saved the rest of the army.
> (fr. 83P)

Cato's sentences do not entirely lack deliberate shape. The *ita*, as a kind of verbal punctuation, introduces the narrative. Correlated *cum . . . tamen* and the hyperbaton of *cognovere* heighten the drama by putting the details of Caedicius' condition before the main verb that explains his rescue. Yet, though there are thirteen verbal ideas in this passage, there are only two participial constructions and three subordinate clauses. Cato treats each action as a discrete verbal unit, and this leads to difficulties. Take the *cum . . . tamen* sequence. What is the relationship among its parts? If *vulnus capiti* means simply "a head wound," the phrase goes closely with *cognovere*; if it means "a mortal wound," the first link is with *inter mortuos*. Is the key point that they found Caedicius alive among the dead, or that they recognized him because his face was uninjured? Is the connection causal or concessive? Cato does not establish a clear relationship among the facts of his narrative. Because his organization is sequential, he relies primarily on independent clauses and must constantly change subject among the tribune, his rescuers, and circumstances themselves to tell the story. The syntax cannot focus attention on any one subject, and Cato's narrative therefore lacks the coherence and point we think typical of the later language.

In less than a century the quality of literary prose changed dramatically. Consider by way of contrast the duel between Titus Manlius and an insolent Gaul as told by Quintus Claudius Quadrigarius in the time of Sulla.[3]

> ita, ut ante dixi, constiterunt: Gallus sua disciplina scuto proiecto cantabundus, Manlius, animo magis quam arte confisus, scuto scutum percussit atque statum Galli conturbavit. dum se Gallus iterum eodem pacto constituere studet, Manlius iterum scuto scutum percutit atque de loco hominem iterum deiecit; eo pacto ei sub Gallicum gladium successit, ne Gallus impetum in ictu haberet, atque Hispanico pectus hausit, deinde continuo humerum dextrum eodem congressu incidit neque recessit usquam, donec subvertit. Ubi eum evertit, caput praecidit, torquem detraxit eamque sanguinulentam sibi in collum imponit. Quo ex facto ipse posterique eius Torquati sunt cognominati.

> They came together, as I said above, like this: the Gaul, as was their practice, singing with his shield before him, Manlius, trusting more to courage than to skill, struck shield with shield and threw the Gaul off balance. When the Gaul tried to close

---

[3] For Claudius as historian, see E. Badian, "The Early Historians" in T. A. Dorey, ed., *Latin Historians* (New York 1966) 18–21, and as stylist, A. D. Leeman, *Orationis ratio*, vol. 1 (Amsterdam 1963) 78–81. M. Zimmerer, *Der Annalist Qu. Claudius Quadrigarius* (Diss. Munich 1937), offers a complete discussion.

again in the same way, Manlius again struck shield with shield and again hurled his man from position. In his fashion he slipped beneath the Gaul's sword so he could not strike back and stabbed him in the chest with his Spanish sword, then immediately pressed against his right shoulder in the same way and did not stop until he overturned him. Once he overturned him, he cut off his head, removed his torque, and put the bloody thing around his own neck. That is why he and his descendants are nicknamed "Torquatus."

(fr. 10b P)

Norden's "Cicero" might well have preferred "eo everso, torquem sanguinulentam de capite praeciso detractam sibi in collum imponit" for the penultimate sentence, but in context neither this sentence nor the passage as a whole is in any way naively constructed. The duel involves a sequence of actions carefully arranged for dramatic effect. Manlius and the Gaul begin as equals, and the syntax reflects this equality (*Gallus cantabundus* ~ *Manlius confisus*). The balance ceases as Manlius seizes the initiative (*percussit, conturbavit*). The tense to-and-fro of the combat is reflected in the repetitions of *iterum . . . iterum . . . iterum, eodem pacto . . . eo pacto, scuto scutum percussit . . . scuto scutum percutit*. Claudius' repetitions heighten the sudden shift to historic presents, while his use of subordination shapes the sequence of actions into a tighter whole than Cato's parataxis would allow. We find verbal adjectives (*proiecto, cantabundus, confisus*) and subordinating conjunctions (*dum, ne, donec, ubi*) imposing an order and pace on events. The focus throughout is clearly Manlius. The parataxis at the end is a matter of choice to heighten the drama, and thus the significance of the moment.[4]

---

[4] Contrast Livy's version of the same action (7.10): "iacentis inde corpus ab omni alia vexatione intactum uno torquo spoliavit, quem respersum cruore collo circumdedit suo." Livy's emphasis, and therefore his syntax, is different. Periodicity entails sacrifices as well as gains. Other famous and

Though Claudius Quadrigarius is not an author of the first rank, the fragments of his history reveal time and again the characteristic structures of mature Latin prose narrative. Here he describes the approach of the Gallic chief who duels with Valerius Corvinus (fr. 12P):

> Dux interea Gallorum, vasta et ardua proceritate armisque auro praefulgentibus, grandia ingrediens et manu telum reciprocans incedebat perque contemptum et superbiam circumspiciens despiciensque omnia venire iubet et congredi, si quis pugnare secum ex omni Romano exercitu auderet.

> Meanwhile the Gallic chief, standing erect and very tall, his weapons shining with gold, stepping boldly and waving a spear in his hand approached and, looking about and down with contempt and complete arrogance, bid to come and do battle, if anyone from the entire Roman army dared fight him.

The sentence structure is paratactic (*Dux . . . incedebat . . . [et] iubet . . . si quis . . . auderet*), but Claudius stretches his clauses to include additional information by using two ablative phrases and four nominative participles. The present participles, including a comparatively rare one in the ablative absolute, cause the sentence to ramble as details pile up without apparent direction, but Claudius works to avoid monotony by varying their complements: an adverbial accusative (*grandia*), a direct object (*telum*), a prepositional phrase (*per . . . superbiam*).[5] We may not especially

---

equally instructive parallels with Quadrigarius include fr. 12~Liv. 7.26 (the tale of Corvinus) and fr. 57~Liv. 24.44 (the Fabii, consul and proconsul). For the matter of style and emphasis in such passages, see A. H. McDonald, "The Style of Livy," *JRS* 47 (1957) 155–172, esp. 158–159 and 167–168, and P. T. Eden, "Caesar's Style: Inheritance and Intelligence," *Glotta* 40 (1962) 74–117, who relates the difference in style between Claudius and Livy to a difference in genre (pp. 78–81).

[5] The prominence of these participles is especially striking. Claudius seems to be experimenting not so much with the syntax of the present par-

like this sentence, but we cannot deny its author's literary design. A difference more of talent and taste than of linguistic resources explains the superiority of Caesar's prose, as in his story of Piso Aquitanus (*BG* 4.12):[6]

> hic cum fratri intercluso ab hostibus auxilium ferret, illum ex periculo eripuit, ipse equo vulnerato deiectus quoad potuit, fortissime restitit; cum circumventus multis vulneribus acceptis cecidisset atque id frater, qui iam proelio excesserat, procul animadvertisset, incitato equo se hostibus obtulit atque ⟨item⟩ interfectus est.

> This man, while bringing aid to his brother cut off by the enemy, snatched him from danger. He himself, thrown from his wounded horse, fought very bravely for as long as he could. When he fell, surrounded and having received many wounds, and his brother, who had by now escaped the fight, saw this from afar, he spurred his horse, threw himself on the enemy, and was likewise killed.

Where Claudius' effects appear labored and sometimes shapeless, Caesar writes tautly, yet seemingly without effort. He moves deftly from the one brother to the other as his consummate economy compresses fifteen discrete verbal ideas into a short passage with only three main clauses. Yet more significant

---

ticiple (only the absolute construction is truly unusual in early Latin) but with its ornamental value. The parallel passage at Liv. 7.26 replaces the participles with subordinate clauses. For the development of the present participle, see J. Marouzeau, *Quelques aspects de la formation du latin littéraire* (Paris 1949) 153–159, and E. Laughton, *The Participle in Cicero* (Oxford 1964) 19–45, and, for the ablative absolute, 100–117.

[6] With Caesar's famous remark, "ut tamquam scopulum sic fugias inauditum atque insolens verbum" (Gel. 1.10.4, quoted by Eden, above, n. 4) compare Zimmerer's comment on Claudius (above, n. 3) 109: "sein Ziel war offenbar die klare, knappe und ungekünstelte Form des Geschichtswerkes die in seiner Zeit schon verloren zu gehen drohte."

than the manipulation of these particular participles and subordinate clauses is the process of thought they represent. Caesar takes greater pains than either Claudius or Cato to impose a subtle order on the events of his narrative. He may work his participles very hard, e.g., the time sequences created by *cum fratri intercluso auxilium ferret* and *equo vulnerato deiectus*, but the resulting clarity of description suggests ease and inevitability of expression rather than strain on the medium. His special talent as a stylist involves the skillful matching of thought and grammatical structure. The tendency of ancient critics—and not only of *ancient* critics—to discuss style largely in terms of diction, figures, and phraseology unfortunately obscures its foundation in syntax. The organization of sentences precedes their ornamentation. The other things, as W. R. Johnson observes of Cicero, "are not style but the accidents of style. Prose style means not merely the ability but almost the necessity to shape thoughts and feelings, which were otherwise hidden, into intelligible patterns."[7] A stylist like Caesar brought formidable tools to this work of patterning thoughts in language, but he neither invented the tools himself nor took them directly from Greek workshops. The establishment of Greek rhetorical schools at Rome certainly made Romans of his age more sensible to what style could do, but the advance in the writing of prose between Cato and Caesar is essentially a Latin phenomenon. How did the language come to develop so?

The record of change is unfortunately in tatters. Surviving fragments of early prose show signs of structural and ornamental experiments, but the passages are too brief to reveal the organization of their author's thoughts. For a more complete record of accomplishment, we must look in a different direction. Cicero

[7] W. R. Johnson, *Luxuriance and Economy: Cicero and the Alien Style* (Berkeley 1971) 6–7. "Style," he observes a little earlier, "is not so much a thing as a process. . . ."

and Caesar themselves point the way in a famous passage from Suetonius' life of Terence.

> Cicero in Limone hactenus laudat:
> Tu quoque qui solus lecto sermone, Terenti,
> conversum expressumque latina voce Menandrum
> in medium nobis sedatis motibus effers,
> quiddam come loquens atque omnia dulcia dicens.
> Item C. Caesar:
> Tu quoque, tu in summis, o dimidiate Menander,
> poneris, et merito, puri sermonis amator.
> Lenibus atque utinam scriptis adiuncta foret vis,
> comica ut aequato virtus polleret honore
> cum Graecis, neve hac despectus parte iaceres!
> Unum hoc maceror ac doleo tibi desse, Terenti.

> Cicero praises him this much in his *Limo*:
> You too, who alone with careful speech, Terence,
> brings Menander among us, translated and
> formed in Latin with gentle measures,
> always speaking finely and saying everything sweetly.
> Caesar says the same:
> You too will be ranked with the highest, O half-sized Menander,
> and rightly so, lover of pure speech.
> If only some vigor had joined with your gentleness,
> so that your strength as a poet would rival
> the Greeks, and you did not lie faulted on this score!
> This alone I lament and regret you are lacking, Terence.

These highly formal epigrams are not concerned with theatrical merit.[8] Caesar puts *comica virtus* squarely in the context of stylis-

---

[8] The text is that of A. Rostagni, ed., *Suetonio, De Poetis e Biografi minori* (Turin 1944). In discussing the formality of these epigrams, Rostagni compares Domitius Marsus' epigram on Tibullus, which begins, "Te quoque

tic achievement, and neither critic mentions such essential elements of drama as plot and characterization. Even the references to Menander reflect the interests of the study more than the stage. Though he was of course Terence's primary model, he was never a seminal influence on Roman drama. At the time Aristophanes of Byzantium launched the scholarly study of Menander, Plautus was looking primarily to Diphilus and Philemon to inspire his living theatre. "Menandros" as a symbol of comedy is a literary conceit of a later generation.[9] Terence's own stature also increased as interest in stage comedy waned. At the beginning of the first century B.C., when its memory was still fresh, Volcacius Sedigitus had rated Terence only sixth in a list of ten comic poets headed by Caecilius and Plautus. Half a century later, as antiquarian and literary interests came to the fore, Varro raised him to the level of these two.[10] Thus Cicero and Caesar

---

Vergilio comitem non aequa, Tibulle." Ausonius 13.58–60 later imitates the form: "tu quoque, qui Latium lecto sermone, Terenti. . . ." Note too the formulaic critical vocabulary. Cicero, for example, applied similar terms to Caesar's *Commentarii*: "nihil est enim in historia pura et inlustri brevitate dulcius" (*Brut.* 262). The fullest discussion of these epigrams is W. Schmid, "Terenz als Menander Latinus," *RhM* 95 (1952) 229–272; also see Leo, *GRL* 253–255.

[9] Thus Ovid's famous line, "fabula iucundi nil est sine amore Menandri / et solet hic pueris virginibusque legi" (*Tr* 2.369–370), better suits his own argument than the extant Menander. And note *legi*. The other famous Ovidian statement, "dum fallax servus, durus pater, improba lena vivent et meretrix blanda, Menandros erit" (*Am.* 1.15.28–29), is more appropriate to the Roman adaptations. The situation was different for Hellenistic Greeks, for whom literary and theatrical traditions survived side by side. Contrast the differing natures of the ancient testimonia discussed by W. G. Arnott in the Loeb Menander, vol. 1 (Cambridge 1979) xix–xxvi. Also see E. Fantham, "Roman Experience of Menander in the Late Republic and Early Empire," *TAPA* 114 (1984) 299–309.

[10] Volcacius' famous canon is preserved at Gel. 15.24. Cf. Varro, *Men.* 399B: "in quibus partibus in argumentis Caecilius poscit palmam, in ethesin Terentius, in sermonibus Plautus." See J. Blänsdorf, "Das Bild der Komö-

were attracted to the *lectus* and *purus sermo* that had preceded their own efforts to write Latin with the subtlety of Greek. It was Terence's stylistic contribution that won their admiration and secured his place in the development of literary Latin.

Though it is common and convenient to speak of *the* style of Terence, however, some distinctions must be made. A dramatist, like an orator, always has a live audience to keep attentive. Effective communication requires his language to vary with the burden it must bear: how much and what needs to be said? in monologue or dialogue? accompanied by lively or sedate stage action? presented broadly or subtly? Not all syntactic structures suit all dramatic occasions. The dramatist must pick and choose among them, and for Terence the result is three quite distinct stylistic levels.[11] First is the rhetorical style of the prologues, which adapt the techniques of contemporary oratory to the requirements of theatrical polemic. Second is the style of dramatic dialogue, where interjections, questions, verbal echoes, and frequent changes of speaker suggest the rhythms of ordinary conversation. Third, and I think most significant for later generations, is narrative, the style of exposition and explanation. Terence's aesthetic goals and the dramatic decisions they involve imposed special requirements upon such passages. Plots built upon complex situations, delicate personal relationships, and intrigues require careful exposition, but Terence forfeited both the license of formal prologues to expound plots directly and the repetitions, sometimes at the expense of the dramatic illusion, that enabled dramatists to emphasize crucial details at key moments.

---

die in der späten Republik," *Musa Iocosa*, ed. U. Reinhardt and K. Sallmann (Hildesheim 1974) 141–157.

[11] Compare the findings of J. Marouzeau, "Quelques particularités de style Térentien," *Charisteria Thaddaeo Sinko* (Warsaw 1951) 211–219, and Chapter 2 above. A major limitation of J. Straus, *Terenz und Menander, Beitrag zu einer Stilvergleichung* (Diss. Bern 1955), is the failure to relate stylistic mannerisms to their dramatic context, but see the chapter on dialogue, pp. 38–54.

Terence sought instead to develop exposition as the seemingly natural consequence of dialogue by incorporating narrative passages in staged conversations, a technique requiring both maximum clarity and sufficient economy of expression to maintain the dramatic pace. He met these self-imposed requirements by fashioning a new narrative style for himself that fused traditional and innovative techniques.

The traditional manner of dramatic exposition built upon the leisurely parataxis familiar from early prose narrative. Thus Plautus, *Mercator* 11–13:

> pater ad mercatum hinc me meus misit Rhodum;
> biennium iam factum est postquam abii domo.
> ibi amare occepi forma eximia mulierem.

> My father sent me from here on business to Rhodes;
> it's been two years since I left home.
> There I fell in love with a really beautiful woman.

Such narrative is hardly artless. Plautus spices this potentially tedious story with contrived alliteration (note the hyperbaton of *meus*) and softens the artificiality of the formal prologue by having young Charinus deliver his own exposition. Yet Plautus preserves the old style: a single thought in each line, each thought a sentence, a simple order to the thoughts. Relations of time and space, not logic, link these statements into a narrative. His most common variations involve not syntactic innovation but a pacing and manipulation of the content by surrounding formal exposition with jokes (*Pseudolus*), setting a delayed exposition to music (*Mostellaria*), or combining the two (*Epidicus*). His is a technical rather than strictly stylistic virtuosity. Terence's variations on the traditional form of narrative are different. Here is Menedemus explaining his son's romance to the inquisitive Chremes.

> est e Corintho hic advena anus paupercula;
> ei(u)s filiam ille amare coepit perdite,
> prope iam ut pro uxore haberet: haec clam me omnia.

> ubi rem rescivi, coepi non humanitus
> neque ut animum decuit aegrotum adulescentuli   100
> tractare, sed vi et via pervolgata patrum.
> cotidie accusabam: "hem tibine haec diutius
> licere speras facere me vivo patre,
> amicam ut habeas prope iam in uxoris loco? . . ."

There is a poor old woman here, a foreigner from Corinth.
He came to love her daughter madly,
almost as a wife. None of this I knew.
When I found out, I started acting harshly
and not as a lovesick boy requires,   100
but with force, taking the common course of fathers.
Every day I let him have it: "Do you hope to carry on
this way much longer while I your father am alive,
to keep a girlfriend as if she were a wife? . . ."

(*HT* 96–104)

The first three lines use the old pattern of simple ideas simply expressed. Lines 99–101, however, constitute a single, far more elaborate sentence marked by chiasmus (*rescivi, coepi*) and hyperbaton (*coepi . . . tractare*). Menedemus employs three distinct constructions to describe his conduct (adverb, subordinate clause, ablative phrase) and keeps the relationship among them clear with the sequence *non . . . neque . . . sed*. Then the narrative takes still another turn with the shift to direct speech, which Menedemus continues for ten lines (102–112). The colloquial, indignant *hem* signals the change and lends vividness and special emphasis to what is really the central part of Menedemus' exposition, the breach between himself and his son. Menedemus' sentences continue to be long, but tightly organized. Here *haec* anticipates *ut*, and the sequence *licere speras facere* reflects a deliberate pattern of emphasis. There are also devices to suggest the spontaneity of natural discourse. The repetition of *prope iam ut pro uxore* and *prope iam in uxoris loco* captures the essence of Menedemus' outrage and helps tie the sections of his speech together. Note, too, the order *amicam ut habeas*. Terence frequently thrusts one element ahead of its proper unit to simulate the everyday tendency to rush key thoughts to the front of an utterance. This tendency probably explains the hyperbaton at 101. Though *tractare* would more naturally follow closely on *humanitus*, Terence displaces it by a line so Menedemus can complete the first, essential part of his thought.

In nine lines Terence has employed an impressive variety of stylistic devices, but he has not used all of those at his disposal. Here is the slave Parmeno explaining how Pamphilus, though still in love with the *meretrix* Bacchis, was compelled to marry.

> hanc Bacchidem
> amabat ut quom maxume tum Pamphilus
> quom pater uxorem ut ducat orare occipit
> et haec communia omnium quae sunt patrum,
> sese senem esse dicere, illum autem unicum:
> praesidium velle se senectuti suae.
> ille primo se negare; sed postquam acrius
> pater instat, fecit animi ut incertus foret
> pudorin anne amori obsequeretur magis.

> Pamphilus then
> was madly in love with this Bacchis,
> when his father started pressing to marry,
> saying all those things that fathers do:
> that he himself was old and Pamphilus an only son,
> that he wanted some insurance for old age.
> Pamphilus at first said no, but as his father
> pressed him, he came to be uncertain whether
> love or honor had the greater claim.
> (*Hecyra* 114–122)

This passage incorporates a remarkable variety of stylistic features. There are the familiar signposts *tum . . . quom* and *haec*, introducing three infinitive clauses. We find five types of subordination in these nine lines: clauses of time, command, result, and indirect question and statement. The narrative shifts between the expected imperfect and perfect tenses of narrative in the past to the more vivid historic present and infinitive. Sentence length varies artfully. Lines 114–119 are a single sentence. Line 120 has both a single short sentence and the beginning of a third sentence that extends through line 122. There is also that colloquial tendency to rush an idea to the front of its clause (116, 117, 121). Yet this is no idle display of linguistic facility. Terence has carefully considered the relationships among Parmeno's thoughts, and his mastery of syntax gives those thoughts a deliberate shape. This passage, like Claudius' description of Manlius and the Gaul, describes the conflict of two individuals, but Terence has brought much greater subtlety to their relationship. The emphasis might seem to lie with the father, Laches. He is the subject of most of these verbs, but Pamphilus is the subject of the three main clauses. This is *his* story as told by *his* slave, though Laches forces himself on the narrative just as he forces his will upon his son. Terence's syntax not only conveys content, but helps form our impression of that content. Doing so requires a full range of subordinate clauses and complete control over tense, sentence length, and grammatical subject. Complex ideas seem neither to tax nor to belabor the linguistic resources. Like Caesar, and unlike either Cato or Claudius Quadrigarius, Terence hides his art in the appearance of ease. How did he acquire such verbal mastery?

It did not come from Plautus. Terence's departure from the style of his Latin predecessors is well known. Though certainly mannered, his language is less flamboyant and less overtly stylized than theirs.[12] Nor did he simply copy the style of his Greek models. There are of course passages where a Greek stylistic pat-

---

[12] Thus, *inter alios*, Wright, *DiC* 131–138, and L. R. Palmer, *The Latin Language* (London 1951) 74–94.

tern was easy to assume. The fawners of Menander, for example, have a distinct way of explaining their technique. Here is Sikon, the cook of *Dyskolos*, describing how to borrow a pot.

> εὕρηκ' ἐγὼ τούτου τέχνην·
> διακονῶ γὰρ μυρίοις ἐν τῇ πόλει
> τούτων τ' ἐνοχλῶ τοῖς γείτοσιν καὶ λαμβάνω
> σκεύη παρὰ πάντων. δεῖ γὰρ εἶναι κολακικὸν
> τὸν δεόμενόν του. πρεσβύτερός τις τῇ θύρᾳ
> ὑπακήκο'· εὐθὺς πατέρα καὶ πάππα[ν λέγω.
> γραῦς· μητέρ'. ἂν τῶν διὰ μέσου τ[ις ᾖ γυνή,
> ἐκάλεσ' ἱερέαν.

> I've found the craft for this.
> I cater to the millions in this town,
> pester all their neighbors and borrow
> things from all. A man who needs a thing
> must be a flatterer. Suppose an older man comes
> to the door. At once I call him "Father," maybe "Dad."
> An older woman? "Mother." A woman of uncertain
> age? "Priestess."
>
> (*Dyskolos* 489–496)

In *Eunuchus*, Terence's parasite Gnatho explains an analogous skill with the same progression from grand generalization to rapid examples in asyndeton.[13]

> ego adeo hanc primus inveni viam.
> est genus hominum qui esse primos se omnium rerum volunt
> nec sunt: hos consector; hisce ego non paro me ut rideant,
> sed eis ultro adrideo et eorum ingenia admiror simul.
> quidquid dicunt laudo; id rursum si negant, laudo id quoque;
> negat quis: nego; ait: aio; postremo imperavi egomet mihi
> omnia adsentari. is quaestus nunc est multo uberrimus.

---

[13] For the dramatic effect of this speech, see Denzler, *Monolog* 65–69.

> I was first to find this route.
> There is a kind of man who wishes to be first in everything
> but isn't. That's the kind I follow. I arrange not that he laughs at me
> but that I do the laughing and admire all his talents.
> No matter what he says, I praise it. A change of mind? I praise that, too.
> He says no. I say no. He says yes. I agree. I finally trained
> myself to approve everything. That's the richest way to go.
>
> (*Eunuchus* 247–253)

Such structural similarities, however, are isolated phenomena. Far more often, fundamental differences between Greek and Latin sentence structure assert themselves. Here, for example, is how the slave Daos of *Aspis* describes the setting of a military ambush in Lykia.

> ἐγὼ μὲν ἐξώρμων ἔωθεν, ᾗ δ' ἐγὼ
> ἀπῆρον ἡμέρᾳ λαθόντες τοὺς σκοποὺς
> τοὺς ἡμετέρους οἱ βάρβαροι λόφον τινὰ
> ἐπίπροσθ' ἔχοντες ἔμενον, αὐτομόλων τινῶν
> πεπυσμένοι τὴν δύναμιν ἐσκεδασμένην·
>
> I was setting out at dawn, but on the day
> I left, avoiding all our scouts
> the natives seized a hill above us
> and lay low, having learned from some deserters
> that our forces had been scattered.
>
> (*Aspis* 40–44)

Note the sequence λαθόντες ... ἔχοντες ... πεπυσμένοι and the economy of τὴν δύναμιν ἐσκεδασμένην, which in Latin would probably require a subordinate clause.[14] This reliance on

---

[14] For example, *Hec.* 483: "te postputasse omnis res prae parente intellego" and *Ph.* 674–675: "quantum potest me certiorem, inquit, face, / si illam dant, hanc ut mittam, ne incertus siem."

participles to organize information is characteristically Greek, though their arrangement here is artful as Menander makes a deliberate contrast between this gradual disclosure of the enemy advance and the rapid statement of Daos' own actions (ἐγὼ μὲν ἐξώρμων . . . δ' ἐγὼ ἀπῆρον) which fix it in time.

Terence cannot reproduce such effects. His first recourse is simply to adapt the familiar form of paratactic Latin narrative. Here is old Demea of *Adelphoe*, who has just returned from an especially irksome wild-goose chase.

Ne ego sum infelix: primum fratrem nusquam invenio gentium;
praeterea autem, dum illum quaero, a villa mercennarium
vidi: is filium negat esse rure. nec quid agam scio.

I really am unlucky. First I couldn't find my brother anywhere;
then, while seeking him, I met a worker from the farm.
He said my son's not in the country. I don't know what to do.
(*Ad.* 540-542)

Despite its Greek ring, *ne ego* introduces a Roman comic formula, and the rest of the speech is thoroughly Latin in form.[15] Terence takes care to express the logical as well as purely chronological relationship between Demea's two actions (*primum . . . praeterea autem*), and keeps his clauses short to prevent confusion. The essentially chronological structure, however, and the pronoun of 542 with its obligatory change of subject are typical of early Latin narrative. So is the asyndeton. Menander would have put a γάρ in 540 to connect the clauses and would probably have replaced *mercennarium . . . is* with a participial phrase. Latin does not, and though the content is hardly altered, the stylistic effect puts Terence's lines squarely in the Latin tradition of narrative.

The difference between Latin and Greek styles shows most clearly where Menander himself is essentially paratactic. At *Dyskolos* 666ff., for example, Sostratos delivers a monologue explain-

[15] *Most.* 564: "ne ego homo sum miser"; *HT* 825: "ne ego homo sum fortunatus." Other examples include *Amph.* 325, *Most.* 562, *Vid.* 63.

ing how he, his helper Gorgias, and the girl he loves have rescued old Knemon from the well.

> τῆς γλυκείας διατριβῆς·
> ὁ Γοργίας γάρ, ὡς τάχιστ' εἰσήλθομεν,
> εὐθὺς κατεπήδησ' εἰς τὸ φρέαρ, ἐγὼ δὲ καὶ
> ἡ παῖς ἄνωθεν οὐδὲν ἐποοῦμεν· τί γὰρ
> ἐμέλλομεν; πλὴν ἡ μὲν αὑτῆς τὰς τρίχας
> ἔτιλλ', ἔκλα', ἔτυπτε τὸ στῆθος σφόδρα,
> ἐγὼ δ' ὁ χρυσοῦς, ὡσπερεὶ νὴ τοὺς θεοὺς
> τροφὸς παρεστώς, ἐδεόμην γε μὴ ποεῖν
> τοῦθ', ἱκέτευον, ἐμβλέπων ἀγάλματι
> οὐ τῷ τυχόντι.

> How sweet an occupation!
> Gorgias, as soon as we arrived,
> at once dropped down the well. I and
> the girl above did nothing. Well,
> what could we do? She just tore
> her hair, cried, and beat her breast quite hard;
> I, the golden boy, stood by her like
> a nurse. I urged and begged her not
> to act like that, while gazing on
> that marvelous sight.
>
> (*Dyskolos* 669–678)

There are rapid changes of subject here and verbs in asyndeton at 674 and 676–677. Sostratos is very excited, but not so excited that he forgets the logical connection among the figures of his narrative. The sequence ὁ Γοργίας γάρ . . . ἐγὼ δὲ καὶ ἡ παῖς followed by ἡ μέν . . . ἐγὼ δέ not only makes clear that the narrative is intended to explain his current rapture (γάρ), but also reveals his point of view. The result is not a staccato, piecemeal account, but a gradual narrowing of focus from the three young people to the two—Gorgias is soon and almost fatally forgotten in the well (682–683)—and from the two to the girl as seen and addressed by her admirer. The particles create a subtle but deliberate ordering of thought as Sostratos displays the naive egotism so characteristic of him.

Rapid narration in Terence takes a different form. Here, in a passage probably based rather closely on its Menandrean model, old Simo describes the funeral of Chrysis:[16]

> funus interim
> procedit: sequimur; ad sepulcrum venimus;
> in ignem inpositast; fletur. interea haec soror
> quam dixi ad flammam accessit inprudentius,
> satis cum periclo. ibi tum exanimatus Pamphilus
> bene dissimulatum amorem et celatum indicat:
> adcurrit; mediam mulierem complectitur:
> "mea Glycerium," inquit "quid agis? quor te is perditum?"
> tum illa, ut consuetum facile amorem cerneres,
> reiecit se in eum flens quam familiariter!

> The funeral march
> proceeds. We follow. We reach the grave.
> They put her on the pyre. There's weeping. Then that sister
> I mentioned came too close to the flames,
> dangerously close. Then Pamphilus at once, breathless,
> shows that love so carefully concealed and masked:
> he runs up, grabs the woman at the waist.
> "Glycerium, dear," he says, "what are you doing? Why seek death?"
> Then she—you could easily see the love's not new—
> drew back to him, weeping how familiarly!
>
> (*Andria* 127–136)

---

[16] Büchner, *TT* 31–44. Unfortunately, no fragment assigned to one of Terence's Greek originals is long enough to allow the kind of stylistic comparison now possible between Plautus' *Bacchides* and Menander's *Dis Exapaton*. *TT* 506–515 assembles what we have.

Terence, like Menander, employs asyndeton to create a lively pace—five unconnected verbs in the first three lines—and frequent changes of subject throughout the passage. Yet the impression made by Simo's narrative is quite different from Sostratos', though each describes an impressive offstage scene. Sostratos presents an ordered account of events at the well that clearly reflects their effect upon him. His sentence structure reveals not only his excitement but also his perspective. Simo does not yet know what he thinks; the ostensible purpose of this narrative, which also serves as the play's expository prologue, is to sort out his thoughts and announce a course of action. His account is therefore a series of vignettes not only in the short opening sentences, but even as the sentences lengthen. Because his linking adverbs reflect only sequence in time (*interea, ibi tum, tum*), we receive separate images of the funeral, of the girl, and then of Pamphilus that we must assemble for ourselves into a coherent whole just as Simo has already had to do. Our mental process is therefore analogous to his, and the narrative thus succeeds in putting us into his own position and coming to see things his way. Early Latin's dearth of logical particles has not troubled Terence. He makes the traditional style of paratactic narrative serve his dramatic needs, not by emulating an alien Greek form, but by building on native linguistic features to create his effects.

Taken together, these examples display an array of stylistic devices and a skill in their use to organize thought that are nearly a century ahead of developments in prose. In the generations immediately after Terence's death, orators and annalists alike experimented continuously with the organization of ideas in a sentence but had difficulty controlling the resulting complexities. Thus the participles in Claudius' description of the Gallic chief (fr. 12P), though vivid and succinct, stretch the sentence out of shape and lead it only to anticlimax. Terence's precision and economy, what later critics were to call his *elegantia* and *lectus sermo*, put his sentences beyond both the lumbering quality of

THE *purus sermo*

Cato and the exuberant excess of Claudius Quadrigarius. But, to repeat the earlier question, what fostered that skill if it was not the example of Latin or Greek predecessors? At the heart of his stylistic innovation lies the ability to shape sentences effectively, and the matter of shape brings us at last to the fact of meter.

Meter, by its very nature, gives shape to utterances. The line of verse, with its established pattern of heavy and light syllables, functions as the metrical equivalent of the sentence and generally becomes a primary unit of the poet's meaning.[17] Poetic sentences therefore automatically have a distinctive shape, metrical if not syntactic, though the two usually coincide since lines of verse tend to end with grammatical boundaries. The continuation of Parmeno's expository narration in *Hecyra* will show what this means for Terence.

> usque illud visum est Pamphilo ne utiquam grave
> donec iam in ipsis nuptiis, postquam videt
> paratas nec moram ullam quin ducat dari,
> ibi demum ita aegre tulit ut ipsam Bacchidem,
> si adesset, credo ibi eius commisceresceret.
>
> Pamphilus didn't think the matter serious
> until the wedding day. When he saw
> things were prepared and nothing would delay his
>   marriage,
> then at last he got so frenzied even Bacchis,
> had she been there, would, I think, have pitied him.
>   (*Hecyra* 125–129)

The metrical line here is more central to the organization of Parmeno's statement than the grammatical sequence.[18] His four

---

[17] For these observations, see W. S. Allen, *Accent and Rhythm* (Cambridge 1973) 113–122, and further references there.

[18] Note the ambiguity of Kauer and Lindsay's punctuation, which reflects the difficulty of imposing modern orthographic conventions on the Latin.

main ideas are all marked by conjunctions: *usque, donec, postquam, ibi demum*. Three of these begin lines. There is special emphasis on *donec* because it explains the important change in Pamphilus' thinking and on *ibi demum* because it introduces the main clause. The lesser boundaries after *videt* and *Bacchidem* pace the narrative by creating an alternation of main and subordinate ideas in successive lines. Parmeno speaks in sentences, but Terence has organized those sentences as iambic senarii.

This tendency of meter to pattern thought enables Terence to write complex sentences that remain clear and economical, a skill as valuable in argument as in narrative. Here, for example, is Phaedria begging indulgence for his cousin Antipho.

> si est, patrue, culpam ut Antipho in se admiserit,
> ex qua re minus rei foret aut famae temperans,
> non causam dico quin quod meritus sit ferat.

> If it's true, uncle, that Antipho's got himself in trouble
> because he made too free with fame and fortune,
> I'll only say he gets what he deserves.
>
> (*Ph.* 270–272)

The lines are again the important units of sense, though the sentence itself contains six clauses. Phaedria's next sentence contains four.

> sed siquis forte malitia fretus sua
> insidias nostrae fecit adulescentiae
> ac vicit, nostra[n] culpa east an iudicum
> qui saepe propter invidiam adimunt diviti
> aut propter misericordiam addunt pauperi?

> But if someone puffed up with malice
> set a trap for our youth and

We might prefer a full stop after *nuptiis*. There is no such ambiguity about the relationship of Terence's thought to the sequence of senarii.

>   won, are we to blame, or is the court,
>   that often out of envy bilks the rich
>   and out of pity pays the poor?
>   (*Ph.* 273–277)

Terence is still structuring his sentence in terms of senarii, capitalizing on the verbal force of *fretus* by isolating it in line 273 and emphasizing *vicit* by thrusting it to the front of 275. Phaedria's meaning could hardly be more clearly expressed, but the organization of his sentences is not simple. Each line adds a new piece of information, and all but two lines (274 and 277) have a new syntactic relationship to what precedes. Contrast Cato's much simpler use of the same form of argument in a speech dated to about 154.

sed si omnia dolo fecit, omnia avaritiae atque pecuniae causa
fecit, eiusmodi scelera nefaria, quae neque fando neque legendo
audivimus, supplicium pro factis dare oportet.

But if he did everything with guile, did everything for the sake of greed and money, heinous crimes of a kind we have neither heard nor read, he ought to pay the penalty for his deeds.
                             (fr. 177 M)

Cato has turned a simple statement into a masterful outburst of rage, but, though his sentence is long, it says little. The two *si*-clauses are parallel and synonymous: *eiusmodi* introduces *quae*. Cato is only embellishing a single idea. Each of Terence's sentences says much more.

In the prologues, such capacity for tight and subtle organization makes a special contribution to the meaning. Remember the famous sentence of *Andria* in which Terence defends himself against the charge of *contaminatio*.

>   qui quom hunc accusant, Naevium Plautum Ennium
>   accusant quos hic noster auctores habet,

> quorum aemulari exoptat neglegentiam
> potius quam istorum obscuram diligentiam.

> Accuse him thus and Naevius, Plautus, Ennius
> all stand accused, whom our poet takes as models
> and whose negligence he'd rather emulate
> than carping critics' abstruse diligence.
>
> *(Andria* 18–21)

Each line is once more a thought; the enjambement at 18 has the effect of strengthening the key identification of the three famous poets with the preceding *hunc*. Where the paratactic style, however, would have also made each line into a separate sentence, Terence's command of relative pronouns leads to a more sophisticated structure. He begins instead with a *quom*-clause and weaves his separate statements into a single, deft line of argument. The relative *quos* allows him to change subjects in the second line. *Hunc* becomes *hic*, and in the process the accusers stand accused. *They* are now measured against Naevius, Plautus, and Ennius—*quorum* set against *istorum*—and are of course found wanting. This facility with sentence structure, used here with special rhetorical point, is unparalleled in the contemporary prose of Cato, while the formal demands of the senarius prevent the prolixity of Quadrigarius.

The ability of a metrical pattern to contribute in this way to the organization of an utterance is the truth behind Cicero's remark that it is easier to write verse than prose, "quod in illis [versibus] certa quaedam et definita lex est, quam sequi sit necesse; in dicendo autem nihil est propositum, nisi ut ne immoderata aut angusta aut dissoluta aut fluens sit oratio" (*Or.* 198). Much early prose is indeed *immoderata* and *dissoluta*, precisely because there was no governing *lex*. Metrical patterns, however, were not the answer to the organizational problem of early prose, though there were experiments along those lines. Some of Cato's cola seem to scan, as in the famous remark, "Antiochus epistulis bēllūm gĕrĭt x calamo et atrāmēntō mīlĭtāt" (fr. 20M), but the articulation of this sentence depends at least as much on its syntactic parallelism.[19] Coelius Antipater, probably the finest prose stylist between Cato and Cicero, certainly sought metrical effects, but he also felt the need to apologize for manipulating word order to create his cadences.[20] Prose rhythm was a difficult tool for early writers to control, and it really came into vogue only after syntactic developments had brought their discipline and flexibility to the Latin sentence. Thus, for Cicero, the question of rhythm involved the aesthetics more than the mechanics of sentence structure.[21] Terence's contribution lay outside this later debate; the lesson he had to teach was syntactic rather than rhythmic.

[19] The scansion, as well as the identification of metrical clausulae in Cato, is that of E. Fraenkel, *Leseproben aus Reden Ciceros und Catos* (Rome 1968) 130, who observes that "die Wiederholung der Klausel – – – ‿ – dient der Hervorhebung des Parallelismus." Fraenkel notes the same pattern in fr. 28 and 163; also see J. Solodow, "Cato *Orationes*, Frag. 75," *AJP* 98 (1977) 359–361. Is the metrical pattern deliberate or only an epiphenomenon caused by the parallelism? As Cicero reminds us: "Formae vero quaedam sunt orationis, in quibus ea concinnitas est ut sequatur numerus necessario. nam cum aut par pari refertur aut contrarium contrario opponitur aut quae similiter cadunt verba verbis comparantur, quidquid ita concluditor, plerumque fit ut numerose cadat . . ." (*Or.* 220). A quantitative analysis of relative frequencies leads A. Primmer, "Der Prosarhythmus in Catos Reden," *Festschrift Karl Vretska* (Heidelberg 1970) 174–180, to doubt Fraenkel's interpretation of the data.

[20] "Quod se L. Caelius Antipater in prooemio belli Punici nisi necessario facturum negat. O virum simplicem qui nos nihil celet, sapientem qui serviendum necessitati putet!" Cic., *Or.* 230 = fr. 1P. A notorious example is fr. 24b: "In priore libro has res ad te scriptas, Luci, misimus, Aeli," with which compare the Saturnian epitaph for P. Cornelius Scipio (augur 180 B.C.), "qua re lubens te in gremiu, Scipio, recipit / Terra, Publi, prognatum Publio, Corneli" (CIL i² 10 E 15). Badian (above, n. 3) 33 n. 76 catalogues Antipater's rhythms; also see Norden (above, n. 1) 176–177. Zimmerer (above, n. 3) 117–119 identifies metrical clausulae in Quadrigarius, too, but the evidence is insufficient to guarantee that these effects are deliberate.

[21] See J. F. D'Alton, *Roman Literary Theory and Criticism* (London 1931)

But of all the poets of Republican Rome, why was Terence singled out as a model of Latin style?

This final question goes back to the authors who first came to grips with the *patrii sermonis egestas*. By Cicero's day that language had become a medium pliant enough to be molded at will into either poetry or prose.

> Nihil est enim tam tenerum neque tam flexibile neque quod tam facile sequatur quocumque ducas quam oratio. Ex hac versus, ex hac eadem dispares numeri conficiuntur; ex hac haec etiam soluta variis modis multorumque generum oratio; non enim sunt alia sermonis, alia contentionis verba, neque ex alio genere ad usum cotidianum, alio ad scaenam pompamque sumuntur; sed ea nos cum iacentia sustulimus e medio, sicut mollissimam ceram ad nostrum arbitrium formamus et fingimus.

> For nothing is as delicate or as flexible or follows as easily wherever you lead it as speech. Verses and irregular rhythms are made from it; from it come the many styles and various kinds of prose. There is not one vocabulary for conversation and another for oratory, nor is one kind assumed for everyday use and another for public display. We take words up from common life as they lie, and we form and mold them at will like the softest wax.

> (*De or.* 3.176–177)[22]

247–252, with full references to the ancient sources. His long discussion of *Or.* 168–236 is especially revealing.

[22] At *Fin.* 1.3.10, Cicero addresses Lucretius' specific complaint, which involves philosophical terms in Latin: "ita sentio et saepe disserui Latinam linguam non modo non inopem, ut vulgo putarent, sed locupletiorem etiam quam Graecam." The sentiment is repeated at *Tusc.* 1.1; contrast Lucr. 1.136–139, 831–832, 3.260. The change of attitude in the course of this generation is remarkable, whatever the fact of the matter may be.

It was not always so, nor is Cicero's vision entirely historical. The language of prose and the language of poetry followed quite different lines of development. The first poets, their talents honed and disciplined by the requirements of meter and by close study of Greek models, found a suitably precise and often powerful idiom with remarkable speed, but only by moving their language away from the Latin of everyday life. Livius Andronicus, at the very beginning of Latin literary history, deliberately introduced such Alexandrian mannerisms as archaism and the dialect gloss. Though the inventive Ennius brought new dignity and boldness to both epic and tragic diction, his artfulness was by nature and design equally artificial and furthered the separation of popular and poetic language.[23] Even dramatic speech became so highly stylized that its best and most popular practitioners, Caecilius and Pacuvius, are dismissed by Cicero as *male locuti* when the issue involved not dramatic power but *locutio emendata et latina* (*Brut.* 258, cf. *ad Att.* 7.3.10).

Literary prose had a different relationship to the *sermo cotidianus* and a much slower development. There were no prose authors of note in the time of Livius Andronicus. Fabius Pictor, Rome's first historian, was a contemporary of Plautus and apparently found literary composition in Latin so daunting a prospect that he wrote in Greek, where a tradition of historical prose lay ready to hand.[24] Only in the next generation did Cato face the challenge of expository narrative in Latin and initiate the process

---

[23] Palmer (above, n. 12) 97–107, G. Williams, *Tradition and Originality in Roman Poetry* (Oxford 1968) 684–699, G. A. Sheets, "The Dialect Gloss, Hellenistic Poetics and Livius Andronicus," *AJP* 102 (1981) 58–78 and "Ennius Lyricus," *ICS* 8 (1983) 22–32.

[24] For the cultural forces at work on Fabius Pictor and his choice of Greek for his history, see Chapter 7 of E. S. Gruen, *The Hellenistic World and the Coming of Rome*, vol. 1 (Berkeley 1984), and for Pictor's Roman tradition, B. W. Frier, *Libri Annales Pontificum Maximorum: The Origins of the Annalistic Tradition* (Rome 1979) 278–284.

of development we have already traced. Cato's pioneering effort, however, furthered the gap between prose and poetry. Where Livius Andronicus had put poetic language on the path of deliberate artifice, Cato aimed for naturalness. In oratory and even more so in his expository prose, he sought clarity without undue artificiality. *Rem tene; verba sequentur.* Effective simplicity, however, is not easily achieved. As Cicero was to observe,

> Summissus est et humilis, consuetudinem imitans, ab indisertis re plus quam opinione differens. Itaque eum qui audiunt, quamvis ipsi infantes sint, tamen illo modo confidunt se posse dicere. Nam orationis subtilitas imitabilis illa quidem videtur esse existimanti, sed nihil est experienti minus.

> The restrained and plain orator, imitating ordinary usage, differs from those untrained in speaking more than is commonly thought. His hearers, however inarticulate they may be, nevertheless assume they can speak that way. A plain style seems easy to imitate in the thinking, but nothing is harder in the doing.
>
> (*Or.* 76)

Narrative prose requires not true simplicity—there is all too much of *that* in the fragments of early writers—but the illusion of simplicity. Roman authors required the better part of a century to learn this distinction. It finally came to them in large part from the formal study of Greek rhetoric, which became the functional analogue of the poets' Greek models, but also from the Roman dramatist who combined (in Latin) both the syntactic sophistication and the illusion of simplicity that they sought.[25]

---

[25] How soon the study of rhetoric affected the development of Latin literature is perhaps an unanswerable question, but a time soon after Terence's death in 159 seems likely. See M. L. Clarke, *Rhetoric at Rome* (London 1966) 10–22 (now somewhat dated), and G. Kennedy, *The Art of Rhetoric in the Roman World* (Princeton 1972) 90–102.

Comedy was the one genre of Republican poetry that did not cultivate an artificial sound.[26] Though comic verse had its archaisms and metrical formulae, it aimed to suggest rather than to avoid the patterns of everyday speech. It never developed an artful tension between metrical and conversational pulse, and the arrangement of heavy and light syllables within the line often imitated the emphasis and emotion to be found in common speech.[27] Thus the iambic senarius, its common spoken meter, could be so like the rhythm of speech that, as Cicero remarked, "non nunquam vix in eis numerus et versus intellegi possit" (*Or.* 184, cf. 191). Terence, above all dramatists, stressed these "prosaic" qualities of comic verse. At least half of each play is in senarii, and he substituted the recitative of longer iambic and trochaic verse for the polymetric *cantica* of Plautus. He willingly forfeited the richness of Plautine vocabulary.[28] The result,

---

[26] I leave satire aside, sharing with W. S. Anderson the view that "had not Lucilius been succeeded by Horace, who gave the rather amorphous poetry left by Lucilius an entirely new form, it is difficult to imagine how Roman satire would ever have developed a tradition. . . ." ["The Roman Socrates: Horace and his Satires" in J. P. Sullivan, ed., *Satire* (London 1963) 1 = *Essays on Roman Satire* (Princeton 1982) 13]. For Lucilius' style see M. Coffey, *Roman Satire* (London 1976) 58–62.

[27] For these features of comic verse see the *excursus* by A. S. Gratwick in *The Cambridge History of Classical Literature, Vol. 2: Latin Literature* (Cambridge 1982) 86–93, and A. S. Gratwick and S. J. Lightley, "Light and Heavy Syllables As Dramatic Colouring in Plautus and Others," *CQ* 32 (1982) 124–133.

[28] These points are best demonstrated by comparison, e.g., Ballio's instructions for his birthday celebration at *Ps.* 159ff. (a polymetric *canticum*) and Syrus' instructions about the fish at *Ad.* 375ff. (senarii). The talk about food is comic in each case, but with a different point and in a different style. The only examples of lyric *cantica* in Terence seem to be *An.* 481–485 and 625–638, *Ad.* 610–617, and perhaps *Eun.* 560. He apparently had little desire to write song. Quintilian, for what it is worth, much preferred his senarii: "plus adhuc habitura gratiae si intra versus trimetros stetissent" (*Inst.* 10.1.99).

though thin by the traditional standards of the Roman stage—"tenuis oratio et scriptura levis" are the pejoratives Terence put in the mouth of his critics—is ideally suited to model that combination of simple diction and structural sophistication that eventually won him such a following.

In recasting the Latin of his day to serve his own artistic needs, Terence imposed upon it a new discipline that set new standards for concise, logical expression. The great thing that later Latin stylists as diverse as Cicero and Tacitus were to share is the ability to put a good deal of information in a short space without sacrificing clarity and point. This kind of precision is what we miss most in a writer like Cato and is a crucial difference between early Latin prose and the various manifestations of the later language. We find it first in Terence as the fusion of traditional structures, and new talent creates richness without bulk. Terence left behind the diffuse rambles of early prose and the playful verbosity of his comic predecessors, creating instead the kind of Latin that first showed clearly those features from which the great stylists of later times developed their individual voices. His *lectus sermo* was therefore praised both by later authors and grammarians, and their admiration helps explain the final oddity of Terence's career. His plays lived on in library and schoolroom long after stage comedy at Rome was only a memory. His greatest contribution to Latin literature was independent of his literary genre, for the *comoedia palliata* did not long survive him. Why was this so?

[VIII]

THE DEATH OF COMEDY

The lover of Roman comedy eventually confronts a curious fact. Although the roots of modern comedy lie in Plautus and Terence, and although the modern idea of theatre with its secular and professional orientation is itself Roman rather than Greek, comedy comprises only a brief and early chapter in the history of Latin literature. We may admire the genius of Plautus and the skill of Terence, but their art stands removed from the creative mainstream. Comedy at Rome was to die with Turpilius in 103 B.C., a year when Cicero was a toddler in Arpinum and some seventy years before Latin literature reached maturity in the time of Augustus. Its golden age is thus quite distinct from the golden age of Latin literature itself, but something more than a minor genre died with Turpilius. The very interest in stage comedy that had survived the change in conditions from Aristophanes to Menander and the change in culture from Greece to Rome died quietly in the late second century B.C. No further comedy of literary stature was written in antiquity, and the ancient tradition lay dormant until revived by the Italian humanists of our own fourteenth century.[1] Turpilius and his immediate predecessors had ignored Terence's innovations and, by returning to the older comic style, carried its time-worn formulae to oblivion. Subsequent generations found them no match for Plautus, who became the classic master of stage comedy, while Terence's innovations in dramatic tone and structure went unappreciated in the schoolroom.[2] Thus, though Terence brought Roman comedy to a peak

[1] D. Radcliff-Umstead, *The Birth of Modern Comedy in Renaissance Italy* (Chicago 1969).
[2] On Turpilius in general see H. Bardon, *La Littérature latine inconnue*, vol.

of sophistication, he also marks the end of its creative life. Why, though, did Turpilius prefer the old formulae to the newer Terentian forms? What was there about Terence's plays that discouraged Roman imitators? This last problem of Terence involves not just his relationship to the Roman comic tradition, but the different roles of Greek and Roman drama in the intellectual life of their times.

The constant, creative reworking of old myths that gave Athenian tragedy its intellectual tension and vitality established drama as a legitimate medium for serious thought, and tragedy's profound appeal enriched the substance of comedy even as the comic poets aped its mannerisms. The Old Comedy of Aristophanes took not only such useful stage devices as narrative soliloquies and *ex machina* endings from tragedy, but also a sense of urgency that led to the building of comic fantasies around matters of substance. The New Comedy of the following century represented the culmination of dramatic development at Athens and was thus heir to both the technical and intellectual traditions of tragedy and comedy. While Menander's domestic comedies are certainly not pointed fantasies in the old style, neither are they trivial restatements of established *topoi*. They too have a respectable intellectual base, using the romantic plots of lost children and obstructed marriages to explore legitimate problems of social and family relationships. *Perikeiromene* and *Misoumenos* present soldiers who lose their swagger and confront genuine problems of integration into civilian society. The young husband of *Epitrepontes* discovers his own moral failing in a climax that, like Aristotle's best kind of tragic plot, combines a sudden realization with an abrupt reversal in the direction of the play's action.

Such comedies may have many serious moments, and to signal them Menander's characters frequently strike a tragic pose or

---

1 (Paris 1952) 135–138, and for his relationship to the old comic style, Wright, *DiC* 153–181.

speak in tragic style, but the dramatist's purpose then is not parody. Menander aims instead to borrow some of tragedy's seriousness by assuming its manner. The messenger's speech of *Sikyonios*, for example, shares the function and echoes the language of a similar speech in Euripides' *Orestes* without ridiculing the tragic prototype. Meter and staging combine for a different tragic effect in *Dyskolos*, when Knemon is brought out of his house after nearly drowning in a well. His rescue leads him to renounce the misanthropy that had isolated him from society and prevented the marriage of his daughter, and it is crucial to the play's success that we take this scene of recantation seriously. If we do not listen carefully to Knemon's words and perceive both the honesty and the difficulty of his apology, the subsequent action makes little sense. Menander signals the importance of this moment by structuring his scene to recall similar moments in tragedy. After the disaster within, Knemon is wheeled out in tableau like a tragic hero, and, as often happens in tragedy, the meter changes to trochaic tetrameters to mark the coming climax. These are the only devices required to suggest seriousness to an audience steeped in the tragic tradition and attuned to its nuances. Menander draws upon established classics, adding something old and grand to something light and new.[3]

The situation was rather different at Rome, though tragedy and comedy also developed side by side. By the time of Plautus, tragedy also held a secure place at the *ludi scaenici*, and the surviving fragments reveal a powerful and dignified tragic style. Here, for example, is a fragment from Ennius' *Alexander*. Cassandra is about to prophesy to Hecuba.[4]

---

[3] Goldberg, *MMC* 16–20, and for Knemon's tragic pose, 85–87. A. G. Katsouris, *Tragic Patterns in Menander* (Athens 1975) 86–103, compares Knemon's great scene to the Euripidean *lysis*.

[4] Citations of Ennius are from the edition of H. D. Jocelyn, *The Tragedies of Ennius* (Cambridge 1967). My analysis takes much from his commentary. For the stage history of Roman tragedy, see W. Beare, *The Roman Stage*[3]

> mater, optumatum multo mulier melior mulierum,
> missa sum superstitiosis hariolationibus;
> neque me Apollo fatis fandis dementem invitam ciet.
> virgines vereor aequalis, patris mei meum factum pudet,
> optimi viri. mea mater, tui miseret, mei piget.
> optumam progeniem Priamo peperisti extra me. hoc dolet:
> men obesse, illos prodesse, me obstare, illos obsequi.

> Mother, by far the best mother of mothers,
> driven was I by the soothsayer's utterings:
> Apollo with prophecy moves me unwilling to madness.
> I shrink from maidens my age. My deed shames my father
> exalted. Mother, I pity you. Mother, I grieve for me.
> Save me you have borne the best children to Priam. Alas,
> that I oppose, they defend, I obstruct, they concede.
> (Ennius, XVII J)

Ennius' diction combines such familiar devices of early Latin literature as extended alliteration and the *figura etymologica* with such novelties as the four lines of end rhyme and the paucity of elision. A similar address in Plautus, also trochaic, reveals the contrast in speed and sound.

> optumum atque aequissimum oras optumusque hominum
>   es homo.

> You man best of men ask a thing fine and fair.
> (*Captivi* 333)

Ennius' stress on *optumus*, the parallelism of *pudet, miseret, piget*, and *dolet*, and the final anaphora, which was no doubt accompanied by broad and solemn gestures, add to the dignified effect. He also strains his language in the manner of high poetry: simple verbs for complex ones (*missa* for *emissa*, *vereor* for *revereor*), the

---

(New York 1965) 70–84, and for its character, L. A. MacKay, "The Roman Tragic Spirit," *CSCA* 8 (1975) 145–162.

striking image in the second line, which sounds most like Aeschylus' Cassandra (τέχναισιν ἐνθέοις ἠρημένη, *Ag.* 1209), *pudet* constructed with the double genitive. There are also the rare, perhaps archaic, genitives *optumatum* and *meum*, *derepente* for the more common *repente*, and *progeniem peperisti* for the colloquial *puerum parere*.

The Romans loved such sounds and the stirring, sometimes macabre, effects that accompanied them. Crowds roared in excitement when Pylades tried to sacrifice himself for his friend in Pacuvius' *Dulorestes*. When the ghost of Deiphilus roused his sleeping mother to avenge his death in *Iliona*, Cicero assures us that his words, chanted to subdued and tearful melodies, reduced the audience to tears.[5] Scenes of madness were especially popular. Pacuvius, in an unidentified play, showed Orestes beset by the Furies as he left the sanctuary of Apollo, and Ennius' *Alcmaeo* had a similar scene as the Furies appear to Alcmaeon after he has murdered his mother, Eriphyle.

>   incede incede adsunt: me expetunt.
>
>   fer mi auxilium, pestem abige a me,
>   flammiferam hanc vim quae me excruciat,
>   caerulae incinctae igni incedunt,
>   circumstant cum ardentibus taedis.
>
>   intendit crinitus Apollo
>   arcum auratum luna innixus;
>   Diana facem iacit a laeva.
>
>   Come! Come! They are here. They seek me.

---

[5] Cic., *Tusc.* 1.106. This scene immortalized the unfortunate actor Fufius, who once slept through his cue "Catiensis mille ducentis 'mater te appello' clamantibus" (Hor., *S.* 2.3.60–62). For the success of *Dulorestes*, Cic., *Fin.* 5.22.63.

> Bring aid. Drive off the plague from me,
> this flameful force that tortures me.
> Darkly dressed, with fire they come.
> They stand about with glowing torches.
>
> Long-haired Apollo poised
> stretches his golden bow.
> Diana wields a torch on the left.
> (Ennius XV J)

This kind of scene inspires Plautus' Menaechmus II to rout the poor father-in-law of Epidamnus with feigned madness (*Men.* 831ff.). The young man pretends to hear Bacchus and Apollo urging him to violence. Then he sees a chariot before him.

> iam astiti in currum, iam lora teneo, iam stimulum:
> > in manust.
>
> agite equi, facitote sonitus ungularum appareat,
> cursu celeri facite inflexa sit pedum pernicitas.

> Now I've mounted the chariot. Now I hold the reins.
> > Now the whip's in hand.
>
> Off with you horses. Make the sound of your hoofs resound,
> with swift step make unflinching speed of your feet.
> (*Men.* 865–867)

These sequential images are as vivid and the action as lively as the scenes of true madness in Ennius' *Alexander* and *Alcmeo*. Plautus recognized the effectiveness of the tragic style and embraced it with enthusiasm. Menaechmus' vision is comic rather than tragic, largely because it is so incongruous.

Incongruity is central to the effect of all Plautus' tragic echoes, whether they parody specific postures as Menaechmus does, or whether tragic diction simply elevates the tone at moments of high emotion.[6] Then eloquence for its own sake never passes un-

---

[6] Leo, *PlF* 132–137; A. Thierfelder, "Plautus and römische Tragödie,"

challenged. "Ut paratragoedat carnufex!" remarks Charinus when Pseudolus becomes unduly poetic (*Ps.* 707); the maid Bromia loses her own tragic dignity in a moment when she trips over the unconscious Amphitruo, felled on his own doorstep by Jupiter's thunderbolt (*Amph.* 1072). Plautus plays on the outward form of tragedy, borrowing its manner for a momentary effect. Terence may do the same. In *Eunuchus*, for example, Chaerea explains how a picture of Jupiter and Danae encouraged his amorous designs.

> deum sese in hominem convortisse atque in alienas tegulas
> venisse clanculum per pluviam fucum factum mulieri.
> at quem deum! qui templa caeli summa sonitu concutit.
> ego homuncio hoc non facerem?

> A god turned himself to a man and through another's roof
> came in secret to rain a trick on a woman.
> And what a god! Who shakes the heights of heaven with
>   his sound.
> Why couldn't a puny man like I do this?
>
> (*Eun.* 588–591)

The line "qui templa ... concutit" is apparently borrowed from Ennius, an incongruous touch of grandeur in this speech by a fraudulent eunuch about to ape the god.[7] Tragic echoes of this sort, however, are never very subtle and never integral to a play's meaning in the way that Knemon's tragic pose shapes our understanding of *Dyskolos*. Roman comedy could not use tragic diction to enrich the texture of a play as Menander so often did.

Though Roman tragedy had its own distinct vocabulary and

Hermes 74 (1939) 155–166; G. A. Sheets, "Plautus and Early Roman Tragedy," *ICS* 8 (1983) 195–209. Fraenkel, *EPP* 62–67, argues that not all Plautus' tragic echoes originate in his Greek models.

[7] Don, *ad Eun.* 590: "parodia de Ennio ... tragice, sed de industria, non errore." The passage is CLXI in Jocelyn's *Incerta*. See O. Skutsch, *Studia Enniana* (London 1968) 177–181 = *HSCP* 71 (1967) 128–131.

its own type-scenes, the underlying structure of its verse and its stock of technical devices were much like comedy's. Both genres shared the same stage apparatus from the beginning. They also used the same meters. There was no Latin equivalent of Porson's bridge. No clearly felt norms of resolution and caesura distinguished their spoken meters, nor can we identify organic differences between tragic and comic lyrics; Ennius' lyric meters were the same anapests, cretics, and bacchiacs that Plautus favored. Nor did the Latin language offer dramatists the dialectical variation that enriches and distinguishes Greek diction. The difference in sound between the Latin tragic and comic styles was largely on the surface.[8] This made the mannerisms and the melodrama of Roman tragedy easy for comic dramatists to incorporate as parody, but the very similarity of their verse made more subtle allusions difficult to achieve. For the most part, this hardly mattered. Menandrean comedy needed the subtle effects of tragic echoes because it was assuming some of tragedy's seriousness. It represented nearly two hundred years of dramatic development and played before audiences steeped in its traditions. Roman comedy did not shoulder a similar burden. Its sophistication was largely technical, the ability to have characters speak and act effectively on the stage, and it achieved this technical virtuosity and popular success in two generations by developing those elements of Greek New Comedy best suited to a broad, musical idea of theatre. The most elaborate plots of intrigue and mistaken identity, the most clever slaves, most memorable villains, and most brilliant lyrics that survive are thus products of this Roman half of the tradition. Plautus is less subtle than Menander, but much livelier. Yet the very success of Plautine comedy posed a problem for Terence, who sought to capture something of New Comedy's more serious side. Without recourse to

[8] For meter and diction, Jocelyn 32–43; for technical devices, R. J. Tarrant, "Senecan Drama and Its Antecedents," *HSCP* 82 (1978) 216–263.

tragedy for signaling a serious intent, his only alternative was to alter the effect of comic conventions.

Remember Micio, the lenient brother of *Adelphoe*. His disagreement with his brother Demea and his struggle for control of his son Aeschinus embody genuine issues of educational method and social relationships. Yet the serious matter of *Adelphoe* is developed without tragic overtones. Comic elements themselves create the new interest. In Chapter 4, we saw how Terence uses Micio's expository monologue to undercut his pretensions and how the scene interpolated from Diphilus dramatizes his true effect on Aeschinus. Micio is hardly the ideal father of Roman theory. He is, however, the ideal father of every Plautine *adulescens*. Aeschinus admits as much.

> quid hic est negoti? hoc est patrem esse aut hoc est
>   filium esse?
> si frater aut sodalis esset, qui mage morem gereret?
> hic non amandus, hicine non gestandus in sinust? hem?

> Well, what is this? Is this what it means to be father
>   and son?
> If he were a brother or friend, what greater help could
>   he be?
> Here's a man to be loved and cherished. Wow!
>   (*Ad.* 707–709)

Micio embodies values that the lovesick boys of Plautus are more apt to find in their clever slaves and parasites. Terence recasts the relationship between father and son, and in doing so alters its significance.

The battle between the brothers Micio and Demea is the battle waged between generations in the intrigue plays of Plautus. Perhaps the closest parallel to their quarrel is the exchange between Tranio, the *urbanus scurra* of *Mostellaria*, and the rustic Grumio.

In the famous opening of that play, Grumio berates Tranio for abetting the debauchery of their young master, Philolaches.

> haecine mandavit tibi, quom peregre hinc it, senex?
> hocine modo hic rem curatam offendet suam?
> hoccine boni esse officium servi existumas
> ut eri sui corrumpat et rem et filium?
>
> Is this what the old man ordered when he went abroad?
> Is this the way he will find his property treated?
> Is this what you think is a good servant's duty,
> corrupting his master's son and spending his wealth?
>
> *(Most.* 25–28)

Tranio's answer, of course, is yes. This is precisely the duty of the Plautine slave. Philolaches has indeed been corrupted by Tranio and will come to regret that corruption, not because it is wrong, but only because he will fear its consequences. Yet Grumio, though he speaks the truth, is defeated. Tranio, the champion of easy living, is the winner of their exchange, and the winner at play's end, too. In Plautus' comic world a sensible attitude is a wrong attitude. His plays are built upon a conflict of generations that leads to the triumph of youthful values and the evasion of responsibility. The frivolous wining and dining that Grumio condemns are the life-blood of the *palliata*.

In *Adelphoe*, Terence inverts that convention. Demea takes over the complaint of Grumio. As Micio admits,

> venit ad me saepe clamitans "quid agis, Micio?
> quor perdis adulescentem nobis? quor amat?
> quor potat?"
>
> He often comes to me crying, "Micio, what are you doing?
> Why do you ruin our boy? Why does he flirt?
> Why does he drink?"
>
> *(Ad.* 60–62)

Micio, like Tranio, defends the easy life.

> non est flagitium, mihi crede, adulescentulum
> scortari neque potare: non est. . . .
>
> It's not a crime, believe me, for a kid
> to go whoring and drinking. It isn't. . . .
> (*Ad.* 101–102, cf. *Most.* 36–37)

The values of the *servus callidus* have devolved on the *senex*, but with a vital difference. Micio is a loser. The absurdity of Tranio's success was part of his charm. The consequences of Micio's actions and attitudes are brought home to him at the end, and he pays for them with the loss of slaves, money, and finally the loyalty of his adopted son. Micio is always being bested. Terence's two sets of brothers are distinguished not so much by their severity and leniency, but by their strength and weakness. The younger brothers, Micio and Ctesipho, are weak and passive. The older brothers, Demea and Aeschinus, are strong and active. Micio is their victim from the beginning. He opened the play in considerable agitation because he does not know where Aeschinus is, and he must eventually admit to Demea that he has little control over events.[9]

> DE. ceterum
> placet tibi, Micio? MI. non, si queam
> mutare. nunc quom non queo, animo aequo fero.
>
> DE. Are you happy
> with this, Micio? MI. Not if I could change
> it. Since I can't, I take it as best I can.
> (*Ad.* 736–738)

Micio's "philosophy" has consisted, not of guiding Aeschinus, but of yielding to him. He gets nothing his way. Aeschinus, the

---

[9] When issues depend on talk, Micio triumphs, but he is powerless in the face of action. See W. R. Johnson, "Micio and the Perils of Perfection," *CSCA* 1 (1968) 171–186.

self-confessed rapist and thief, is neither honest with him nor gracious toward others. Abandoning the *ius patrium* indulges Micio's passive nature at the cost of his control. When Demea eventually assumes similar lenient principles, however, the effect is quite different. Micio endures what he cannot control; Demea changes in order to control. The famous monologue announcing that change reflects a decision to take the initiative (855ff.). Micio had repeatedly urged him to put aside his harshness (754–755, 794, 838–839). When he finally does so, he initiates the rapid sequence of actions that wins the respect of Aeschinus and teaches Micio a painful lesson. The two strong brothers, Demea and Aeschinus, join forces and compel Micio to surrender his bachelorhood, a part of his income, and two of his slaves.[10] The perennial victim of his son becomes at last the victim of his brother.

His fall thus inverts the logic of Plautus' comic world. Micio is punished for just the values that brought rewards to Tranio. His defeat repudiates the standards of conduct that made Plautine comedy so funny. Yet Roman audiences had laughed easily at Tranio's success. Why now would they be expected to laugh at the defeat of Micio? An answer lies in the changing attitude to the Greek world among Romans of the second century.

After the defeat of Carthage in 202 B.C., Rome turned its attention increasingly to the east. In the next fifty years a succession of political maneuvers and military campaigns imposed Roman *imperium* on the Greek world and brought Romans of all social classes into ever closer contact with Greek culture. Mili-

---

[10] Terence alters his original here to emphasize the extent of Micio's defeat. "Apud Menandrum," says Donatus *ad* 938, "senex de nuptiis non gravatur: ergo Terentius εὑρετικῶς." See J. N. Grant, "Notes on Donatus' Commentary on *Adelphoe*," *GRBS* 12 (1971) 205–209. F. H. Sandbach, "Donatus' Use of the Name Terentius and the End of Terence's *Adelphoe*," *BICS* 25 (1978) 123–145, esp. 140–143, believes that Aeschinus' presence here at the end is also Terence's addition, similarly designed to stress the weakness of Micio.

tary service abroad and the inevitable flow of booty to Italy not only enriched Roman cultural life but made the Greek world itself increasingly familiar. The comic fantasy of Plautus' Greece thus became more difficult to maintain. Greeks were no longer so exotic, and the conflict Plautus exploits between Greek and Roman values was no longer so laughable. A new tension entered the cultural relationship, a tension well illustrated in the writings of Cato, whose long life spanned the careers of both Plautus and Terence. A famous passage addressed to his son reflects the complexity of his attitude.

> Dicam de istis Graecis suo loco, M. fili, quid Athenis exquisitum habeam et quod bonum sit illorum litteras inspicere, non perdiscere, vincam. nequissimum et indocile genus illorum, et hoc puta vatem dixisse: quandoque ista gens suas litteras dabit, omnia conrumpet . . . nos quoque dictitant barbaros et spurcius nos quam alios opicon appellatione foedant. . . .
>
> I shall speak of those Greeks in their proper place, Marcus, my son, as to what I know as the result of my inquiries at Athens, and I shall demonstrate what benefit there is in looking into their literature, but not in studying it thoroughly. Theirs is an utterly vile and unruly race; and consider this as said by a prophet: when that race gives us its literature, it will corrupt everything. . . . They constantly speak of us too as barbarians, and they insult us more foully than others by calling us Opici.
> (*ad M. filium*, fr. 1J)

Cato nevertheless kept a Greek grammarian in his household. He himself knew Greek literature well and especially admired Xenophon and Demosthenes. This passage slights his own knowledge and his own cultural debt because he is advancing a racial rather than a strictly literary opinion.[11] What troubled Cato most

---

[11] A. E. Astin, *Cato the Censor* (Oxford 1978) 170–178, discusses the passage in detail. The grammarian Chilon was not permitted to teach Cato's

about the Greeks was the gap between the excellence of their literary heritage and the decadence of its contemporary heirs. For him, literary facility demanded moral integrity; the ideal orator was, above all, an honest man ("orator est, Marce fili, vir bonus dicendi peritus," fr. 14J). Thus, when the famous Academic philosopher Carneades visited Rome in 155, he drew Cato's anger not simply because one day he captivated the Roman youth, including Scipio Aemilianus, with a brilliant discourse on justice, but because the next day he seemed to refute himself with the help of dialectic subtleties that baffled the Roman mind.[12] Cato despised such mental gymnastics and resented the very thought of so evidently unprincipled a race mocking the Romans as rustic barbarians.

Plautus, who perhaps died in the year of Cato's censorship, had of course made a frequent joke of calling the Romans *barbari*.[13] By the 160's the joke was not so funny. The clash of values had become a serious matter and left the humor of Plautine comedy rooted in an outdated attitude. To revitalize the comic form, Terence had to put the *palliata* tradition on a new footing. His plays lack fantasy because the people who wore the *pallium* were no longer fantastic. A character like Micio, though he faces a traditional comic dilemma, must be presented in the light of contemporary social attitudes. He is therefore eloquent, rational,

---

son, but apparently because he was a slave, not because he was a Greek. Plut., *Cat.mai.* 20.5ff.

[12] The nature of Carneades' discourses and their effect on the Romans are unclear. See J.-L. Ferrary, "Les Discours de Philus et la philosophie de Carnéade," *REL* 55 (1977) 128–156.

[13] G. Lodge, *Lexicon Plautinum* (Leipzig 1904–33) s.v. *barbaria, barbaricus, barbarus*. There are ten citations in all. The words do not appear in Terence, nor does he indulge in those jokes on Greek language and behavior so familiar from Plautus, e.g., *pergraecari* (*Most.* 22, 64, 960). *Graeca fides* (i.e., "no credit," *As.* 199), ναὶ τὰν Πραινέστην (*Capt.* 88off.), and the Greek vocabulary of *Curc.* 284ff. For Cato's response to cultural change, see H. H. Scullard, *Roman Politics 220–150* B.C., 2 ed. (Oxford 1973) 220–226.

and charming, but he wins no more success than a member of Cato's *nequissimum et indocile genus* deserves. Other plays offer the same combination of familiar situations and a newly critical perspective, especially when Terence tinkers with the dramatic balance of his Greek models to emphasize the weakness of their characters. The addition of Charinus to *Andria* increases the social burden on poor, hapless Pamphilus. A new kind of suspense focuses attention on the helpless women of *Hecyra*, and the prominence of Thraso and Gnatho in *Eunuchus* creates an ironic paradigm of the young men's own willing subservience. These plays thus present such uncomic sights as a weak boy cowed by a forceful father, the selfishness of men as revealed by their women, and lovers made foolish by their love. Terence's response to the new interests and demands of his time has turned the comic conventions upside down. These *adulescentes* remain foolish to the end, while their fathers generally keep their dignity. Women command our sympathy and respect. Clever slaves are ineffective, for plots are resolved more by rightness than by wit. A coldly logical light shines on the antics of characters who are, after all, only *graeculi*. The plays are still amusing, but the new perspective was to take its toll on the genre's appeal.

Though in different ways, both Menander and Plautus had treated their characters with affection. Stage events challenge Menander's men and women, forcing them to change and grow. We learn to like them as the plot unfolds, and, because we like them, we become engrossed in their problems. The double tradition of Athenian tragedy and comedy allowed Menander to expand New Comedy's range and transcend its harsh, formalized plots. Plautus, writing with no such tradition of serious comedy, substituted a boundless enthusiasm for its conventions. Characters like Ballio and Pseudolus may come very close to caricature, but audiences did not mind. Laughter was what they expected. Terence substituted irony for that Plautine affection. He never lets us forget that his dramatic material is built upon the self-indulgence, obtuseness, and moral failings of his characters. We may sympathize, for example, with the problems of *Adelphoe*, but not with its characters. We tolerate Micio's fall precisely because we have been taught to distrust him. Demea is no more likable in triumph than he was in defeat. The willful, spoiled Aeschinus enjoys the fruits of his misdeeds without ever facing the fact that they *were* misdeeds. Ctesipho escapes our moral scrutiny only because his weak personality largely escapes our notice. Terence's irony is clever and incisive, but it makes the comic devices seem contrived and unpleasant. His success in manipulating the old formulae to yield these new results necessitated the end of both comic fantasy and comic exuberance.

His genre could not endure this double loss, nor could it accept his substitution. The new kind of seriousness that Terence brought to comedy was not a Roman seriousness, and, ultimately, his comedy failed to be a Roman comedy. One cause of that failure is technical. Like many artists, Terence is more inclined to raise important questions than to answer them, but his presentation of those questions sometimes fails to take a suitably theatrical form. Thus the shift of focus from youth to age and male to female in *Hecyra* is both touching and bold, but was too abrupt for an audience coming to the play with more traditional expectations. A similar problem of dramatic preparation is less apparent but no less real in *Adelphoe*. The brief appearance of Sostrata and the nurse Canthara in that play (288ff.) is an example of quite effective dramaturgy, a deft way to impress Aeschinus' thoughtlessness upon the audience by demonstrating the needless suffering he has brought these innocent people.[14] The

---

[14] J. N. Grant, "The Role of Canthara in Terence's *Adelphoe*," *Philologus* 117 (1973) 70–75, suggests that the nurse is Terence's addition here to enliven the scene. It is not sufficient, however, to conclude with W. Ludwig, "The Originality of Terence and his Greek Models," *GRBS* 9 (1968) 169–182, esp. 180–181, that the point of such alterations is to enrich the action. It also enriches the *meaning* of that action.

stage time devoted to them thus contributes to our understanding of him. The larger issues of the play, however, are not always so clearly represented on the stage. Terence's refusal to choose between Micio and Demea may be intellectually sound, but it is dramatically difficult. Demea's *volte-face* happens so quickly that audiences are more prone to be amused by it than to recognize its deeper significance, and Aeschinus' transfer of allegiance is at best undermotivated. Neither fault spoils the play in performance. Audiences caught up in the developing action readily accept such reversals uncritically. Yet Terence's very subtlety in depicting these important shifts in his characters' positions provides insufficient material for the kind of second thoughts necessary to bring their meaning home to thoughtful spectators.[15] The dramatist has made insufficient use of the dramatic form to convey his meaning.

A second, more pervasive difficulty is a consequence of Terence's ironic probing of social relationships. By inverting the comic forms, he also took the fun out of them. Terentian comedy thus gained a certain inner tension, but fun lay at the heart of the *ludi scaenici*. Those substantive issues that gave Greek drama intellectual content were not, for the Romans, the essence of public entertainment. Terence's addition of a certain seriousness to the Roman tradition could only come at the expense of its most fundamental appeal. He was always able to write the kind of traditional comic scenes that would make his plays saleable. His Thraso is a worthy sucessor to Pyrgopolynices. Phormio rivals Curculio, and his lovers, fathers, and whores are hardly new creations. Yet the values Terence assigns these familiar figures, their abiding significance after the laughter has stopped, are indeed new and had an unsettling effect on his successors.

[15] And readers. This is why the ending of *Adelphoe* has been such a problem for so long. Cf. N. A. Greenberg, "Success and Failure in the *Adelphoe*," *CW* 73 (1979/80) 221–236, with ample reference to previous scholarship.

Terence's spiritual heirs were not dramatists. Within a generation, the poet Lucilius had adapted the bite of Terentian irony to the new genre of satire. A century later, Latin elegy returned to the theme of love and its consequences. These were both, however, essentially private forms of literature to be enjoyed at home or read before comparatively small, educated groups. Stage comedy was left with only the shell of art. Plautus had made it too absurd, and Terence had made it too alien to be taken seriously by subsequent poets. Turpilius kept Roman audiences laughing a little longer, but no dramatist emerged to keep them thinking. Terence became the last pioneer of the ancient stage. Within a century of his death Latin literature entered its golden age, but ancient comedy as a creative genre was gone for good.

SELECTIVE BIBLIOGRAPHY

G. Cupaiuolo, *Bibliografia terenziana (1470–1983)* [*Studi i testi dell' antichità XVI* (Naples 1984)] provides an exhaustive and beautifully indexed inventory of Terentian scholarship. Critical discussion of this secondary literature can be found in the earlier bibliographical studies of H. Marti, *Lustrum* 6 (1961) 114–238 and 8 (1963) 5–101, 244–264, K. Gaiser, *ANRW* 1.2 (1972) 1027–1113, W. G. Arnott, *Menander, Plautus, Terence* [*Greece and Rome New Surveys in the Classics, No. 9* (Oxford 1975)], and S. M. Goldberg, *CW* 75 (1981) 77–115. Serviceable English translations include B. Radice, *The Comedies* in the Penguin series (Baltimore 1976) and especially P. Bovie *et al.*, *The Complete Comedies of Terence* (New Brunswick, N.J. 1974). The following list aims simply to identify some particularly helpful works in this extensive and rather formidable bibliography.

CULTURAL BACKGROUND

Beare, W. "The Life of Terence," *Hermathena* 59 (1942) 20–29.
Blänsdorf, J. "Das Bild der Komödie in der späten Republik" in U. Reinhardt and K. Sallmann, ed., *Musa Iocosa* (Hildesheim 1974) 141–157.
Calboli, G. "La retorica preciceroniana e la politica a Roma" in *Fondation Hardt Entretiens XXVIII: Éloquence et rhétorique chez Cicéron* (Vandoeuvres-Geneva 1982) 41–99.
Earl, D. C. "Terence and Roman Politics," *Historia* 11 (1962) 469–485.
Garton, C. *Personal Aspects of the Roman Theatre* (Toronto 1972).
Horsfall, N. "The Collegium Poetarum," *BICS* 23 (1976) 79–95.
Jory, E. J. "Associations of Actors in Rome," *Hermes* 98 (1970) 224–253.
Kindermann, H. *Das Theaterpublikum der Antike* (Salzburg 1979).
Martina, M. "Terenzio e i nobiles: sul prologo dell' *Eunuchus*," *QS* 9 (1983) 161–167.
Waszink, J. H. "Anfangsstadium der römischen Literatur," *ANRW* 1.2 (1972) 869–927.

GENERAL

Blänsdorf, J. "Die Komödienintrige als Spiel im Spiel," *A&A* 28 (1982) 131–154.
Büchner, K. *Das Theater des Terenz* (Heidelberg 1974).
Croce, B. "Terence" in *Philosophy, Poetry, History*, tr. C. Sprigge (London 1966) 776–801.
Denzler, B. *Der Monolog bei Terenz* (Zurich 1968).
Fantham, E. "Adaptation and Survival: A Genre Study of Roman Comedy in Relation to its Greek Sources" in *Versions of Mediaeval Comedy* (Norman, OK 1977) 297–327.
Gilula, D. "The Concept of the *Bona Meretrix*. A Study of Terence's Courtesans," *RFIC* (1980) 142–165.
Glücklich, H.-J. *Aussparung und Antithese. Studien zur terenzischen Komödie* (Diss. Heidelberg 1966).
Görler, W. "Doppelhandlung, Intrige und Anagnorismus bei Terenz," *Poetica* 5 (1972) 164–182.
Gratwick, A. S. "Drama" in E. J. Kenney and W. V. Clausen, ed., *The Cambridge History of Classical Literature, Vol. II: Latin Literature* (Cambridge 1982) 77–137.
Gratwick, A. S. and S. J. Lightley. "Light and Heavy Syllables as Dramatic Colouring in Plautus and Others." *CQ* 32 (1982) 124–133.
Haffter, H. "Terenz und seine künstlerische Eigenart," *MH* 10 (1953) 1–20 and 73–102, reprinted as a monograph (Darmstadt 1967) and as *Terenzio e la sua personalità artistica*, tr. with additional notes by D. Nardo (Rome 1969).
Hunter, R. L. *The New Comedy of Greece and Rome* (Cambridge 1985).
Juhnke, H. "Terenz" in E. Lefèvre, ed., *Das römische Drama* (Darmstadt 1978) 223–307.
Lefèvre, E. *Die Expositionstechnik in den Komödien des Terenz* (Darmstadt 1969).
Leo, F. *Analecta Plautina II* in *Ausgewählte kleine Schriften*, vol. 1 (Rome 1960) 123–162.
Leo, F. "Terenz" in *Geschichte der römischen Literatur I* (Berlin 1913) 232–258.
Ludwig, W. "The Originality of Terence and his Greek Models," *GRBS* 9 (1968) 169–182.

Marti, H. *Untersuchungen zur dramatischen Technik bei Plautus und Terenz* (Zurich 1959).
Straus, J. *Terenz und Menander. Beitrag zu einer Stilvergleichung* (Diss. Bern 1955).
Wright, J. *Dancing in Chains: The Stylistic Unity of the Comoedia Palliata* (Rome 1974).

THE PLAYS

Andria

Calboli, G. "Terenzio, *Andria* 481–88," *Philologus* 124 (1980) 33–67.
McGarrity, T. "Thematic Unity in Terence's *Andria*," *TAPA* 108 (1978) 103–114.
Ronconi, A. "Analisi del prologo dell' *Andria*," *RCCM* 20 (1978) 1129–1148.

Heauton timorumenos

Brothers, A. J. "The Construction of Terence's *Heauton timorumenos*," *CQ* 30 (1980) 94–119.
Fantham, E. "*Heautontimorumenos* and *Adelphoe*. A Study of Fatherhood in Terence and Menander," *Latomus* 30 (1971) 970–998.
Lefèvre, E. "Der *Heautontimorumenos* des Terenz" in his *Die römischen Komödie: Plautus und Terenz* (Darmstadt 1973) 443–462.
Primmer, A. "Zum Prolog des *Heautontimorumenos*," *WS* 77 (1964) 61–75.
Primmer, A. "Die homo-sum-Szene im *Heautontimorumenos*," *WS* 79 (1966) 293–298.

Eunuchus

Gilmartin, K. "The Thraso-Gnatho Subplot in Terence's *Eunuchus*," *CW* 69 (1975) 263–267.
Lowe, J.C.B. "The *Eunuchus*: Terence and Menander," *CQ* 33 (1983) 428–444.
Ludwig, W. "Von Terenz zu Menander," *Philologus* 103 (1959) 1–38, reprinted with *addendum* in Lefèvre's *Die römische Komödie*, 354–408.
Saylor, C. "The Theme of Planlessness in Terence's *Eunuchus*," *TAPA* 105 (1975) 297–311.

Phormio

Arnott, W. G. "*Phormio parasitus*. A Study in Dramatic Methods of Characterization," *G&R* 17 (1970) 32–57.

Blanchard, A. "La composition du *Phormion* et l'originalité de Térence," *REL* 58 (1980) 49–66. [Review of Lefèvre, below.]

Konstan, D. "*Phormio*: Citizen Disorder" in his *Roman Comedy* (Ithaca 1983) 115–129.

Lefèvre, E. *Der Phormio des Terenz und der Epidikazomenos des Apollodor von Karystos* (Munich 1978).

Lowe, J.C.B. "Terentian Originality in the *Phormio* and *Hecyra*," *Hermes* 111 (1983) 431–452.

Segal, E., and C. Moulton. "*Contortor legum*: The Hero of the *Phormio*," *RhM* 121 (1978) 276–288.

Hecyra

Gilula, D. "Terence's *Hecyra*: A Delicate Balance of Suspense and Dramatic Irony," *SCI* 5 (1979/80) 137–157.

Gilula, D. "Who's Afraid of Rope-Walkers and Gladiators? (Terence, *Hec.* 1–57)," *Athenaeum* 59 (1981) 29–37.

Konstan, D. "*Hecyra*: Ironic Comedy" in his *Roman Comedy* (Ithaca 1983) 130–141.

McGarrity, T. "Reputation v. Reality in Terence's *Hecyra*," *CJ* 76 (1980/81) 149–156.

Sandbach, F. H. "How Terence's *Hecyra* Failed," *CQ* 32 (1982) 134–135.

Sewart, D. "Exposition in the *Hekyra* of Apollodorus," *Hermes* 102 (1974) 247–260.

Adelphoe

Fantham, E. "Terence, Diphilus, and Menander. A Re-examination of Terence, *Adelphoe*, Act II," *Philologus* 112 (1968) 196–216.

Grant, J. N. "The Beginning of Menander, *Adelphoi B'*," *CQ* 30 (1980) 341–355.

Grant, J. N. "The Ending of Terence's *Adelphoe* and the Menandrian Original," *AJP* 96 (1975) 42–60.

Greenberg, N. A. "Success and Failure in the *Adelphoe*," *CW* 73 (1979/ 80) 221–236.
Johnson, W. R. "Micio and the Perils of Perfection," *CSCA* 1 (1968) 171–186.
Lefèvre, E. "La structure des *Adelphes* de Térence comme critère d'analyse," *Théâtre et Spectacles dans l'Antiquité: Actes du Colloque de Strasbourg* (Leiden 1983) 169–179.
Lord, C. "Aristotle, Menander, and the *Adelphoe* of Terence," *TAPA* 107 (1977) 183–202.
Pöschl, V. *Das Problem der Adelphen des Terenz*, *SHAW* no. 4 (1975) 1–24.
Rieth, O. *Die Kunst Menanders in den Adelphen des Terenz* (Hildesheim 1964).

INDEX

PASSAGES CITED

Caesar, *BG* 4.12: 178
Cato
 de Agricultura 134: 173
 Origines
  fr. 83 P: 174–175
  fr. 2 P: 101
 ad M. filium
  fr. 1 J: 215
  fr. 14 J: 216
 Orationes
  fr. 58 M: 40–42
  fr. 158 M: 44–45
  fr. 163 M: 42–43
  fr. 164 M: 43–44
  fr. 169 M: 49–50
  fr. 177 M: 195
  fr. 193 M: 172
Cicero
 Brut. 294: 46
 de Or. 3.176–177: 198–199
 Or. 76: 200
  77–78: 51
CIL i² 614: 173
Q. Claudius Quadrigarius
 fr. 10b P: 175–176
 fr. 12 P: 177–178
L. Coelius Antipater, fr. 24b P: 197n

Ennius
 Alexander XVII J: 205–207
 Alcmaeo XV J: 207–208
Eupolis, fr. 159 K: 107–108

Horace, *Ep.* 2.1.182–186: 167

Menander
 Aspis 40–44: 188–189
 Dys. 45–46: 60n
  489–496: 187
  669–678: 189–191
 Epitr. 908–910: 151
 Sa. 206–210: 24–25
 fr. 11 K–T: 26
 fr. 127 K–T: 11

P. Argent. 53: 32n
Phrynichos, fr. 18 K: 27n
Plautus
 As. 1–15: 33–35
 Aul. 688–695: 19
 Cas. 17–20: 36–37
  18–20: 4
  1012–1014: 125
 Curc. 280–282: 16–17
 Men. 72–76: 91
  865–867: 208
 Trin. 16–17: 32
 Merc. 11–13: 183
 Most. 25–28: 212

Quintilian 8.3.87: 51

Rhetorica ad Herennium
 1.9.14: 45
 1.11: 171–172

Terence
 Ad. 8–11: 98
  12–14: 93–94
  15–21: 9
  42–47: 25
  51–52: 102
  60–62: 212
  65–67: 103
  101–102: 213
  173–176: 105
  311–319: 18
  540–542: 189
  707–709: 211
  733–737: 73
  736–738: 213
  855–859: 24
  863–868: 26
  872–874: 26
  877–880: 23
  985–988: 27
 And. 1–27: 47–52
  13–16: 92
  18–21: 195–196
  127–136: 191–192
  128–129: 79
  220–224: 45
  330–332: 133
  333–335: 134
  471–476: 20
  490–492: 20
  625–638a: 131–133
  709–713: 131
 Eun. 7–8: 29, 58
  19–20: 58
  19–24: 93
  30–33: 106
  35–41: 16
  147–149: 118–119
  197–198: 118
  197–201: 22
  232–233: 108
  247–253: 187–188
  261–264: 109
  391–394: 110

228   INDEX

Terence, *Eun. (cont.)*
    425–429: 110
    440–444: 111
    588–591: 209
    772–774: 112
    868–871: 119
    1037–1040: 119–120
Hec. 1–8: 37–40
    52–54: 58
    114–122: 185–186
    125–129: 193–194
    277–278: 153
    355–358: 164
    516–517: 154
    556–559: 156

866–868: 152
HT 1–3: 54
    11–15: 54
    16–19: 92
    24–27: 55
    31–32: 17
    35–36: 56
    53–60: 170–171
    61–64: 11
    75–77: 137
    84–86: 135–136
    96–104: 184–185
    136–139: 137
    155–158: 143
    213–216: 138
    225–227: 138

    915–925: 141–142
    1020–1022: 143
    1059–1066: 149–150
Ph. 26–28: 76
    136–139: 78
    270–277: 194–195
    317–318: 77
    384–390: 83–84
    639–641: 74
    738–747: 85
    754–755: 85
    792–794: 86
    884–893: 75–76
    1012–1013: 88
    1040–1042: 88

GENERAL

Accius, 4n
adulescens, see stock types
Aemilius Paullus, 7, 9, 13, 167, 173
Ambivius Turpio, 14, 55–58, 167n
anguish in comedy, 159–160
Antiphanes, 111n
Apollodorus of Carystos, 21, 89, 90, 150, 157n, 159–160, 168n
Apollonius of Tyre, 146
Aristophanes, 31, 90, 123n, 203
Aristotle, 123

Caecilius, 4, 5, 57, 167n, 181, 199
Caesar, opinion of Terence, 180–181; style of, 172n, 178–179, 181n, 186
cantica, 201, 210; in Terence, 131
Carneades, 216
Cato, 5, 10, 13; and Ennius, 6–7; attitude towards Hellenism, 215–217; narrative style, 174–175, 186, 196, 197n, 199–200, 202; oratorical style, 40–46, 172, 195; *Origines*, 45, 101, 174
character revelation in comedy, 163–165
childbirth in play, 18–20, 115
Cicero, 10, 51, 102, 110, 179, 197, 198–199, 200, 207n; admiration for Terence, 169, 180; opinion of Livius, 4; of Cato, 46
Claudius Quadrigarius, annalist, 175–179, 186, 192, 193, 196, 197n
Coelius Antipater, annalist, 197
collegium poetarum, 5
contaminatio, 50, 50n, 55, 59, 126, 130, 140, chap. 4 *passim*

dialogue style, 164–165, 182
Diomedes, grammarian, 123
Diphilus, 21, 32, 53, 93, 104, 124n; model for Plautus, 135, 181
Donatus, 28, 28n, 39, 53, 59, 78, 94,

95n, 106, 109, 111–112, 116, 127, 128, 129, 153n, 159, 160, 209n
Dryden, John, 123–124

Ennius, 26, 199, 205–208, 209; patronage of, 5–7
Eubulus, 141n
Eugraphius, 59n
Euhemerus, Ennius' translation of, 45
Eupolis, 107–108, 124n
Euripides, 33n, 160
expository style, 45, 182–186, 188–192

Fabius Pictor, 199
Feydeau, G., 63, 90, 148
Fraenkel, E., 71
Freytag, G., 70
Fulvius Nobilior, M., 8, 14; patronage of Ennius, 5–7

Gellius, Aulus, 46, 50
graeculus, see stock types
Greek drama, conditions different from Roman, 35, 204–205
Guarini, Battista, 128

Hermogenes, rhetorician, 49n
Horace, 10, 117, 118n, 167, 207n
humanitas, 10, 14, 152n

Ibsen, 65
industrious maiden, *see* stock types

Laelius, 9
leno, see stock types
Leo, F., 28, 71, 95–96, 148n
Lessing, G. E., 61–63, 69, 98
Livius Andronicus, 3–5, 199–200
Livy, style, 176n, 177n

ludi scaenici, 3–8, 14, 21, 60, 167, 205, 219
Luscius Lanuvinus, 10, 14, 53, 59–60

madness, on Roman stage, 207–208
Menander, model for Terence, 11–12, 21, 26–27, 186–192; narrative style, 188–191; plot construction, 66n, 68–69, 72, 123–124, 134; prologues, 32–33, 60; reputation in antiquity, 181; tragic echoes in, 204–205, 209, 210; use of conventions, 204, 217;
– individual plays:
Dyskolos, 66–69, 129–130
Epitrepontes, 150–151, 168n
Kolax, 12, 15, 106–107, 116–117
Perikeiromene, 12, 32–33, 60, 123
Samia, 69, 99–100, 103
meretrix, see stock types
meter, effect on style, 193–198, 201; shift for emphasis, 26–27, 153, 205; tragic and comic compared, 210
miles gloriosus, see stock types
Molière, 61; *Les fourberies de Scapin*, 80–81
monologues, in Menander, 22–23; in Terence, 23–28, 155–156

Naevius, 5–6
neglegentia in Terence, 50–51, 171–172
Norwood, G., 80, 113, 139n, 148, 152n

otium, 101–102
Ovid, 181n

Pacuvius, 199, 207
parabasis, 31, 108
parasite, *see* stock types

parody, tragic, 205, 208–210
Philemon, 21, 181
philhellenism, 9–11, 13–14
Phrynichos, 27n
Plautus, 3, 4, 5, 90, 93, 101, 181, 183, 201; legal language in, 52–53; plot construction, 69–72, 124–126; prologues, 31–37, 60; tragic parody in, 208–209; use of conventions, 91, 214, 216–218;
— individual plays:
   Amphitruo, 147, 159, 209
   Captivi, 61, 114, 145
   Casina, 4, 125
   Menaechmi, 146–147, 208
Postumius Albinus, A., 13–14
prose rhythm, 196–197
pura oratio, 56, chap. 7 *passim*

Quintilian, 46, 51n, 201n

rape, in play, 115
recognition in comedy, 158–159, 161
rhetoric at Rome, 179, 200; Terence's knowledge of, 59n; Terence's use of, 42–60, 171
Rhetorica ad Herennium, 45, 52, 171
Ritschl, F., 61, 62n, 70–71

Sardou, V., 63–65, 68, 69
satire, 201n, 220
Schlegel, A. W., 62–63, 66, 71
Scipio Aemilianus, 9, 13, 216
Scipio Africanus, 7
Scipionic circle, 9–10, 13–14
Scribe, E., 63–64, 72, 148
senex, *see* stock types
servus callidus, *see* stock types
servus currens, *see* stock types

Shakespeare, xi–xii, double plot in, 146–148
social class in comedy, 144–148
socrus, *see* stock types
stataria, 56
stock types, *adulescens*, 115, 127, 152, 211, 217; *graeculus*, 102, 217; industrious maiden, 140n; *leno*, 104; *meretrix*, 22, 117–121, 151n; *miles gloriosus*, 12, 16, 107, 112–113; parasite, 76–77, 107–109, 111, 113, 121, 187–188; *senex*, 136–137, 153, 155; *servus callidus*, 16, 79–80, 157, 211–213, 217; *servus currens*, 16–18, 21, 55, 78, 158; *socrus*, 153n
Suetonius, *vita Terenti*, 9, 95n, 103, 180

Terence, alteration of models, 11–12, 28–30, 89n, 106, 140n, 157n, 159, 160n, 214n, 218n; character in, 73–74, 144; chronology of plays, 167n; ironic use of conventions, 15–16, 157–159, 216–219; metrical change in, 27; patronage of, 8–10, 14; putative weaknesses in, 161–166, 218–219; style, 164–165, chap. 2 *passim*, chap. 7 *passim*;
— individual plays (major discussions):
   Adelphoe: change of ending, 214n; *contaminatio* in, 97–105; contrast of Demea and Micio, 73–74, 144; Demea's change of heart, 23–28, 219; reversal of comic roles in, 211–214, 218–219
   Andria: alternative ending, 129; *contaminatio* in, 126–135
   Eunuchus: 105–122
   Heautontimorumenos: 135–148, 149–150

Hecyra: 150–169; problems in staging, 39n, 57, 167–169
Phormio: 75–90
tragedy, Greek, 204; Roman, 205–211
translation, ancient standards of, 29
Turpilius, 203, 204, 220

Udall, N., 113

Varro, 4n, 103, 181
Volcacius Sedigitus, 181

Weise, K. H., 69–71
Wilde, O., *Lady Windermere's Fan*, 65, 67, 68, 83, 162
Winckelmann, J. J., 61–63

LIBRARY OF CONGRESS CATALOGING-IN-PUBLICATION DATA

GOLDBERG, SANDER M.
UNDERSTANDING TERENCE.

BIBLIOGRAPHY: P.
INCLUDES INDEX.
1. TERENCE—CRITICISM AND INTERPRETATION. 2. COMIC,
THE, IN LITERATURE. I. TITLE.
PA6768.G65 1986   872'.01   85-43285
ISBN 0-691-03586-5 (ALK. PAPER)

GPSR Authorized Representative: Easy Access System Europe - Mustamäe tee 50, 10621 Tallinn, Estonia, gpsr.requests@easproject.com

www.ingramcontent.com/pod-product-compliance
Lightning Source LLC
Chambersburg PA
CBHW061441300426
44114CB00014B/1779